Critical Acclaim for This Book

'A timely contribution to the debate on Africa's future in the age of globalization. In this penetrating analysis, Fantu Cheru analyses Africa's marginal position in the new global hierarchy and then proceeds to offer important but pragmatic pointers that African governments, in consultation with their populations, must undertake to navigate successfully the cold currents of globalization. This book is a must-read for African policymakers, civil society leaders, and donor organizations.'

CARLOS LOPES, *Deputy Assistant Administrator, Bureau of Development Policy, United Nations Development Programme*

'Globalization, with its contradictory tendencies, poses a great challenge to the African continent. Despite gloomy predictions about Africa's future, however, Cheru argues that globalization can offer a great opportunity for the continent, but only if African leaders are prepared to manage it carefully and with greater concern for empowering the poor. Africa can and must compete in a rapidly changing global economy. But this will require fundamental change in African attitudes, institutional arrangements, orientation to governance and economic management – a conclusion broadly in line with UNECA's "Compact for African Development".'

K.Y. AMOAKO, *Executive Secretary and Assistant Secretary-General, United Nations Economic Commission for Africa*

'Dr Fantu Cheru's new book provides an insightful evaluation of Africa's political and economic points of origin, as well as its desired Renaissance destination. Most importantly, it offers clear directions for all those joining the fight against global apartheid!'

SALIH BOOKER, *Executive Director, Africa Action*

About the Author

The author is a Professor at the School of International Service, The American University, Washington DC. Ethiopian by birth, Dr Fantu Cheru is a specialist in policy analysis, rural development and urban and regional planning. He has acted as a consultant to a wide range of institutions including UN agencies – the United Nations High Commission on Human Rights, the United Nations Development Programme (UNDP), and the United Nations Centre for Human Settlements (Habitat) – as well as various development agencies including SIDA and DANIDA. His research and consultancy activity has enabled him to spend periods of time in a wide range of African countries.

In addition to writing a large number of scholarly articles and chapters, as well as monographs and official reports, he is the author of the following books:

The Silent Revolution in Africa: Debt, Development and Democracy

Ethiopia: Options for Rural Development (with Siegfried Pausewang and others)

Dependence, Underdevelopment and Unemployment in Kenya: School Leavers in a Peripheral Capitalist Political Economy

From Debt to Development: Alternatives to the International Debt Crisis (with John Cavanagh and others).

AFRICAN RENAISSANCE

Roadmaps to the Challenge of Globalization

FANTU CHERU

ZED BOOKS
London & New York

DAVID PHILIP
Cape Town

African Renaissance was first published in 2002 by
Zed Books Ltd, 7 Cynthia Street, London N1 9JF, UK,
and Room 400, 175 Fifth Avenue, New York, NY 10010, USA

Distributed in the USA exclusively by Palgrave, a division of
St Martin's Press, LLC, 175 Fifth Avenue, New York, NY 10010, USA

Published in South Africa by David Philip, an imprint of New Africa Books,
PO Box 23408, Claremont 7735, Tel. 27 21 674 4136, Fax 27 21 674 3358

Designed and typeset in Monotype Bembo by Illuminati, Grosmont
Cover designed by Andrew Corbett
Printed and bound in Malaysia

A catalogue record for this book is available from the British Library

Library of Congress Cataloging-in-Publication Data applied for

ISBN 1 84277 086 1 (Hb)
ISBN 1 84277 087 X (Pb)

In South Africa: ISBN 0 86486 592 9 (Pb)

Contents

Acknowledgements

The 1980s and 1990s were characterized as the 'lost development decades' for Africa. Much of the Western media and academic commentary dwelled on the depressing economic and political slide of the continent, and few commentators paid any attention to how to pull Africa out of the economic and political morass it is in. Robert Kaplan's article in the *Atlantic Monthly*, 'The Coming Anarchy', and the June 1999 *Economist* headline, 'Hopeless Africa', cemented the prevailing negative view in the West about Africa. It was in this negative climate, and in response to the pessimistic view of Africa's future, that I ventured to write a book that tries to chart out a pragmatic strategy to deal with the structural crisis of the continent. This undertaking would not have been possible without the support of many individuals who believed in the capacity of Africans for self-transformation.

The idea of writing a book that challenges the negative Western stereotype about Africa was conceived in the campus of the University of Toronto. While attending a conference there in 1995, my colleague Professor Mustafa Pasha prodded me to put together a number of critical writings I had done and to turn them into a book. On closer examination, however, the material I had on hand at that time was not adequate to produce a credible book. It took many years of research and more than two dozen trips to the continent under the auspices of various United Nations bodies to put together this volume.

At American University, a number of graduate assistants who worked with me contributed immensely to the present project. Among them were Rachel Yousey, Erin McCandeles, Christopher Bennett, Sara Bouchie, Tara Williams, Kubby Rashid and Andrea Bretnich. I also benefited from valuable comments from Gunilla Eitrem, Margaret Lee, Joyce Malombe, Annika Tornqvist, David Hirschmann, Betew Hagos, Catalina Trujillo, Guy Martin, Doug Hellinger, Patrick Bond, Steven Hellinger, Tadesse Zerihun, Reinaldo Figueredo, Genene Zewge, Henrik S. Marcussen. Special thanks also go to my publisher Robert Molteno and to the staff at Zed Books, who did a marvellous job in the preparation of this book from beginning to end.

I also want to thank hundreds of graduate students who passed through my courses at American University and who willingly allowed me to test many of my ideas on them. Their critical questioning in class helped me sharpen my analysis. In dozens of African countries where I travelled and researched, countless numbers of ordinary Africans were willing to share with me their hopes, aspirations and disappointments. There is no word that would capture my gratitude to them.

Finally, I would like to thank my wife Annika and our two kids, Malkom and Hanna Makeda, for allowing me to pursue this project to the end. They have endured my frequent long absences from home during the preparation of this book. Without their understanding, support and love, I would not have been able to bring it to fruition.

List of Tables and Boxes

Introduction

The notion of an 'African Renaissance' has been around in African political discourse since the colonial period. The Senegalese intellectual Cheik anta Diop first used the term in the context of the struggle against colonial rule, intending to capture the dreams and aspirations of the people of Africa in their quest for self-determination. With the end of apartheid in 1994 and the resurgence of democratic ideals throughout Africa, South African president Thabo Mbeki resurrected the term as his country aspired to take a leading role in the economic and political transformation of the continent. It is still too early to tell whether Mbeki's vision of the African Renaissance is a specifically South African hegemonic project or whether it truly captures the sentiments of the majority of Africans.

The 'African Renaissance' was also the term used recently by former IMF managing director Michel Camdessus to describe the recent turnaround of several African economies after two decades of 'scorched-earth' neoliberal economic reform by the Bretton Woods institutions. Camdessus credited his institution with single-handedly engineering this so-called African economic renaissance. Despite these exaggerated claims by the IMF, many African countries still find themselves at the lower end of the human development index.

Clearly, Thabo Mbeki's African Renaissance is the expression of desire, need and hope rather than a plan for the future. Indeed, this might be the most disquieting facet of the so-called renaissance: the absence of any coherent, continent-wide agenda or framework for change. And if one closely follows the neoliberal economic model being implemented by the ANC government, Mbeki's vision of the 'African Renaissance' is more in line with the much-discredited neoliberal project of the 'Washington

Consensus' than what the idea actually implies. The kind of renaissance that Camdessus talked about neither brings equitable development nor strengthens the foundations for democratic governance or the enhancement of human rights culture at national and global levels. Regressive economic and political conditionalities by donor governments and multilateral financial institutions cannot be liberating and empowering when the rights of countries to determine their development autonomously have been significantly eroded.

The basic premiss of this book is that globalization, with its contradictory tendencies, is an irreversible process and that any vision of an 'African Renaissance' must, at the very least, provide a coherent strategy on how to navigate this complex process successfully. While the possibility of developing a counterhegemonic strategy to global neoliberalism is unthinkable in the near future, African countries must be prepared to manage globalization to their own advantage through the adoption of key reforms at national and regional levels, without heavy-handed intervention by the institutions of the world system. This approach, developed throughout the book, seeks to identify and examine the local dimensions of global reform in Africa.

For almost two decades, an interesting but contentious debate on Africa's economic and political future has been flourishing in the corridors of international organizations and at academic conferences. The debate has centred on the merits and pitfalls of state-led development versus market-driven approaches. As the African economic and social crisis has deepened, the number of international initiatives purportedly designed to cure the continent's ills have also multiplied. In spite of this, the vast majority of the African poor continue to lead a rather isolated existence, oblivious to the numerous initiatives being undertaken on their behalf.

This book attempts to go beyond the simple approach to Africa's development: namely, should it be state-led or market-driven. The author argues that there is no simple solution to Africa's economic and social crisis, and that both state and market approaches are relevant, providing they take into account the particular circumstances of each African country. Two important lessons from Africa's development experience follow. The first is that failure to mobilize the resource-allocative functions of the market can only contribute to the inflexibility of the economy. Second, failure to recognize the weakness of market forces in a number of fundamental areas can lead to failed adjustment, and a serious undermining of badly needed human development. What is needed in Africa today are more 'common sense' approaches that open up new avenues for increased productivity, by laying the conditions for development through improved governance, increased investment in education and infrastructure, and improved access of the poor to productive assets and information. Finally, a 'common sense' approach to eradicating poverty will require political stability and rule-based political order mediated by an impartial and independent judiciary, with particular emphasis on transparency, accountability, and greater citizen participation in decision-making. Dogmatic faith in either planning or markets will simply not do. A nexus of truly developmental state–society arrangements will enable Africa to address successfully the numerous economic, social, political and ecological challenges of the new century.

Ironically, many of the reform proposals discussed in this book are also central in neoliberal thinking. The point of departure for neoliberals in explaining the African crisis, however, is very narrow and does not place the crisis in historical context. Needless to say, critics of neoliberalism tend to dismiss the need to provide greater scope for the market (because it supports right-wing conservatism) and to demarcate the specific roles of state and market in national development. As Colin Leys reminds us:

> national success in the global marketplace depends on coherent long-term strategic action by states and the construction and maintenance of a dense web of 'intermediate' institutions (banks, financial and technical services, training, and infrastructure of all kinds) and sufficient social protection for the poor that the market needs but does not itself provide. (1996: 195)

The experience of the newly industrializing countries of East Asia (NICs) demonstrates that the state has an important role to play in national development, and that the state is not necessarily or inevitably parasitic or corrupt. Indeed, the policies of the IMF and the World Bank actually require a strengthening of key aspects of the state apparatus, although the rhetoric of structural adjustment and 'systemic transformation' suggest otherwise. Areas in need of state capacity building and/or strengthening include policy analysis and development management, research and development across all sectors, and legal and regulatory mechanisms and operation, which would also serve to strengthen the productivity of the domestic private sector. The quality of the labour force must be improved, as well as that of the transport and telecommunications infrastructure. Moreover, the sustainability of a transformation strategy will depend on an equitable distribution of income, extensive land reform, and provision of safety nets for those who cannot produce because of old age or chronic sickness.

In contrast to the East Asian countries, many governments in Africa have tried to respond to the challenge posed by globalization in two ways.

The first response has been to embrace globalization uncritically as a development strategy. 'If you can't fight globalization, you may as well join it' is the slogan most used by aspiring countries such as South Africa. The state becomes a conduit to capital, as opposed to being an arbiter and enforcer of social equity. However, this strategy will do nothing to reduce dependence and marginalization. As the 1994 Mexican peso crisis and the 1997 financial meltdown in East Asia demonstrated, such a strategy is not sustainable politically or economically in the long run.

The second response by developing countries, including some in Africa, has been to resist indiscriminate market liberalization and 'coerced' integration into global markets. A handful of Third World countries have tried to defy openly the policies of the institutions of the world system, particularly the policies of structural adjustment and repressive reintegration. These feeble efforts were successfully resisted (or repulsed) by the World Bank and Western donors through cross-conditionalities and the threat of trade and aid sanctions. The agitators were brought back into line one by one, without defaulting a cent on the debts they owed to creditor nations.

This book charts the contours of a third option: *a guided embrace of globalization with a commitment to resist* through pre-emptive national or regional development strategies and economic policy coordination. African countries must be prepared to develop alternative formulations and conditions under which to engage themselves in beneficial global economic exchanges. Africa can and must compete in a rapidly changing global environment. To get to this stage, however, African governments must work hard to overcome a series of obstacles, such as renewing democracy and improving governance (Chapter 2); investing in African education (Chapter 3); revitalizing agricultural production and reducing poverty (Chapter 4); strengthening regional economic cooperation (Chapter 5); managing fast-growing cities and strengthening the urban–rural interface (Chapter 6); and preventing conflicts and building the foundations for peace (Chapter 7). Only when African governments are able to overcome these major hurdles can they realistically take advantage of the opportunities available in the global economy. Addressing these internal problems in a timely fashion is an absolute necessity if the dream of the 'African Renaissance' is to become a reality, and if Africa is to become a serious and respected player in the global political economy. The dream of the African Renaissance should have the following core elements: self-determination over economic and political development; unwavering dedication to the promotion and protection of all human rights; and a commitment to democracy and international solidarity.

CHAPTER 1

Africa and the Globalization Challenge

Globalization, a phenomenon brought about by technological revolutions, is an increasingly important dimension of international economic relations in terms of its implications for trade, productive investment and finance. In both mainstream media and corporate boardrooms, the rapid integration of national markets with one another is presented as the only means to bring unprecedented world prosperity and freedom in the post-Cold War era (Barnet and Cavanagh, 1994; Barber, 1994). This rapid interpenetration of economies is facilitated by a global drive for liberalization of markets and a rapid reduction of the commanding role of the state in national planning. The state itself, therefore, facilitates globalization, acting as an agent in the process.

By contrast, critics of globalization characterize it as the greatest threat to potential human development. The primary emphasis of globalization has been economic liberalization, with very little attention paid to the importance of international equality and solidarity. As the remote forces of globalization hobble governments and weaken the bonds of social solidarity, anger is growing among those whose existence is being threatened (Mittelman, 1996). Moreover, the rise of globalization has also seen a greater degree of economic differentiation among developing countries, a factor which has further undermined the ideals of South–South co-operation (Nhalapo, 2000: 19). Whatever the merits of these divergent points of view, it is clear that globalization is here to stay. Managing it successfully in order to promote human development and eradicate mass poverty remains the greatest challenge.

As Africa entered the twenty-first century, it faced mounting challenges. Widespread poverty, rapid population growth, ecological degradation, large-scale unemployment, fragile political institutions and weak public administration still hamper the continent's quest for economic and social transformation. The process of economic globalization further compounds these problems. While African governments increasingly recognize the importance of private initiatives for economic growth, they are being pressed to integrate their economies with world markets in the absence of a transparent trading system in which rules are respected by all. Competitiveness in the global economy will not be maintained or enhanced merely by the steady devaluation of state sovereignty or by erecting barriers against African products once they have penetrated other markets.

African uneasiness about globalization is not without justification. The continent is no stranger to globalization and its deleterious effects. More than any region in the world, Africa has paid a high price for the globalizing policies of rival capitalist powers as they have striven to expand the geographic bounds of capital. Starting with the slave trade in 1650, and continuing under colonial rule after the Berlin Conference of 1884, the continent was heavily drawn into the centres of capitalist accumulation, but always as a subordinate partner whose primary role was to contribute to the development of the metropolitan powers (Rodney, 1982; Fanon, 1963). The present globalization process, much like nineteenth-century globalization under colonialism, could again end up leaving the continent permanently marginalized unless African governments redirect their efforts to manage it successfully to their own advantage. For Africa, this is an absolute necessity if the continent wants to avoid a repeat of the degrading and inhumane treatment its peoples received from the colonial state and capitalist forces. The globalization of the twentieth and twenty-first centuries should not be allowed to leave behind the same terrible economic, political and social legacies.

The process of globalization is by no means complete. Most developing countries with favourable initial conditions – such as a good skill base, sound infrastructure, and solid research and development capacity – will gain more economically from the globalization process than countries with less favourable initial conditions. For example, East Asia has gained the most to date from globalization. The situation of sub-Saharan Africa appears less promising, however. This is because the basic institutional, infrastructural and human resources required for initiating meaningful transformation are missing. Strengthening the capacities of African countries to manage the cold currents of globalization in ways that promote democracy and human development, therefore, remains perhaps the most critical contemporary challenge. The main goal of this book is to explore ways to reverse Africa's marginalization and to examine key areas of reform that must be undertaken quickly as a precondition for Africa's successful insertion into the global economy. These broad-based political and sector-based reforms should serve as the building blocks for Africa's 'renaissance'.

A Continent in Despair

The 1980s and 1990s have been billed as Africa's 'lost development decades'. Many African countries experienced either stagnation or a reversal of the gains made in the 1960s and 1970s. Between 1965 and 1985, sub-Saharan Africa's GDP per capita increased less than 1 per cent a year on average. And, despite positive economic indicators in some parts of the continent since the mid-1990s, growth in the region slowed down after 1998, and poverty is increasing rather than stabilizing. In 2000, incomes for nearly half of the continent's 760 million people averaged less than 65 US cents a day. The average GNP per capita for the region in 2000 was US$492. But in twenty-four countries, GNP per capita was $350, with the lowest incomes found in Ethiopia ($100), the Democratic Republic of the Congo ($110), Burundi ($120) and Sierra Leone ($130) (World Bank, 2001). Reversing this decline is perhaps the most pressing challenge facing African governments and the international community in the coming years.

Since the early 1980s almost all African countries have embarked on a course of World Bank- and International Monetary Fund (IMF)-sponsored structural adjustment. This involved a reduced role for the state, macroeconomic stabilization, economic policy reforms and public sector restructuring with the goal of reviving economies and eradicating poverty. Greater macroeconomic stability and removal of large price distortions in key areas have no doubt made an important contribution to economic recovery in some countries. Fourteen countries have grown on average by 4 per cent a year during the 1990s, with rising annual incomes of 2–3 per cent and even higher, with another ten countries following close behind with growth rates above 3 per cent a year (Camdessus, 1998: 194; World Bank, 2001). A small but significant band of countries, such as Ghana, Uganda, Tanzania and Mozambique, which have embraced reforms in the face of significant erosion of the social position of their citizens, have sustained significant real per capita economic growth.

The slow but incremental economic growth in a handful of African countries in recent years, however, does not warrant euphoria or represent a solid indication of the beginning of an 'African Renaissance'. The supply response of farmers and of the nascent private sector has not been commensurate with the scope of the reforms and few countries in the region have successfully completed adjustment programmes with a return to sustained growth. According to the latest edition of *African Development Indicators 2001*, published by the World Bank, growth in the region slowed significantly after 1998, with average per capita GDP falling by almost 1 per cent in 1998–99 (World Bank, 2001). The Bank attributed the slowdown in growth to civil wars, poor governance in some countries, and serious external shocks such as the rapid hike in oil prices at the same time that export earnings from primary commodities collapsed. Moreover, the report warns that growth is below the 5 per cent annual level needed to prevent a rise in the numbers of poor people in the continent. Africa's recovery is still fragile and as vulnerable as ever to fluctuations in commodity prices, bad weather, sudden economic collapse in distant lands, or the outbreak of war.

Even in those cases that have shown increased economic success, something the international financial institutions take credit for, the causal links between economic recovery and the implementation of structural adjustment policies remain weak. Moreover, the moderate economic recovery has not been underpinned by greater investment or increased development assistance. The World Bank estimates that official aid to sub-Saharan Africa fell from $32 per head in 1990 to $19 by 1998 despite the evidence of effective development results in those countries with sound social and economic policies (World Bank, 2001). Aid in 1999, for example, stood at $10.8 billion compared to $17.9 billion in 1992, when development assistance to sub-Saharan Africa reached its highest-ever level. Even if the positive growth registered in a handful of African countries could be sustained throughout the next decade, the marginalization of the continent and the poverty of her peoples would not be reversed. At best, it would constitute some recovery of what has been lost in the past twenty years (UNCTAD, 2000a: 1).

Limited Progress in Human Development

Poor economic performance, exacerbated in many countries by political instability and violent conflict, has translated into limited progress in human development. Outside of Africa, it is often difficult to appreciate what the continent's economic crisis has meant in human terms. For the majority, economic recession means increasingly inadequate diets, income insufficient to clothe children and to buy fuel for heating and lighting homes, and mounting susceptibility to diseases. One out of four Africans has access to clean water. Infant mortality rates, already the highest in the world, will

Table 1.1 Human poverty in sub-Saharan Africa

	% of total pop.	'Low' human development
Illiterate adults (1998)	40.6	50.8
People lacking access to:		
health services (1990–95)*	47	
safe water (1990–98)	46	39
sanitation (1990–98)	52	59
Malnourished children under 5 (1990–98)	31	39
People not expected to live to age 40	34.6	31.9

* Adapted from UNDP, 1997: 27, Table 2.2.

Source: Adapted from Human Development Indicators, UNDP, 2000: 171.

continue to rise. Vulnerability to hunger will increase. In the year 2000, more than 300 million Africans – half of the continent's population – were estimated to be living in poverty (UNDP, 1997: 4).

Surveying human development on the African continent, a visible collapse can be noted in the following critical areas:

Decline in African education

Demand for education at all levels is outstripping the supply of educational facilities and resources. This has a particularly adverse effect on female enrolment rates, which remain low despite improvements over the past three decades. Female enrolment numbers decrease as girls move up the education ladder. Prospects for increasing the access of women and girls to education have been undermined by economic crisis, budgetary cuts, debt-servicing burdens, and unsustainable levels of military expenditure in many conflict-prone African countries.

With the introduction of structural adjustment programmes in the 1980s, the education sector experienced the sharpest cut in resource allocation. Average per capita education spending declined from $41 in 1980 to only

$26 in 1985 and was $25 in 1995. Meanwhile the proportion of foreign aid allocated to education declined from 17 per cent in 1975 to 9.8 per cent in 1990, increasing slightly to 10.7 per cent in 1994 (Manuh, 1998: 10). These cuts have resulted in a dramatic shortage of books and instructional materials. Teacher salaries have also fallen to desperately low levels. Attempts by governments to recover costs have simply driven parents to pull their children out of school.

Limited access to health services

Deprivation in health starts with lack of access to health care and other services. Despite considerable improvements over the past twenty-five years, nearly 50 per cent of the people in sub-Saharan Africa do not have access to adequate health care. In many countries, the exodus of doctors, nurses and technicians, compounded by declining or stagnating public expenditure on health, has culminated in a virtual collapse of the health infrastructure. There is only one doctor per 18,000 people, compared to one per 1,000 in Latin America and the Caribbean (UNDP, 1997: 28). In 1999, the infant mortality rate in Africa was estimated at 92 deaths per thousand. The average expenditure on the health sector in sub-Saharan Africa rarely exceeds about 5 per cent of GDP (UNECA, 1996: 65). Because the health policies of most member governments are yet to be grounded in preventive and primary health care, a large proportion of public expenditure on health, sometimes as high as 60 per cent, goes toward curative services in a few teaching hospitals. Similarly, the majority of nurses and other essential health workers are concentrated in a few urban areas. Rural communities are highly disadvantaged.

Health is also affected by lack of access to clear water and sanitation. Inadequate potable water, sanitation and waste disposal in urban and rural areas leave populations vulnerable to water-borne and other environmental diseases. Malaria, lung and other respiratory diseases are still major killers in Africa. High levels of maternal, child and infant mortality and low rates of immunization are symptomatic of the gross neglect of Africa's rural communities. Now HIV/AIDS poses the greatest threat to human development in the continent. At the current level of Africa's economic development, focusing on primary health care is the only viable strategy for achieving health for all in the foreseeable future.

HIV/AIDS as a development crisis

According to a report by UNAIDS, there are now 34.3 million people infected with HIV/AIDS worldwide. Of these, 24.5 million are in sub-

Saharan Africa. The current number of people infected in Africa is about three times higher than demographers predicted (UNAIDS, 2000). It is estimated that each day in Africa more than 5,000 people die from AIDS or HIV-related illness, with the figure expected to climb to almost 13,000 by 2005 (UNAIDS, 2000). About 13.2 million children (the vast majority in Africa) have lost either their mother or both parents to the disease. The area of greatest concern is Southern Africa. In the seven countries of Southern Africa, 20 per cent of adults are infected with HIV, which eventually causes AIDS and death in nearly all cases. South Africa has more HIV-infected people than any other country. The current estimate is about 4.2 million, or 20 per cent of the adult population. The nation with the highest prevalence is Botswana, where 36 per cent of adults are infected.

The AIDS epidemic is already measurably eroding economic development, educational attainment and child survival – all key measures of national health – in much of sub-Saharan Africa (Cheru, 2000: 519–35). The demographic effects will only get worse in the coming years. For example, demographers predict that two-thirds of Botswana's 15-year-olds will die of AIDS before the age of 50. It is estimated that 20 per cent of the adult population between the ages of 15 and 49 in Zambia is currently HIV positive (UNAIDS, 1997). In Zambia alone it is expected that more than 40 per cent of primary-school teachers will die of HIV/AIDS by 2005. Zambian Ministry of Education data shows that 680 teachers died in 1996, 624 in 1997, and 1,300 in the first ten months of 1998. Deaths in 1998 were equivalent to the loss of about two-thirds of the annual output of the newly trained teachers from all training institutions combined (Government of Zambia, 1997).

Already the disruptive effects of the epidemic are myriad. For example, in urban areas of Ivory Coast, households containing an adult with AIDS spent half as much on education and four times as much on health care as unaffected households. In a study of farm workers' families in Zimbabwe, 48 per cent of the 'AIDS orphans' of primary-school age had dropped out of school. The Central African Republic has only two-thirds of the primary schoolteachers it needs. From 1996 to 1998, as many teachers died as retired.

The negative effect of HIV/AIDS on macroeconomic performance through the loss of large numbers of the economically active population, the creation of unschooled children (as most AIDS orphans are likely to become) who will lack competitive skills in the job market, and the national cost of treating victims, make the disease Africa's number one development disaster.

The demographic challenge

The demographic explosion compounds the challenge of meeting basic needs and eradicating poverty. Of all the regions of the world, Africa has the youngest population, with roughly 50 per cent of its people below 15 years of age, compared with 20 per cent in the mature market economies. Africa's youthful demographic profile imposes a disadvantage, in terms of the heavy burden of young dependants. This taxes the already crowded and inadequate school systems and health services. It also manifests itself in massive rural-to-urban migration, fuelling an urban explosion.

The race between population growth and economic development is on, and its outcome will shape the economy and society of African countries in the twenty-first century. To attain reduction of poverty by half in 2015, according to a major consensus at the World Summit for Social Development, will require a 4 per cent annual reduction in the number of people living in poverty and an average economic growth rate of at least 7 per cent per annum. But Africa's economy recorded only an average of 3.3 per cent growth in 1998 and 1999, while the population grew at an average rate of about 2.4 per cent. The economic growth rate needs to be increased substantially at the same time as population growth rate is decreased.

A growing refugee problem

The African continent currently hosts about half of the world's displaced people. About 7 million Africans are directly categorized as refugees. This figure does not include many internally displaced persons forced to flee their homes, those unregistered in camps, or persons who have privately sought asylum in other countries. Twelve countries are responsible for over 6 million refugees, most of them from Eastern Africa. No one will ever know the exact number of displaced populations from recent conflicts in nations such as Sierra Leone, Guinea and the Democratic Republic of the Congo.

The primary causes of this phenomenal wave of human displacement are political in nature (ethnic conflicts, civil wars), or associated with drought and famine. While a great many refugees have been repatriated back to their countries following the end of conflicts, millions remain in refugee camps uncertain about their future. Only the ending of hostilities can provide permanent relief to people on the run.

The Causes of Africa's Economic, Social and Political Crisis

The reasons for the persistent decline of African economies are numerous and complex, emerging and transforming through historical and modern contexts. The interactions of both internal and external factors have made the prospect of managing Africa's development in a sustainable way more complex, as globalization ensures that destructive processes traverse borders as quickly as those that are constructive. For example, economic crises that have reduced living standards in many countries have in some cases catalysed social, civil and regional conflicts. The domestic and internal factors that underlie Africa's economic and social crisis will now be considered in turn, although it should be rememebered that they are not always readily separable.

Domestic factors

The internal reasons for Africa's economic problems vary, but include inherited colonial legacies and the transition from colonialism to undemocratic (and often corrupt), highly militarized neo-colonial regimes. These regimes have very often adopted development strategies that benefit a few urban elites at the expense of the majority. Among the indices of such failed strategies are the following:

Inhospitable political climate and inappropriate economic policy environment

The task of reviving African economies involves not only getting socio-economic policies right but also creating a hospitable political environment. The key elements of such an environment are political stability, rule-based political order mediated by an impartial and independent judiciary, and good governance, with particular emphasis on transparency and accountability (Ake, 1996). Poor governance – especially corruption, bureaucratic harassment and a lack of checks and balances – continues to hamper prospects for self-sustained growth in many parts of Africa (Sandbrook, 1986: 319–32; Callaghy, 1990: 257–66). Notwithstanding the recent shift in many African countries, democracy in Africa is still in profound trouble. The task of strengthening the key institutions of the state, such as the judiciary and the legislative and executive branches of government, remains problematic. Decentralization of decision-making to local structures and the meaningful involvement of civil society in the political process have not taken root.

Good governance and political stability enable governments to develop conducive economic policy frameworks. Experience from East Asia, Latin America and, increasingly, the successfully reforming countries in Africa shows that restoring and maintaining stable macroeconomic conditions – low inflation and manageable fiscal and external deficits – are prerequisites for achieving the increases in private investment and savings that are required to accelerate growth. In the case of Africa, the task of maintaining a conducive macroeconomic framework has consistently been held hostage to protracted political instability and the undemocratic nature of the state. Eliminating corruption and red tape, and establishing a transparent system in policy decisions and contractual arrangements remain challenges. Without a stable macroeconomic environment, the likely result is continued economic stagnation.

Persistent decline in agricultural productivity

Economic decline has been particularly evident in the productive sectors. Agriculture, the backbone of African economies, has done comparatively worse than other sectors. For the most part, there has been no Green Revolution in African agriculture. Between 1965 and 1980, agricultural growth rose only 2 per cent a year – less than the rate of population growth – and between 1981 and 1985, it fell 0.6 per cent a year. Compare that with agricultural growth of 3.2 per cent a year in East Asia, 2.5 per cent in South Asia, and 3.1 per cent in Latin America. Stagnant and declining yields in the face of rising population growth rates have led to a long-run decline in food production per capita. This has led to growing dependence on expensive imported food.

Poor performance in agriculture over the last three decades should not be attributed only to droughts and civil strife. The long-term decline in agricultural production and exports has been largely due to the pervasive and significant taxation of agriculture in most countries, combined with the crowding out of private investment and production activities through restrictions on market entry and controlled input and commodity pricing. Reforms to end the monopoly powers of parastatal corporations in agricultural marketing, importation and distribution of inputs, and exportation of produce should be continued. As an integral part of the region's export drive, the provision of agricultural and extension services to smallholder producers, the development of rural infrastructures, and the improvement of public services in rural areas are also important elements in any strategy to upgrade the agricultural sector in Africa (Bates, 1981; Weede, 1993: 25).

The implications of poor agricultural performance for African countries, however, go beyond weaknesses in food self-sufficiency, which is of critical importance in its own right. With the majority of people in the region deriving daily sustenance from agriculture, neither the modulation of absolute poverty nor attempts at its eradication to bring about substantial improvements in welfare can realistically be contemplated without the modernization of this sector. African governments must come to recognize and accept that without agricultural development there will be neither self-sufficiency in food nor the required resources for diversification into non-agricultural activities and the emergence of a strong service sector. Recovery and sustained growth of agriculture are preconditions for economic revival and social transformation.

Poor manufacturing performance

Poor performance in the manufacturing sector mirrors performance in agriculture. Growth rates in manufacturing, which started out strong in the 1960s, declined rapidly in the 1980s. Manufacturing industry's share of Africa's economic output rose only marginally, from 8.9 per cent in 1980 to 10.5 per cent in 1990 (United Nations, 1991b: 33). Only about 9 per cent of the labour force was employed in manufacturing in 1965; this remained virtually unchanged by 1990 (World Bank, 1989c: 223). In 1998, the manufacturing sector grew by 3.2 per cent, down from 3.8 per cent in 1997. The fall in investment was one of the reasons for the drop in the growth of the manufacturing sector (UNECA, 2000: 3). With persistent foreign-exchange shortages and low productivity, capacity utilization in manufacturing is below 20 per cent on average.

The major constraints impeding the full utilization of existing capacity and the rapid industrialization of the continent are well known, and relate to excessive dependence on external sources of technology, capital and know-how. The conspicuous lack of capital goods industry has rendered all industrial investment hostage to the availability of foreign exchange. Inward-looking import-substitution industrialization, which was widely promoted throughout the continent, was misguided, for it typically did not foster linkages between mass consumption and mass production. Ironically, this made these countries even more dependent on external sources of machinery, parts and raw materials than they had been hitherto. Even manufacturing industries such as textiles and food processing, where the backward linkage with the domestic economy is very well advanced, have remained dependent on critical and vital imports to complete their production processes.

The challenge to African policymakers lies in reducing the structural dependence of African economies on external resources as the engine of development. And this they can do through intensive mobilization of domestic resources, diversification of the economic base and enhancement of foreign exchange earning capacity.

Inadequate skills base

With the implementation of structural adjustment programmes since 1980, governments across the continent have cut resources for education, resulting in an insufficient supply of books and materials, and inadequate infrastructure. Teacher salaries have also fallen to desperately low levels. These reductions have contributed to low educational quality. Most alarmingly, an outcome of the economic and political crisis has been the dramatic growth in the brain drain involving middle- and high-level manpower that Africa needs for its recovery and development. According to the UN Economic Commission for Africa, some 27,000 African intellectuals emigrated to developed countries between 1960 and 1975. Between 1985 and 1990 the number jumped to 60,000, and has averaged 20,000 annually ever since.[1] The unprecedented flight of skilled Africans has enormous impact on the functioning of the institutions of higher learning, industry, government and enterprises. The African Renaissance cannot be realized in an environment of depleting skill levels and the loss of the professional class (Africa Institute of South Africa, 2000). Reversing this trend is a precondition for a well-functioning society.

Lack of peace and stability

The last decade of the twentieth century was marred by unprecedented levels of political violence amidst ongoing and emerging crises in the Third World. The African continent has in particular been affected by protracted conflicts claiming the lives of millions of civilians. While the roots of these conflicts date back to the colonial period, they were reinforced by the Cold War machinations of both East and West. With the end of the Cold War, however, the ethnic pieces put together by colonial glue and reinforced by the old world order are now pulling apart and reasserting their autonomy. The persistence of civil strife continues systematically to divert scarce national resources from human development (United Nations, 1997a). As a result, infrastructure – schools, hospitals, roads and communication networks – which takes decades to build is wantonly destroyed. Food production and marketing systems are also a common casualty. Some of the most talented and skilled people are forced to seek their livelihood in more favourable environments in other countries.

Exogenous factors

The world economy has not been kind to Africa. The current monetary, trade and investment regimes reward the developed countries disproportionately and create unmet human needs in the underdeveloped countries. Despite this fact, however, Africa is being advised by the key institutions of the world system to export its way out of poverty by actively participating in global trade. The prescriptions offered are based on a positive scenario that world trade will grow, commodity prices will stabilize, and protectionist barriers will not be erected by the Western powers. The reality has been quite different, as described below.

Deteriorating terms of trade

At the heart of Africa's trade crisis has been a protracted depression in world commodity markets. The rates at which goods are exchanged, or the terms of trade, have not favoured Africa, where most of the region's economies failed to diversify their export base and continue to rely on one or two commodities. A survey carried out by the UN Economic Commission for Africa (UNECA) in 1995 indicates that forty African countries derive more than 70 per cent of their export earnings from the sale of commodities (UNECA, 1996).

Meanwhile, exports of agricultural products became even more concentrated. Nine major commodities accounted for 76 per cent of the region's agricultural exports in the 1980s – up from 70 per cent in 1960. Countries elsewhere, by contrast, diversified their export base and increased their shares in world exports of primary commodities. The protracted depression in world commodity markets had a devastating impact on African economies. During the 1980s, prices for most commodities fell dramatically, in some cases to their lowest levels in real terms since the Great Depression, while import prices continued to rise (Brown and Tiffen, 1992). This caused a sharp deterioration in Africa's terms of trade; the purchasing power of the region's exports has fallen by some 50 per cent since the early 1980s. As a result, Africa's share of developing country exports fell from 12 per cent in 1961 to 5.8 per cent in 1990 (IMF, 1991: 120–21; UNDP, 1997). Other estimates maintain that Africa's terms of trade fell by more than one-third of their value in the period 1977–93, as opposed to other developing countries, where they fell 20 per cent during the same period (UNCTAD, 2000a: 10).

The regional average obscures the marked deterioration suffered by individual countries. In 1986, for example, coffee provided Uganda with $365 million in foreign-exchange earnings and financed about 70 per cent

Table 1.2 World primary commodity prices, 1996–2000 (% change over previous year)

Commodity	1996	1997	1998	1999	2000
All commodities	−4.2	0	−13.0	−14.2	−1.0
Coffee	−19.1	54.7			
Cocoa	1.2	11.2	3.7	−32.1	−.08
Tea		35.1	4.3	−7.0	9.1
Sugar	−9.9	−4.9	−21.2	−30.0	0.02
Beef	−6.4	4.0	−7.0	6.1	1.3
Bananas	7.5	4.3	−3.1	−9.9	24.3
Hides and skins	−23.7	−19.8	−22.7	−27.6	−0.09
Cotton	−14.8	−8.9	−8.3	−22.9	36.7
Tobacco	15.6	15.6	−5.5	−7.0	−3.4
Rubber	−11.9	−28.3	−29.8	−12.6	7.8
Iron ore	6.0	1.1	2.8	−9.2	2.6
Copper	−21.8	−0.08	−27.3	−4.9	−4.9

Source: Adapted from UNCTAD, 2000: 34.

of its imports. By 1991, it yielded only $115 million, and financed less than a quarter of imports. Overall, the slump in commodity prices cost Africa $50 billion in lost earnings between 1986 and 1990 – more than twice the amount the region received in aid.

The persistent decline of commodity prices, despite rapid expansion in production, is influenced by many factors. Many primary resource products are facing mounting competition from substitutes such as synthetics for cotton, aluminium for copper, and sugar beet and corn syrup for cane sugar. Moreover, the Common Agricultural Policy of the European Union restricts market access to African agricultural products. The break-up of the Soviet Union, a major market for African products, is also partly to blame for the commodity glut (Wall, 1992: 14–19).

Another factor contributing to the fall in prices is the oversupply of commodity production as countries try to make up for price declines by producing even more. This, in turn, contributed to oversupply and a further fall in prices. Yet the World Bank, which through its structural adjustment programmes has been advising African countries to export their way out of the crisis, expects no significant upturn, in real terms, in the foreseeable future (Laishley, 1992: 8). At the same time, discriminatory tariffs continue to grow while market access for African products remains limited. Neither commodity price stabilization agreements nor assistance in diversifying agricultural export bases have been forthcoming.

Notwithstanding falling prices and market shares, African economies have not made the necessary switch from reliance upon primary export commodities. One reason is that state marketing boards are mandated to conduct foreign trade at ridiculously low prices (even at a loss) simply to acquire the necessary foreign exchange to service large foreign debt and pay for essential imports. This issue is taken up next.

Uneven pattern in foreign direct investment flows

One of the key elements of the new world economy is the volume of foreign direct investment (FDI), which has now replaced exports as the fastest growing component. Foreign direct investment has overtaken official development finance (ODF) transfers as a channel of development resources. According to UNCTAD's *World Investment Report 2000*, foreign direct investment by transnational corporations was due to surpass one trillion dollars in 1999 (UNCTAD, 2000c). The growth in the number of cross-border mergers and acquisitions, driven by technological and competitive forces, has contributed significantly to the rise of FDI. With transnational corporations (TNCs) now numbering over 35,000 with more than 150,000 foreign affiliates, their impact on the world economy is staggering (United Nations, 1991c). In the present global economy, attracting significant flows of FDI and stimulating domestic private investment are of crucial importance to sustained recovery and growth in Africa.

Unfortunately the growth in FDI has not been evenly distributed across continents. The European Union (EU), the United States and Japan (referred to as the Triad) now receive more than three-fifths of total investment flows. In developed countries, FDI rose to $636 billion in 1999 (from $481 billion in 1998), while FDI to developing countries increased to $208 billion (from $179 billion in 1998) (UNCTAD, 2000c). FDI is the largest source of external financing for many developing countries, which have found it to be more stable, particularly during financial crises, than portfolio investment and bank lending. As investment becomes concentrated among these powers, few developing countries benefit, other than some of the NICs and second-tier countries, where there exist a strong developmental state, an educated workforce and good infrastructure. The solidification of investment patterns that exclude Africa means there will

Table 1.3 Foreign direct investment flow by region, 1997–2000 (US$ billion)

Net private capital flows*	1997	1998	1999	2000
Africa/Middle East	15	8	10	12
Asia/Pacific	67	4	40	59
Europe	76	37	34	35
Latin America	108	88	67	92
Total	148	75	81	71
Net direct investment	139	143	150	153
Net portfolio investment	53	9	23	30
Other net investment	−44	−77	−93	−113
Africa	17	12	15	16
Net direct investment	7	5	10	9
Net portfolio investment	4	4	4	3
Other net investment	6	2	1	4

* Remittances and profits not included. First four rows are estimates of the Institute for International Finance; the remainder are estimates of the International Monetary Fund.

Source: Adapted from UNCTAD 2000b: 43.

be little hope for most African nations to attract foreign investment (UNECA, 1991; UNCTAD, 1995).

Despite the fact that many African countries have liberalized their economies and enacted laws to attract foreign private capital, actual FDI inflows have been negligible. FDI flows to the continent rose to $10 billion in 1999 from $8 billion in 1998. This was in line with the faster growth rate generally experienced by the continent during the decade. Investments by transnational corporations in Africa are still only 1.2 per cent of global FDI flows and 5 per cent of total FDI into all developing countries. About 70 per cent of FDI in Africa in 1999 was concentrated in only five countries – Angola, Egypt, Morocco, Nigeria and South Africa. Many African countries are not trusted as the destination for foreign investment because of potential political instability, corruption and the lack of transparent legal systems. Decrepit transport and telecommunications infrastructure, an underdeveloped monetary and banking system, and the massive brain drain further add to the misperception about doing business in Africa. Attempts to reverse these negative factors are moving very slowly.

The real challenge for Africa lies ahead: integration into the global economy, including integration into the regional or global production networks of transnational corporations. Only then will the continent become a more prominent player in the world market and benefit more from FDI. To reverse the present negative trend, governments must ensure that the needed human capital and institutional structures are in place to carry out the required reforms. Investment in information technology and intellectual capital formation is critical if Africa is to take advantage of the opportunities provided by globalization. Investment in information technology is also important for expanding the information base on democratization. In addition, policies need to be consistent, credible, predictable and transparent – that is, there needs to be good governance.

Unsustainable level of external debt

Compounding Africa's economic woes is its ever-growing external debt, which stood at $341 billion in late 1996. Of this, sub-Saharan Africa owes $167 billion. The North African countries owe the rest (United Nations, 1997: 274). The debt burden remains heavy, accounting for 69 per cent of regional GDP. Actual debt service, which rose from $25.7 billion in 1990 to $26.3 billion in 1996 (close to $10 billion for sub-Saharan countries), absorbed 27.5 per cent of export earnings. This indebtedness is crushing all possibilities for economic growth by diverting scarce resources needed for clinics, schools, and infrastructure and job-creation schemes to the payment of debt.

The problem of indebtedness is especially severe for sub-Saharan African countries. Of the thirty-two countries classified by the World Bank as severely indebted low-income countries, twenty-five are in sub-Saharan Africa. The overall debt of these countries stood at just under $211 billion in 1994, four times higher than in 1980. Over the period 1986–96, Africa paid out a total of $297 billion in debt servicing, $15 billion more than it received in new loans. Over this same period debt servicing to institutions like the World Bank and IMF continued to climb. The IBRD wing of the Bank, along with the IMF, accounted for $28 billion of the region's debt servicing between 1983 and 1994, over $9 billion more than the region received in new loans from these two agencies. The IMF alone has taken almost $5 billion more out of the region than it has provided in new loans over the same period.

In retrospect, Africa was drawn into the debt crisis in entirely unjustified ways. The three most obvious problems were the use to which borrowed money was put, the variable (fluctuating) rate at which most foreign debt was contracted during the 1970s, and the loaning of monies to undemocratic and unaccountable regimes. While some of the debt originated in the need to cope with the 1973 increase in global oil prices, much of the rest was unnecessary, and destined for white-elephant projects, arms expenditures and the import of luxury goods. The creditor countries and institutions that lend the money are obviously at fault for 'loan-pushing'. Some of the money was understood to be lining the pockets of corrupt African elites, but international banks, the World Bank and the IMF ignored the moral implications of lending to a Mobutu or, for that matter, a P.W. Botha.

Moreover, during the initial rise in African foreign debt, through most of the 1970s, the interest rates on dollar-denominated loans were negative in real terms. Then in 1979, the interest payments suddenly increased dramatically when the US Federal Reserve implemented a 'monetarist' (high interest rate) policy. From negative rates in the 1970s, inflation-adjusted interest rates shot up to 5 per cent, 2 per cent above the average annual growth of the world economy (3 per cent) during the 1980s. A related issue was the 'collateral' – also known as security – on such loans. Such security was thought not to be an issue, since sovereign countries in the post-war era were not supposed to default. To this end, the IMF was used during the first part of the 1980s as a vehicle for ensuring African countries repaid Northern commercial bank loans. In exchange for structural adjustment loans, countries were expected to implement IMF-mandated policy reforms, including the liberalization of the domestic trade regime, relaxation of foreign exchange controls, the privatization of basic services, and an end to social subsidies.

Extensive default by African countries has been prevented only by repeated rescheduling operations, in which official creditors, meeting in the Paris Club, have allowed interest and future debt charges to accumulate by deferral payments. More than thirty African governments have been forced to reschedule, many of them repeatedly. However, these merry-go-round exercises have served to fuel rather than alleviate the debt crisis, by contributing to the unsustainable build-up of arrears. Over 40 per cent of the non-concessional debt owed by sub-Saharan Africa to the industrialized countries represents deferred interest payments capitalized by the Paris Club and added to the total debt stock.

Significant debt reduction is necessary for recovery and resumption of growth in Africa. Even for countries not classified as severely indebted, the debt overhang poses a tremendous constraint to growth. Given the variations in the creditor composition of Africa's debt, there is a growing consensus that reducing African debt to sustainable servicing levels will require action by all major creditor sources.

Externalization of decision-making and loss of sovereignty

It has been almost two decades since the widespread application of structural adjustment programmes (SAPs) across the Third World. Enough evaluations have been done to assess their effectiveness on overall social and economic development. A careful review of the literature points to the conclusion that, while there are significant gains to be derived from liberalization of markets as a result of structural adjustment programmes, such reforms do not provide the best outcome for all. The experience of the last twenty years in Africa and Latin America shows that structural adjustment policies are not consistent with long-term development goals. The evidence challenges the assertion by the World Bank and the IMF that structural adjustment policies alleviate poverty and strengthen democracy.

Between 1980 and 1989 alone, thirty-six sub-Saharan African countries initiated 241 structural adjustment programmes. Two decades later, the role of the state in Africa has been significantly curtailed, the dominance of market forces set in place, and economies opened to external competition. However, substantial economic turnaround has not occurred in any of the African countries that implemented structural adjustment programmes. To the contrary: living standards for the majority of Africans have declined and investment in the productive sectors of the economy has dwindled. Budget cuts, often targeted at the poorest segment of the population, depress economies' effective demand, leading to declining growth. Imposed user fees have led to a decline in utilization rates for health and education services, which in turn have reduced 'human capital formation' (Cornia et al., 1987; Cheru, 1989; Sparr, 1994).

The most pernicious aspect of structural adjustment has been the curtailing of the autonomy of African states to guide their countries' development. While market-oriented reforms are arguably necessary and beneficial, donor support for African economic reform efforts has gone far beyond what was initially envisioned. The IMF and the World Bank have de facto usurped the national sovereignty of African countries as they have assumed increasingly a central role in the formulation of national economic policies. The cross-conditionality of bilateral donors, which links assistance to acceptance of IMF programmes, further squeezes African governments to surrender on the economic planning front. As the late Claude Ake succinctly put it:

> When a people must be developed not by themselves but by others, development becomes a benevolence that is largely insensitive to social needs. In Africa, one might say, what currently prevails is development against the people – not of them or for them. The African variet[ies] of structural adjustment break down social consensus, cause violent conflict, anxiety and deep despair, and sometimes cause premature death on a large scale, especially among children. These grim notions of policy reform can be inflicted only by people who do not belong to the adjusting society or by those who are immune to the impact of the reform. (Ake, 1996: 118–19)

This unusually high level of external intervention in the policy decisions of African countries since the early 1980s has meant that African states are increasingly more accountable to foreign creditor nations and international financial institutions than to their own people. In turn, the diminished power of African states decreases their willingness and ability to cope with an expanding social crisis at home. African governments have been unable to take practical measures to alleviate the high unemployment and declining living standards because they are bound by strict spending curbs imposed through externally mandated reform measures.

Consider the role of privatization, a cornerstone of structural adjustment. In many African countries, privatization measures have often not distinguished which state enterprises are strategic in nature. Moreover, the privatization process has too often been accompanied by corruption and foreign takeover of domestic industry, with scant regard for maintaining local employment or production levels (Craig, 2000: 357–66). At the same time, privatization promoted by international financial institutions (IFIs) was not accompanied by consideration of how state agencies could supply services that enhanced 'public goods' – for example, the positive effect of water supply on public health, environmental protection, local economic activity and gender equality. All state services were reduced to mere commodities, requiring full cost-recovery and elimination of subsidies.

The process of neoliberal economic restructuring has intensified polarization between classes and ethnic groups, destroying the possibilities of internal transformation as emphasis is placed on external capital and markets as sources of growth (Mengisteab, 1997: 115; Rodrik, 2001: 55–62). The problems facing leaders are further compounded by the resentment and rebelliousness they provoke in the governed. Many Africans have a sense of uncertainty and a feeling of futility. The losers in global restructuring then try to reassert themselves through organized resistance (Cheru, 1989; Beckman, 1989: 83–105). In some countries, the immediate public response is withdrawal from the political process; in others, there is outrage and criticism. As antagonism increases, energies and efforts towards development are dissipated and leadership is at risk of losing credibility (Barber, 1994).

In the face of widespread public and official resistance to regressive adjustment, the World Bank and its allies held fast, insisting that not only are SAPs working but also that they are a necessary element of long-term transformation. On 12 March 1994, the World Bank released a progress report on Africa, *Adjustment in Africa: Reforms, Results and the Road Ahead*, to defend its failed policy of structural adjustment (World Bank, 1994a). By manipulating selective data of cross-country analysis, and without revealing the significant objection to the report's conclusion from internal Bank economists, the Bank claimed that African countries that implemented SAPs in the 1980s experienced greater positive growth than those that did not. Two years earlier, a draft World Bank study, entitled 'Why Structural Adjustment Has Not Succeeded in Sub-Saharan Africa', stated: 'World Bank adjustment lending has not significantly affected growth and has contributed to a statistically significant drop in investment ratios.'[2] Of the six countries the Bank put forward as adjustment 'successes' – Ghana, the United Republic of Tanzania, the Gambia, Burkina Faso, Nigeria and Zimbabwe – four had deteriorating rates of investment and two had negative GDP growth rates during their respective adjustment periods.

One of the most blatant exaggerations about 'Africa's Renaissance' comes from the IMF. In a paper entitled *Africa: Is This the Turning Point?*, co-authored by Stanley Fisher, the IMF's first deputy managing director, the Fund loudly proclaimed that the economic situation in sub-Saharan Africa had markedly improved in the last few years. It attributed this mainly to improved macroeconomic and structural policies, which the countries implemented under the Fund's guidance. The authors of the report further argued that changes in the external environment in the 1990s, such as increasing globalization and declining official development assistance, have indeed brought sub-Saharan Africa to a turning point. They go on to catalogue a series of institutional and capacity problems that are hampering Africa's capacity to navigate the cold currents of globalization (Fisher et al., 1998).

The Fund's glowing assessment of Africa's reforms has been challenged by a draft report prepared by a team of external evaluators hired by the Fund's Executive Board in 1996. In the report, entitled 'Distilling the Lessons from the ESAF Reviews', the external evaluation team, headed by former Ghanaian finance minister Kwesi Botchway – hardly a leftist – concludes that while ESAF-supported economic reforms generally have positive effects on growth and income distribution, they do entail temporary costs for certain segments of the population (IMF, 1998). The report calls for appropriate compensatory measures to be built into programme design to protect such groups, including the provision of well-targeted assistance and the allocation of adequate resources for the social sector. In addition, the report concludes that, in implementing ESAF, the IMF failed to reinforce strategies to foster country ownership, particularly with a view to assessing the social impact of the reform programme. As the evaluators point out, attention to fostering ownership and to the social impact of reform could help policymakers build domestic consensus in favour of important but difficult reform measures. The report emphasizes the need by the IMF to engage in intensive and informal dialogue with a country's political leadership to understand that country's political constraints and possibilities.

While the reintegration of the African continent into the world economy should not be ignored, it is only achievable if infrastructure is upgraded, trade and financial linkages are restructured, and trading patterns and products are diversified. More importantly, national governments must have the autonomy to guide their countries' development independently and without heavy-handed intervention by the institutions of the world system. Africa's ability to exploit the growing trade and investment opportunities that exist in the world economy is hampered by poor transport and communication systems, a shortage of skilled people, and weak and fragile institutions. These are often made worse by the restrictive trade policies of donor governments, which forbid the easy entry of African products into the markets of the developed countries (Mittelman, 1996). Simply advising African countries to open their economies to outside competition is not a sufficient condition for beneficial integration into the world economy (Mengisteab, 1997: 112–13).

The G7, the HIPC debt relief initiative and the politics of appeasement

After many years of persistent political pressure by a global coalition of NGOs and civil society organizations to cancel the debts owed by many poor countries, the Bretton Woods institutions were finally pressed to recognize the need to address the issue of poor country debts, and approved the Heavily Indebted Poor Countries (HIPC) initiative in the autumn of 1996. The World Bank and the IMF identified forty-one countries as eligible for the HIPC initiative. Under HIPC–1, a country only receives debt relief after jumping two hurdles. First, it must have completed six years of structural adjustment under the IMF's Enhanced Structural Adjustment Facility (ESAF). Second, debt relief itself is a two-step process:

a decision is taken to grant relief, subject to meeting certain additional conditions; when these are met, the debt is actually cancelled.

Less than three years later, however, the IMF and the World Bank concluded at their 1999 spring meeting that the HIPC initiative (HIPC–1) had major shortcomings and there was a need for more substantive steps to address the debt problem. Not surprisingly, only three countries have received actual debt relief by 1999 – Uganda and Bolivia in April and September 1998 respectively, and Mozambique in mid-1999 – almost three years after the programme had started. Four others – Mali, Côte d'Ivoire, Guyana and Burkina Faso – were close to fulfilling the required conditions at the end of 1999. The stringent qualification criteria simply excluded many eligible indebted countries from requesting debt relief (Cheru, 2001).

HIPC–1 and the post-Cologne consensus: old wine in a new bottle?

At the G7 meeting in Cologne in June 1999, the leaders of the industrialized countries announced a major debt reduction initiative that went far beyond what was discussed during the spring meeting of the IMF and the World Bank in Washington. The Cologne Initiative proposed incremental but noteworthy steps towards improving the HIPC Initiative. Chief among these are the proposal to grant larger reductions of the total accumulated debt, quicker reductions in debt service payments, and placing poverty reduction at the heart of an enhanced HIPC (HIPC–2) framework. In launching the enhanced HIPC, a total of $90 billion in debt service was promised for thirty-three countries, with the cost to creditors estimated at just $27 billion, primarily due to heavy discounting of the loans and the advantage of purchasing the debt today as opposed to having it accrue interest over the length of the loan (IMF/IDA, 2000a).

By the time of the IMF/World Bank Annual Meeting in Prague in September 2000, however, there was little substantive progress to report on debt relief under the Cologne Initiative. The incremental, step-by-step approach has delivered some relief ($20 billion out of a total of $90 billion) to only nine countries and has failed to provide relief at the pace and depth required (IMF/IDA, 2000b: 6). In the specific case of sub-Saharan Africa, twenty-two countries had qualified for debt relief by December 2000. However, only $750 million in actual debt relief will be granted each year. At the same time, these countries will be paying $500 million to the international financial institutions alone.

The key impediment to granting deeper debt relief for African countries has been the failure of the G7 governments to dedicate sufficient resources to the HIPC Trust Fund. Both multilateral and bilateral creditors were expected to provide the estimated $28 billion (in net present-value terms) to finance the debt relief programme. Of this amount, four multilateral creditors – the World Bank, the IMF, the African Development Bank and the Inter-American Development Bank – were expected to provide about $14 billion; bilaterals about $13.2 billion; and commercial creditors the rest (Cheru, 2001: 4). However, both multilateral and smaller bilateral creditors are having difficulty securing the funds to cover the cost of their share of financing the HIPC Trust Fund. The rules governing the African Development Bank and the Inter-American Development Bank set a ceiling on the amount of their resources that can be allotted for debt relief purposes for fear of undermining their financial integrity (US General Accounting Office, 2000). Commitments from bilateral creditors have mostly come from Paris Club creditors, many of whom have written off a significant amount of bilateral debt beyond their assistance under HIPC. Parliaments and legislative bodies in the respective bilateral creditor nations have been reluctant to dedicate more funds for debt relief above and beyond bilateral debt relief.

The second impediment has been excessive conditionality for countries to qualify for debt relief. Eligibility for debt relief under the enhanced HIPC is conditional upon 'good performance' in the implementation of IMF and World Bank enhanced structural adjustment programmes (now renamed as the Poverty Reduction and Growth Facility – PRGF) for a period of three years instead of six years under the original HIPC. Having reached the 'decision point' after three years of good economic performance, the country must then demonstrate that its debt servicing is unsustainable, following designated threshold value with respect to the ratio of debt to exports, and the ratio of debt to fiscal revenues.[3] If a country finally qualifies for relief, its debt servicing is brought down to what is deemed within the terms of the initiative to be a sustainable level, but only after reaching the 'completion point', or a further three-year waiting period. However, efforts to comply often take many months or even years and cost applicants scarce resources to develop (Sachs, 2000b). This less than generous arrangement still leaves the country deflecting a sizeable portion of its scarce foreign exchange into debt servicing for an indefinite period of time.

Finally, the enhanced HIPC initiative as it is currently constituted is inadequate since it does not address debts that are owed to non-Paris Club creditors and that have not been rescheduled or serviced for a long period. Consequently, the debt sustainability ratio for these debtor countries is misleading, since the actual debt situation is worse than is apparent. This is because their balance-of-payments reserve accounts include money that should have been paid out to non-Paris Club creditors. In addition, the current approach does not address the relatively little-known problem of intra-HIPC debts, for which no mechanism for resolution exists. For example, Tanzania is a creditor with exposure to Uganda. Similarly, Costa Rica and Guatemala have loans outstanding to Nicaragua. The debts owed by these debtor countries to their neighbours are recorded as part of their respective balance-of-payments reserves, inflating the reserve position of each of these debtor countries. It is more than likely that many HIPC countries with debts to non-Paris Club creditors will fall right back into 'coma' since the current approach is silent on how to address non-Paris Club debts.

The New Protectionism in the Era of Free Trade

Africa's position in the new global economy is unique, for it is at once integrated into and marginalized from that structure. This section examines the theoretical assumptions and the institutional structures that underpin the changing nature of North–South relations and, in particular, the aid and trade regimes through which African development is regulated. Particular attention is paid to the last Uruguay Round of trade negotiations; the new EU–ACP Partnership agreement, which replaced the Lomé Convention; and the Clinton Initiative on Africa. While the central aim of these initiatives is to encourage African countries to open up their markets to outside competition, they do not address themselves to the critical need of opening up Western markets to all products from the world's poorest countries. Moreover, these initiatives fail to address many issues that are crucial to improving the plight of African countries: debt relief, an end to policies that subsidize rich Western farmers, and the removal of trade obstacles in the few sectors – such as textiles and apparel – where Third World products can compete effectively.

The Uruguay Round

The Final Act of the Uruguay Round of multilateral trade negotiations, which entered into force on 1 January 1995, poses the greatest challenge for the continent. While the new trade regime brings significant reductions in the costs of goods and services throughout the world, the benefits will not accrue to all countries equally. The least developed countries start off with challenging handicaps: inadequate productive and entrepreneurial skills base, inadequate science and technology infrastructure, and weak government institutions. Furthermore, the Uruguay Round will have an overall negative impact on Africa's trade prospects, removing trade concessions previously granted by the European Union.

Apart from the liberalization of trade in manufacturing, the main objective of previous rounds, the Uruguay Round brought trade in agriculture and textiles within WTO rules and disciplines. The agreement embraced a number of new issues: services, trade-related investment measures (TRIMs), and trade-related aspects of intellectual property (TRIPs), which had not been covered in previous GATT rounds. The last round established a timetable to phase out, over a ten-year period, the Multi-fibre Arrangement (MFA) that has governed OECD trade in textiles and clothing for three decades.

Many GATT provisions have ambivalent effects when applied to Africa. The trade-related investment measures, for example, are designed to make foreign investment more attractive to foreigners, an objective widely shared by both sides. At the same time, some of the TRIMs provisions may be viewed as an affront to national sovereignty and an unwarranted effort to repeal local legislation designed to provide protection or subsidy to local firms. Thus, while African countries may open their economies more widely to imports and investments from other countries, they may lack the capacity to take advantage of new opportunities for export in sectors beyond primary commodities unless they deepen their technological base and improve the competitiveness of local firms. However, the TRIMs agreement restricts the right of countries to develop certain measures to increase the contribution of industries to their national development (such as those designed to encourage the use of local materials in manufacture or to export a fixed proportion of output) (Raghavan, 1991).

Africa's access to beneficial technology is further blocked by the trade-related intellectual property rights agreement, which sets global rules on patents, copyrights and licensing. Except for the short grace period provided for developing countries, these obligations would be at the same level as those for the industrialized countries. African countries would also have to adopt strict domestic enforcement legislation to ensure full compliance, in default of which they could face sanctions including the withdrawal of concessions in the area of trade in goods. Noteworthy is the TRIPs effect on access to medicines, making health a market commodity (Cosbey, 1998: 12–15). The WTO permits compulsory licensing and parallel importing of specific drugs, which opens the door to cheaper access. With US government support, pharmaceutical corporations fought South Africa's efforts to provide affordable HIV/AIDS medications. Besides medicine, farmers are also concerned about the patenting of plants that could be necessary for their future production and food security. They want to see that indigenous knowledge is not 'stolen' away by patent restrictions.

Of all the issues addressed in the last Uruguay Round negotiations, agricultural reform was the key area of concern for many developing countries, particularly in Africa (Watkins, 1991: 38–50). Among other things, the treaty requires countries to cut export subsidies to farmers. In consequence, African countries may find it more difficult to provide needed support for their agricultural sectors (in the form of trade restrictions such as quotas and tariffs) without violating GATT rules. Moreover, African countries could become victims of 'dumping', such as occurred when European C-grade beef entered the South African market, undermining Namibian beef exports to South Africa. In the meantime, African countries face increased protection in their export markets through 'contingent' protection mechanisms such as sanitary and phytosanitary measures, technical barriers to trade, anti-dumping and safeguard measures. These instruments are being used as substitutes for the old-fashioned protection. The cost of abiding by the requirements of these measures is very high, as firms are expected to restructure their production and distribution infrastructure.

On the other hand, a number of African countries that grow and export commodities stand to gain from increased agricultural export – for example, beef. This will only occur if they can overcome the more stringent regulations on phytosanitary standards which are part of the new agreement. These gains must be balanced, however, against the erosion of marginal preference that African countries have enjoyed under the Lomé Convention (Ritchie, 1990). For example, Tanzania and Mauritius export almost 90 per cent of their sugar exports to the European Union under the Sugar Protocol. Similarly, Botswana and Zimbabwe export large volumes of beef to the European Community under the Beef Protocol. The process was completed in April 2000 with the signing of a new post-Lomé agreement between the European Union and the African, Caribbean and Pacific (ACP) countries, which officially ended preferential treatment to the ACP countries (Watkins, 1991: 44).

Hegemonic bilateralism: the Clinton Initiative on Africa

The Clinton administration proposed the Partnership for Promoting Economic Growth and Opportunity Act in 1997. The Partnership Initiative (the African Economic Growth and Opportunity Act), which was voted into a law in April 1999 by the US Congress, is essentially no different from the Reagan administration's Caribbean Basin Initiative Plan. Reciprocal free-trade arrangements are central to the new trade agreement. Sub-Saharan African countries will be able to sell raw materials and light manufactured products to the USA with little or no duty. In return, African countries will have to privatize industry, cut corporate taxes, open their economies to foreign goods and pursue economic reforms similar to those required by the World Bank and the International Monetary Fund. The economic reforms should include strict budgetary and tax controls that will protect private property, reduction of the state's participation in the economy, support for the growth of the private sector, and removal of restrictions on foreign investment.

Besides requiring massive liberalization, the trade act requires beneficiaries to guarantee intellectual property rights, protect foreign investment, and ensure internationally recognized workers' rights, as well as adhering to US-style democratic governance. The trade agreement also provides for technical assistance to strengthen trade and investment, and establishes a $500 million facility in equity and infrastructural funds for Africa (Buhera, 2000).

While the Clinton Initiative appears positive on the surface, it will mostly benefit US corporate interests. It will provide new markets for US products and services, as well as investment opportunities for US companies seeking cheap raw materials, cheap labour reserves and markets for manufactured products. The market access offered by the USA to African products, in turn, will have no negative impact on the US economy. The US Congress concluded that, given the 'lack of competitiveness of sub-Saharan Africa in the global market, and its limited capacity to manufacture and export textiles and apparel, African countries' expanded access to the US market will not represent a threat to the United States workers, consumers or manufacturers'.

The EU–ACP post-Lomé trade agreement

In February 2000, the European Union and Ministers of the seventy-one African, Caribbean and Pacific countries concluded a new twenty-year Partnership Agreement that replaced the Lomé Convention. The Agreement effectively scraps the Lomé concessions in favour of liberal principles of open markets and global competitiveness. The EU is now characterized by a marked shift from aid to trade as the main instrument of cooperation. Unlike the original Lomé Convention, which was underpinned by the value of North–South solidarity in the context of decolonization, the new

Partnership Agreement has been restructured to reflect dominant neoliberal multilateral norms of international relations. This was particularly the case with the introduction of economic and political conditionality, during Lomé IV and VI, but is also apparent in the new agreement (Brown, 2000: 367–84). The main elements of the agreement in the area of trade and economic cooperation include the following (Tekere, 2000: 7):

- Rolling over the non-reciprocal Lomé trade preferences for eight years to 31 December 2007 under a waiver from the WTO.
- No improvement in market access for the ACP into the European Union market during the transitional period.
- No firm commitment on maintenance during the transitional period of any protocol product, except sugar, which has a life of its own.
- Introduce reciprocity from 2008 in the form of free trade areas between EU and ACP regions.
- Start negotiations about these free trade areas in September 2002 and finish in 2007.
- Cooperate in multilateral trade.
- Produce trade agreements that are WTO-compatible.

An end to non-reciprocal treatment is the more fundamental meaning of the new Partnership Agreement – that is, a rebalancing of obligations and benefits, the subordination of Lomé and all African regional trade and integration arrangements to the WTO. The introduction of reciprocity in trade between unequal economic partners, which the EU and African economies are, will undoubtedly impact adversely on the economies of most African countries (Lambrechts, 1999: 1–3).

Both the United States and the European Union recognize that many developing countries have antagonistic suspicions about the world trading system. And since the collapse of the Seattle trade talks in 1999, both the EU and the USA have struggled to convince Third World nations and their advocates that they are serious about bridging the gap in living standards between the world's rich and poor. Nevertheless, many poor countries have balked at global trade talks until they see major progress on debt, agricultural subsidy by rich countries, and progress in financing for development. To deal with Third World antagonism and buy new converts, the European Union took the unprecedented decision in late February 2001 to open its markets to almost all products from the world's forty-eight poorest countries, with the exception of military weapons (Drozdiak, 2001: E1). Whether such a dramatic policy move by the EU will convince developing countries to endorse a new round of global trade negotiations remains to be seen. Humanitarian aid agencies have criticized the EU plan as a feeble compromise that delays duty-free access for such sensitive products as bananas, rice and sugar. EU officials explained that opposition from Europe's powerful farm lobbies is the reason why such products are not included in the new trade proposal.

In addition to the above three trade agreements, the EU also concluded a special bilateral trade agreement with South Africa, which will have a major impact on the member states of the Southern Africa Development Community (SADC). The agreement will in effect liberalize some $20 billion worth of annual EU–South Africa trade. The agreement commits the EU to remove barriers to 99 per cent of South Africa's industrial exports and 75 per cent of its agricultural exports over ten years. South Africa is to reciprocate over twelve years on about 86 per cent of EU exports. On the other hand, South Africa's partners in the South African Customs Union (SACU) will end up losing a significant proportion of customs union revenues as a result of the removal of duties on imports from South Africa, as well as increased competition from the European Union (Mbekeani, 1999: 25–6).

The homogeneity of new rules governing global economic relations, development cooperation in particular, poses a fundamental challenge to the autonomy of African countries and the kind of development strategy they may want to follow. Given the pervasiveness of neoliberal ideology in trade, aid and development cooperation, African countries have two choices: to embrace globalization as a development strategy or to resist globalization and liberalization. Realistically, however, neither strategy is sustainable. To embrace globalization and liberalization uncritically will do little to reduce dependence and marginalization. To resist globalization – by defying the policies of the institutions of the world system – will amount to economic and political suicide unless such a strategy represents a collective Third World response. The latter course is unlikely given the limited power of developing countries in general vis-à-vis the G7 governments.

Conclusion

This book proposes a third option: *the guided embrace of globalization with a commitment to resist.* African countries must be prepared to come up with alternative formulations and conditions under which they will engage in global economic exchanges. This will mean fully exploiting investment and trade opportunities made available by economic globalization while taking the necessary measures, such as capital controls and expanded South–South trade, to shield their economies from the ill effects of market shifts.

To survive and succeed in this volatile global economic environment, African governments will need to expedite the process of democratization; improve the legal regulatory environment necessary for domestic entrepreneurship and productivity; and invest heavily in education, research and development (R&D), and infrastructure.

The challenges confronting Africa are many and there are no ready-made solutions. The majority of African countries are involved in one form of transition or another: from war to peace; from dictatorship to democracy and respect for human rights; from state domination to market-based and private-sector-led initiatives. The task of simultaneously undertaking economic and political transformation is exceedingly difficult. The success of Africa's transformation agenda will, therefore, depend largely on how quickly the continent successfully completes these transitions and starts putting together sensible national policies to take advantage of the growing economic opportunities in the global economy.

Globalization indeed offers great opportunities, but only if it is managed carefully and with concern for social justice and empowering the poor. This entails the following: enabling poor people to be more productive; achieving universal access to basic services (health, education, water, sanitation); improving basic infrastructure; and providing safety nets for those who cannot produce due to old age or chronic sickness. Human development and transformation must be viewed as a *sine qua non* for self-sustained development (UNECA, 1990).

In the final analysis, the solutions to Africa's economic and political crisis can only be found within Africa. Regrettably, the current African leadership seems to accept 'external direction' as given, denying the possibility of self-transformation. While Western governments and aid institutions can play a constructive role in Africa's transformation, the ultimate responsibility should remain firmly in African hands. Instead of relying on outside actors to solve Africa's problem, Africans must harness the energies and entrepreneurship of their people by adopting policies that make good economic and political sense. This will require fundamental change in African attitudes, institutional arrangements, orientation to governance and economic management. This can only happen with the establishment of a viable, active and democratic state, and the strengthening of social institutions.

The chapters that follow explore the key challenges that African states must confront in the coming decades. The various topics covered in the book are the most important bridges that African governments must build and strengthen if they are ever to arrest the vicious circle of marginalization. Translating words into deeds will require vision, commitment and hard work. While the reintegration of Africa into the new global economy is a necessity, it must be done on terms determined by Africans themselves and with broad consultation with civil society, the private sector and the key institutions of the state.

Notes

1. Communiqué issued in Lusaka on 26 June 2000 by African finance ministers at a regional meeting sponsored by the African Capacity Building Foundation (ACBF).

2. The report was subsequently issued under a new title, *World Bank Adjustment Lending and Economic Performance in Sub-Saharan Africa in the 1980s: A Comparison with Other Low-income Countries* (World Bank, 1992).

3. The enhanced HIPC stipulates that in order to qualify for relief, a country must have a debt/exports ratio of 150 per cent and a debt/tax ratio of 250 per cent or more, combined with tax/GDP and exports/GDP ratios of at least 15 per cent and 30 per cent respectively.

CHAPTER 2

Renewing and Restoring Democracy in Africa: A Herculean Task

> Africa's rebirth depends on individual countries and regional groupings committing themselves to democracy and respect for human rights.
>
> President Nelson Mandela at the 1997 SADC meeting

Africa's economic, social and political crisis since the mid-1970s can be traced to the problem of governance. While external actors have contributed enormously to the governance deficit, particularly during the Cold War period, a significant portion of the blame lies with African governments themselves, who have managed successfully to suppress the avenues of democratic expression, participation and self-government of their citizens. The absence of political freedom has stifled the prospects for sustained economic growth, the deepening of democratic institutions, and the rule of law, and has prevented the emergence and development of a culture of tolerance. Before 1990, only seven African countries – Morocco, Senegal, Botswana, Zimbabwe, Tunisia, Egypt and Mauritius – had multiparty systems. Most of these were limited in some way. Only Botswana and Mauritius allowed open elections. The rest of the countries in the continent were ruled by military dictatorships.

Since 1989, however, democracy as an idea has triumphed in much of Africa. Popular discontent with military or autocratic regimes found vent in mass demonstrations in favour of individual freedoms and multiparty government. We have witnessed substantial regime change in major portions of the continent. Between 1990 and 1997, in more than forty-two countries a peaceful change of government took place as a result of competitive multiparty elections. Several others have had reasonably fair elections, which have resulted in the governing party retaining power

(Africa Institute of South Africa, 1998: 101–9). In others, such as Uganda and Ethiopia, some degree of managed democratization has taken place under the leadership of political parties created by former guerrilla insurgencies.

This remarkable progress notwithstanding, democracy in Africa is in profound trouble and has not moved beyond the holding of multiparty elections. Recent conflicts and political crises in countries like the Democratic Republic of the Congo, Togo, Zambia and Gabon serve as sobering reminders of how tentative and fragile the current attempt at political reform is when basic conditions for democracy are not met. Elections where the incumbent president secures 99.8 per cent of the vote are still embarrassingly common.[1] That a country like Côte d'Ivoire, once considered a success story, can succumb to political turmoil and violence is a barometer of how tentative democracy in Africa is at the present time.

While the task of democratic consolidation in Africa faces great challenges, the most pertinent factor that will ultimately determine the continent's future will be the quality of political leadership. In his acclaimed 1968 book *The Beautyful Ones Are Not Yet Born*, Ghanaian novelist Ayi Kwei Armah lamented: 'Why has there not emerged in Africa since independence, a new generation of political parties and leadership, which are committed to the interest of the mass of the people?' (Armah, 1968). Almost forty years later, a clear answer to the central question raised by Armah has remained elusive. While scholars and politicians continue to debate the appropriate democratic route that Africa should follow, how to produce and nurture Armah's 'Beautyful Ones' – a new generation of leaders not corrupted by money and materialism – remains the greatest challenge to renewing and sustaining democracy in the continent.

Indeed, the prospects for further democratization of African countries present a very mixed picture, with entrenched hierarchical and repressive structures vying with a wide assortment of new initiatives. This is largely because democratic institutions – legislatures, local governments, electoral bodies, political parties, the judiciary, the media, and civil society – remain weak and unable to act as countervailing forces to an often powerful executive branch of government. The overall orientation of opposition political parties has been the removal of incumbent regimes; as a result, they have paid scant attention to the important task of strengthening the key institutions of the state, such as the judiciary, and the legislative and executive branches of government (Bratton and van de Walle, 1997). In some respects, opposition parties, like the former ruling parties, lack interest in genuine institutional reform and empowerment of the masses. Their quest for power is a means of creating their own lines of patronage. Real and enduring change, therefore, will depend on increasing public participation, access to resources, and the building of strong democratic cultures and institutions.

Africa's embryonic democratic experiment is also being thwarted by simultaneous and unrealistic external donor demand for political reform and market-oriented economic reform. There is an inherent contradiction between the two. The economic reforms, coming under the rubric of IMF/World Bank structural adjustment programmes, have, in their political consequence, tended to encourage or reinforce authoritarian political forms that negate the ideals that the same donor community seeks to promote through the 'new' political conditions (Beckman, 1991: 83–105). The economic reform programmes, which have resulted in increased poverty and decreased expenditure on vital social services, are not the outcome of an internal process of dialogue. This in turn has compounded the weakness of the state, engendered hostility from the citizenry, and undermined the state's limited legitimacy. For democracy to take root in Africa, there must be significant social reform and reduction of inequalities as well as the decentralization of political power and decision-making. This will increase the legitimacy of the state; the people will make major decisions and feel involved in decision-making and in the promotion of economic reform.

Africa's challenge in the next decade will be expediting the democratization process, creating the conditions for committed political leadership to emerge while revitalizing the economy at the same time. This will be difficult given Africa's marginal role in a rapidly globalizing economy. If anything, neoliberalism as a development strategy, in the context of inflexible domestic and international political structures, is likely to result in a decisive change in the productive powers and balance of social forces in Africa, further opening up new avenues of conflict (Plank, 1993: 407–30; Soto and Castillo, 1994: 69–83).

The Political Legacy of Colonialism and the Challenge of Democratization

The term 'governance' – which implies responsible, accountable, transparent, legitimate, effective democratic government – is of recent origin in political science discourse. More appropriately, it has become used much more frequently in discussing how governments are to perform in undertaking public changes, innovations and processes that should bring about social, economic and political progress in Africa. If these words and phrases are to be meaningful in the actual process of bringing about change in Africa, then we need to delve deeper into the colonial legacy and the performance of post-independence governments in the continent.

When examining political change in Africa since 1989, one observes a striking similarity between the contemporary movement for democracy and the mass mobilization campaign for independence that took place in the 1950s and early 1960s. In the 1950s, the majority of Africans joined the independence movement to reclaim political freedom taken away from them by the colonial state. Fundamental to the anti-colonial struggle was the pursuit of democracy, equal justice and national autonomy (Ake, 1996: 4–6). However, once 'flag independence' was achieved, the new African leaders turned their back on the masses whose support they actively had sought in order to end colonial rule.

In an effort to give substance to the inherited state, the nationalist leaders who took over the mantle of power from the colonial state quickly brought the various ethnic groups under the authority of the central state. These national entities were allowed little space for autonomous cultural development, much less for self-rule. In the process, post-independence African leaders ended up sacrificing vital principles of self-government on the altar of an imposed national unity. Federalism was viewed as a divisive arrangement that would lead to secessions. Instead, a unitarist centralizing strategy of state building was widely adopted in the continent (Mengisteab, 1997: 120). This often meant that the different nationalities were expected to give up their identity and to adopt some common national culture, which essentially meant the culture of the dominant group in control of the new state. Like the colonial system, neither participation nor accountability has been passed on to local structures by post-independence governments. Africa's pervasive problems with tribalism and ethnic conflicts are, therefore, rooted in the failed strategies of state building following decolonization (Uvin, 1997: 91–115).

The colonial state imposed its boundaries without creating the economic, political and social conditions necessary for consolidation. The newly independent African states lacked the administrative structures, personnel and culture necessary for the efficient management of society. With very little room to manoeuvre, African nationalist leaders felt compelled by circumstances to adopt and legitimize the institutions left behind by the departing colonial powers (Davidson, 1983; Fieldhouse, 1986: 27–63). In response to the inherited institutional handicap, centralization of decision-making became the preferred mode of economic and political management, greatly undermining the constitutional importance of courts, legislatures and subregional governments. Thus, policies came to be determined solely by the concern with stability, order and nation-building rather than by conditions for development. Leaders believed themselves to be above the law, using political office to confer economic privileges on themselves and their supporters.

A major feature of the centralized state is the preoccupation with bureaucracy and planning, and hence the preference for concentrated structures rather than institutions that emphasize grassroots empowerment of the people. This has often meant control of political and economic power by groups who come from a particular ethnic group. This in turn has encouraged a top-down approach to management of public affairs, even when decentralized structures were created. Rural administrative structures lacked adequate resources or discretionary authority. This approach did not increase efficiency. As the state became the principal industry for patronage, it became a burden to society, requiring more and more resources to maintain it.

Some political analysts refer to this type of political system as 'neo-patrimonialism' (Medrad, 1982; Callaghy, 1984). According to Weber, patrimonialism can be defined as a system of rule in which all governmental authority and economic rights tend to be treated as privately appropriated economic advantages and where governmental powers and the associated advantages are treated as private rights (Weber, 1947). Lacking any legal–constitutional foundation and legitimacy to govern, elites in Africa became more and more preoccupied with defining power relations while simultaneously seeking legitimacy from outside. Along with the decreasing ability of the state to respond to the most pressing social issues, a siege mentality set in and, consequently, concern for elite security took precedence over development and improving the welfare of the population.

On the economic front, raising productivity and reducing widespread poverty was never the priority of 'neo-patrimonial' African governments. Right from the start in 1960, what was presented as a 'development strategy' by most governments was simply a much-improved version of top-down colonial extractive policy designed to beef up the coffers of central governments to pursue patronage politics. This implied maintaining the colonial division of labour and a dependent trade relationship. Rural development policy has, by and large, been geared towards the production of primary commodities for the export market to pay for prestige development projects (Bates, 1981). Public investment policies have been oriented to support either urban projects or export agriculture. Peasants are expected to provide the bulk of the resources required for national development through increased taxes and coercion to engage in the same primary resource production during the colonial period. The top-down development approach stifled peasant autonomy, productivity and entrepreneurship.

As the state extended its administrative and regulatory wings to the furthest rural outposts, the capacity of peasants to initiate grassroots development autonomously on the basis of local reality was severely circumscribed. Under the guise of 'development and nation building', corrupt elite bureaucrats and party loyalists, far removed from the reality of rural life, began to dictate what peasants could and could not produce, to whom they could sell their outputs and at what price (Bates, 1981; World Bank, 1989c: 2). Prices paid to farmers for food crops were kept artificially low, thus providing cheap food to people in the cities. Insecure tenure systems, inadequate marketing and storage facilities, and weak extension services all compounded this. Contrary to the popular notion that 'one should not bite the hand that feeds', African governments have consistently pursued policies that are anti-peasant. Consequently, they have succeeded in 'killing the goose that lays the golden egg' (Barraclough, 1991).

By the mid-1970s, the euphoria of independence had long disappeared, independent constitutions and parliaments were discarded, and the military had entrenched itself as the sole conductor of state politics in many parts of Africa. The capacity for state repression was reinforced and any remaining avenues for political expression were closed. State-orchestrated development strategies contributed further to agricultural stagnation, poor export performance and growing indebtedness, and a significant erosion of living standards (World Bank, 1989c: 2). Not only were the development policies pursued by undemocratic elites anti-peasant; the projects and programmes designed to help peasants with assistance from the new external donors ended up marginalizing them (Hancock, 1989). It is no exaggeration to say that the much-publicized war against poverty (i.e. development) has in fact turned out to be a war against the poor.

At the beginning of the 1980s, new demands were made of a largely impoverished and disillusioned peasantry. Since the demands of the post-colonial state for more revenues had steadily increased in order to repay foreign debt, fund expensive oil imports, and sustain bloated military expenditures and presidential looting of the public treasury, peasants and the urban poor were expected to make sacrifices once more for the extravagant mistakes of the powerful as many countries were obliged to implement harsh structural adjustment programmes. Needless to say, the demand by donors for fiscal discipline and 'market liberalization' was rarely accompanied by a similar demand for liberalization of the 'political market'. External policy intervention focused primarily on getting African countries onto a sound financial footing so that they could continue to service their external debts. The urgent need to introduce democratic forms of governments in Africa never featured prominently in the foreign-policy agendas of either East or West.

In practice, the flip side of structural adjustment has been further repression of the very producers that it was supposed to liberate from state direction (Beckman, 1989: 83–105). However, exclusive focus on market reform has helped consolidate citizens' resistance to structural adjustment. As many people began to draw a direct connection between their economic plight and the paucity of basic liberties, local grievances very quickly escalated into popular challenges to the established systems of government and the draconian economic policies they were implementing under IMF direction. Since structural adjustment programmes breed repression, interest groups seek to secure greater autonomy from the state. In short, the resistance to the SAP, rather than the SAP itself, offers a source of democratization. Ordinary people now want to construct a new political and economic future based on democratic participation, local control of decision-making, and the meeting of basic needs.[2] This has created a fundamental tension between peoples and states (Chazan and Rothchild, 1988).

In response to popular demand for 'democratization from below', the state has tried to keep control over informal organizations through co-optation of their key spokespeople, intimidation or outright banning. Progress towards democratization has also been hampered by the weakness of civil society groups. The vibrancy of these new institutions of civil society contrasts with the paucity of their strategic power and resources. Organizing around daily subsistence increasingly consumes too much of people's energy and meagre resources, thus making the task of developing a counter-project exceptionally difficult and slow (Joseph, 1997). Therefore, if the territorial integrity of many African countries is to be preserved, the prevailing gross economic and political disparities must be addressed.

What Type of Democracy for Africa?

Although democracy as a concept is difficult to define in a way that is applicable to all societies, there are a number of attributes that could be universalised in what one could characterize as 'good governance', the ultimate goal in the democratization process. Schmitter and Lynn define modern political democracy as 'a system of governance in which rulers are held accountable for their actions in the public realm by citizens, acting directly through the competition and cooperation of their elected representatives' (Schmitter and Lynn, 1991). These fundamental elements of democracy include the following:

Pluralism

This is generally seen as one of the important elements in 'good governance'. It entails, essentially, a system that facilitates the participation of civil society in social and political processes. Thus, the degree to which people are allowed to express themselves freely either as individuals or through established civic organizations, such as trade unions, political parties and pressure groups, indicates the level of democracy in a given country and the ability, real or potential, of civil society to influence government action. Such participation is guaranteed by the constitution.

Accountability and transparency

These fundamental elements of good governance relate to the need to create a public administration that is transparent, predictable, efficient and accountable to the people. But this must be buttressed with a good information base able to make accurate decisions.

Sanctity of the rule of law

A third major element that defines 'good governance' refers to sanctity of the rule of law and individual citizens' security. Citizens have a right to express themselves on political matters without the risk of punishment. Citizens also have the right to form independent associations or organizations, including independent political parties and interest groups. Violations of human rights are often an expression of either the existence of constitutional provisions that were made in 'bad faith' in order to safeguard the political interests of a certain group, or a clear case of abuse of authority (Zakaria, 1997: 22–43).

Decentralization of authority and responsibility

The generally held view is that the closer decisions are to the grassroots, the more likely is the state to respond meaningfully, positively and promptly to the people's demands. The concept of decentralization can apply to both the political and the economic level.

At the *political level*, it concerns the form of representation and the system's ability to facilitate a positive flow of information from the bottom upwards. It is also concerned with the problem of the tendency of central ministries and agencies to assume a monopoly of political decision-making at the expense of organs outside the centre. The main goal of decentralization is, therefore, to provide ways and means for the majority of the people to control the political and economic machinations of the state effectively through participation.

At the *economic level*, the call for decentralization in governance not only concerns itself with the need for grassroots organs and people to participate effectively and actively in development programmes and budget deliberations, but should also entail particularly the achievement of fiscal parity between rural and urban areas in education, health, housing, and local government. Democratizing the economy also implies, among other things, some form of redistribution of wealth, and would thus call for a period of sustained high economic growth. What is important in linking sustained economic growth and democratization is that this growth is in some way directed towards social uplift and empowerment of especially the poorest sectors of society.

The central themes of the democracy debate in Africa have focused primarily on multiparty competition and free market economic reform (Sandbrook, 1988). While these are important formal criteria, they are by no means sufficient to judge the democratic qualities of a society (Harbeson, 2000: 235–57). Political reform and participation cannot be divorced from other kinds of freedom. There is an organic link between political freedom and freedom from hunger, ignorance and disease. Therefore, for democracy to take root in Africa there must be significant social reform and a reduction of economic inequality (Gills and Rocamora, 1992). Moreover, democracy cannot take root when political parties and leadership lack a deep commitment to promote the interests of the vast majority of African poor. In the absence of real change in people's lives, zero-sum mentalities and destructive competition will prevail instead of moderation, thus undermining the chances of democratic transition.

Economic Reform and the 'New' Political Conditionality: A Confusion of Agenda

With the end of the Cold War, free elections and free markets have assumed greater importance in the foreign policies of Western powers and in the programmes of both bilateral and multilateral aid agencies; it was argued that political liberalization must be accorded priority if donor-supported economic reform programmes in Africa were to be sustained. Consequently, the donors began to promote a second generation of structural adjustment programmes in the name of liberating civil society from an oppressive state. Governance, transparency and accountability were the new watchwords. This shift in donor policy coincided with the dramatic demand for democratic change in Eastern Europe and the collapse of the Soviet Union in 1989. The new climate began to favour those who espoused and practised liberal democracy – that is, elections, a free press and a market economy. Many African leaders quickly jumped on the multiparty bandwagon.

Some scholars, however, have challenged claims that market-driven economic growth and democracy are linked, pointing to the fact that undemocratic states have been as likely to achieve growth as democratic ones. Rueschemeyer, Stephens and Stephens, for example, argue that democracy depends not only on economic growth, but on the concomitant growth and influence of the urban working class, in particular, as well as of civil society more generally (Rueschemeyer, Stephens and Stephens, 1992). The major success stories of economic growth in the developing world – South Korea, Taiwan, Singapore and, more recently, Thailand and Indonesia – have not occurred under conditions of democracy. Their economic success can be attributed to the fact that they represent 'developmental states' – states led by elites that utilize state autonomy to pursue national economic growth as their central objective, to the exclusion of other priorities (Wade, 1992; Onis, 1991).

Others take the position that politics, not simply governance, is the key to development and that it is necessary to consider the nature of the interaction between economic growth and democratic politics. According to Leftwich, democratic outcomes depend on a number of preconditions: the legitimacy of the state; broad-based consensus on the rules of the political game; an avoidance of the 'winner takes all' approach on the part of victorious interests following elections; the capacity for accommodation and compromise among competing interests in society; a strong and diverse civil society; tolerance where diverse ethnic, regional and religious interests coexist; no threats to the authority of the state from, for example, private armies; and the absence of economic crises that exacerbate social inequalities (Leftwich, 1993; Ake, 1996). In other words, a democratic project can only be sustained when there are political forces that not only accept it but also are prepared to defend it against attacks and where possible extend it. This condition does not exist in Africa at the present moment. A new generation of Africans who are committed to putting the interest of the collective good ahead of narrow personal and ethnic interests have yet to be born.

Given such an understanding of the conditions under which democracy emerges, the prospects for democratization in Africa would appear to be bleak. Some have taken stock of these realities and concluded that democratization will not address Africa's sluggish economic growth, and that in fact attempts to strengthen democratic forces and civil society under such circumstances will lead to social unrest and undermine sound economic reform and growth (Ihonvbere, 1996).

The great irony is that, in the African context, democracy is simultaneously being encouraged and limited by external forces. Economic reforms in many African countries have been carried out independent of substantive political reforms and greater concern for social justice. If the logic of a market economy is to free individual market forces as actors in the market place, then it should be accompanied by political reforms which also free individuals to participate in the political marketplace. Yet, the new 'political conditionality' of Western donors pushes a version of democracy that carries its own specific ideological load. Given the extensive links that tie the leading Western powers to Africa and African regimes, the proponents of the new political conditionality have an interest in ensuring that democratization does not upset existing socioeconomic arrangements and donor-supported economic reform programmes (Harbeson, 2000). Therefore donor pressure for democratization is likely to remain at the level of effecting minimal political reform that leaves intact existing power structures and relations.

The Limits of Democratization from Above

Since 1989, virtually every country in Africa has been faced with the need to alter the structure of its regime. Despite the fact that such change took place in the context of a call for political liberalization and democratization, the direction of change has not necessarily bolstered democratic aspirations. While the slogan 'second liberation' implies a vision of social development and political change fundamentally different from the 'first liberation', the lack of broad-based programmes of economic and social transformation points to the limitations of the present democratization project (Bratton and van de Walle, 1997). What explains the demand for democracy on the one hand, and the relative difficulty in sustaining and consolidating it on the other?

First-hand observation tells us that the creation of new parties has not directly involved many citizens from outside the existing political elites, and particularly not those in grassroots organizations and interest groups in rural areas. Election results in many African countries show the main party to be overwhelmingly dominant in a core region. The system of winner-takes-all seems to create permanent losers and permanent winners. In such a situation, groups that are numerically small can never gain representation. They therefore remain permanently aggrieved. Opposition parties have no clear strategy on how to sustain the involvement of grassroots organizations in a substantial way to help them build local democratic capacities that will endure over time. Instead, both economic and political reforms in Africa over the past decade have been carried out 'from above' rather than being the outcome of an internal process of dialogue.

The crucial factor in the transition to democracy has been the inability of political parties to avoid ethnic manipulation. This is a pervasive problem throughout Africa; political contenders try to consolidate their ethnic base for fear of losing out to an opponent's ethnic mobilization (Diamond, 1983). Electoral politics tends to exacerbate communal divisions as politicians pursuing power and profit appeal to ethnic identities using bargaining, manipulation and deceit. The vertical solidarity of tribalism and extended family linkages remains intact almost everywhere in Africa, sustaining nepotism and favouritism in bureaucracies. That makes governments ill-equipped to act as economic agents and arbitrators. The decline into communal violence in Kenya, for example, is largely attributable to the weakening of the elite's commitment to the rule of peaceful competition.

Second, representative political parties with agendas for the nation as a whole are still in short supply. Differential power and influence of civil society groups determine the nature and form of democratic transitions. The groups that are most vocal and best organized within civil society tend to be elite-dominated. These groups generally have very little in common with rural folk and poor people although they claim to represent the marginalized sectors in society. Given their strong organizational base and external support, they see themselves as the natural successor of the incumbent regime. If and when they take up the mantle of power, they do so under great handicap since authority is not conferred on them by their role in broad-based mobilization of civil society.

In Kenya, for example, all the opposition leaders – Matiba, Kibaki and Odinga – were close to the centre of power in the two previous governments. They chose the right moment to break with the past and embrace the language of good governance and respect for human rights. Kibaki, who was at one time vice-president, held the post of health minister until his resignation in 1991, three weeks after the formal introduction of pluralism. Matiba also was a staunch KANU minister until he joined the voices of dissent in 1990, which landed him in detention (Mukalo wa Kwayera, 1993: 8–12).

The third observation is that the collapse of one-party states is rarely accompanied by a substantial reorientation of power relations between urban and rural areas. The urban bias remains overwhelmingly strong (Lipton, 1977). As Odinkalu put it succinctly, the current brand of rights and democracy is the agenda of a 'terminally endangered middle and intellectual class'. Amanor-Wilks, Mbogori and McFadden point to the sections of society – farm workers, the poor and rural women – still beyond democracy's reach. Mbogori goes even further to suggest that grassroots people see democracy and human rights as luxuries.[3] African governments can sit and do nothing while whole provinces of peasants starve to death due to official neglect. Yet these governments are able to survive politically. The same could not be said if basic commodities such as milk and sugar were to disappear from shops in the capital for a week. The policy of 'urban appeasement' will remain entrenched even with a multiparty system unless rural people are empowered so that they can effectively defend the democratic project in their respective countries and influence local and national policies.

In many African countries, the institution of formal democracy has failed to broaden popular political participation in a meaningful way. Social reform agendas that could have established the basis for broader popular participation and greater social justice have been completely abandoned. Multiparty government has not fundamentally changed the ubiquitous corruption, the marginalization of rural people, and ethnic identification patterns (Ihonvbere, 1996). The task of building real people's power remains a big challenge. More than simply the modification of state forms and the recognition of parties, civil society groups in Africa have to be given time and space to breathe and for non-state movements to emerge.

Finally, democracy and economic reform cannot be imposed from above. The people must shape both. They must be the outcome of an internal process of dialogue. The fact remains that no democratic system can flower which is not anchored in domestic social forces. Similarly, democracy and economic reform cannot be imposed from outside. It may be easy for outsiders to teach Africans how to speak the English language, but they cannot teach Africans how to govern themselves. That is a task that Africans themselves must figure out on their own through a process of dialogue. That process is already under way in many communities across the continent, occasioned by the growth of new social movements, which have begun to transform aspects of the political culture. What Western donors should be doing is seeking out these indigenous democratic impulses that offer encouragement and support.

The 'Silent Revolution': Democratization from Below

It would be a great mistake to attribute the growth of democracy movements in Africa strictly to the mobilization efforts of elite-led parties that have sprung up in recent years. Rather, the movements owe their success to the debilitating economic impact of the 'silent revolution' on the part of ordinary peasants in protest at the incapacity of African governments to provide even the most basic services to previously protected groups (teachers, civil servants, doctors, etc.). It was the crippling effect of this resistance that created the conditions for opposition. This process dates back to the mid-1970s when peasants began to drop out in large numbers from the formal economy to demonstrate their anger at the perceived hostility of the state towards them (Hyden, 1981; Cheru, 1989). It has almost become a patriotic act to sabotage state policies that continue to marginalize them.

The paradox of the new wave of democratization in Africa is that its 'success' is built upon the failure of 'development' (Ake, 1996). The growing demand for democracy is a response to declining living standards in the face of widespread corruption and mismanagement by political elites. Issues of landlessness, taxation without representation, exploitation of peasants by parastatals, lack of basic services and the denial of basic rights and community control of decisions are all pressing issues today as they were on the eve of independence. Africans, then, do not just want multiparty democracy; they want fundamental economic change as well.

Notwithstanding the hundreds of books and journal articles that have been published since 1989 purporting to know what democratic route Africans should take, new social actors in civil society – far removed from the conventional politics of opposition and elaborate donor-funded conferences – have been transforming aspects of political culture and creating new institutional resources throughout Africa (Cheru, 1997; Monga, 1996). This terrain has increasingly been occupied by civic associations, women's groups, peasant associations, environmental groups, and human rights organizations, pressing demands on the state through the 'politics of claims', non-payment of taxes, open peasant insurrection, urban riots, and collective actions to find solutions to common problems and to transform aspects of African political culture (Pradervand, 1989). The overall consensus among these social movements is that the process of poverty alleviation must go hand in hand with the institution of far-reaching political change.

Initially, many Western commentators on Africa disregarded everyday forms of resistance by ordinary Africans as trivial coping mechanisms, whose impetus was non-political. This view completely misses the point. The impact of such resistance to the policy decisions of governments may not always be visible on the surface; its significance must be measured by long-term effects. In reality, these actions have been effective in eroding the foundations of many autocratic regimes.

Transformation can be perceived in many of the new institutions that have been created to take over the provision of basic services once carried out by the resource-deficient state. Contrary to Robert Kaplan's 'coming anarchy' thesis, in extreme cases where central authority has collapsed, as was the case in Somalia, local communities have proved more resilient, more politically innovative, and less passive in the face of the crisis of governance (Kaplan, 1994: 44–76). The most significant political functions in much of Somalia are carried out at the village or neighbourhood level (Menkhaus, 1998: 220–24). Ken Menkhaus writes:

> While Somalia today is stateless, it is not anarchic. Although repeated efforts to revive a central government have failed, local communities have responded with a wide range of strategies to establish the minimal essential elements of governance.... Indeed, in some parts of Somalia, local communities enjoy more responsive and participatory governance, and a more predictable, profitable, and safer commercial climate, than at any time in recent decades. (p. 220)

The new social movements advance the idea that development is a human right, the achievement of which requires popular participation and local control. The desire to define issues in these terms has forced local social movements to link up with other groups that are grappling with similar problems elsewhere in the world. These global networks are being facilitated by the various forms of communications and transportation hardware, which are also part of the conditions for globalization (Ekins, 1992; Durning, 1989). This has profoundly changed the nature of social mobilization. Among the most promising groups with the capacity to initiate fundamental change are the following:

Peasant organizations

Ordinary peasants know from experience that the post-colonial state has lost its role as an instrument of development. Instead of growing more effective, the state in Africa has become the main obstacle to development (see Chapter 4). Relations between the state and the peasantry are thus characterized by mutual suspicion and distrust.

In many areas, peasants have become aware of their powerless situation and drawn the conclusion that it is better to avoid the state altogether, withdraw within their local communities on a subsistence basis and create new avenues for social and political mobilization (Cheru, 1989 and 1997). In many communities, the emphasis has shifted from export crops to food crops for local consumption. Farmers now market their produce through their own channels, disregarding political boundaries and marketing boards (Cheru, 1989). By involving themselves in such locally initiated projects, peasants are educating themselves in organizational dynamics and self-government at the local level. Such local initiatives are an important starting point for building a more democratic state. In short, social movements are redefining issues in terms that address more fundamental questions of resource distribution and access, political rights and processes (Pradervand, 1989; Rau, 1991).

In Kenya, for example, farmers almost totally abandoned coffee farming in the early 1990s, and tea and sugar growers on occasion neglected their crops to demonstrate their anger at the perceived hostility of official buyers (whether parastatals or other bodies) towards them (Kimenyi, 1993: 47). Something close to agrarian revolt was evident in parts of the country. In Nyeri, Central Province, some 800 members of the troubled Mathira Coffee Farmers' Society joined a boycott by farmers from eleven other processing plants in delivering their coffee to the Kenya Planters' Cooperative Union in late February 1993 demanding that the Society be dissolved.[4]

In the light of the failure of government parastatals to make payments as scheduled, and the large percentage that the government consumes directly, such behaviour by farmers appears quite rational. The result was very low rates of growth in agriculture as farmers sought to escape the 'rent-seeking' state. The effects of negative government policies have also been evident in other fields that directly affect peasant interests, such as credit, provision of inputs and extension. Although the situation in rural Kenya has changed since 1995 with the liberalization of agriculture, how long the policy will remain open is anyone's guess.

The informal economy and self-help associations

The predominance of informality in African urban centres is beyond dispute. The retreat of the state in key areas of social services since the implementation of SAPs has left enormous gaps, which have been filled by local initiatives and survival strategies. From Johannesburg to Dakar, large numbers of people are now engaged in the parallel economy: shelter, employment, law and order, transportation, refuse collection, trade, and even household credit supply (Mabogunje, 1991). In spite of the barriers represented by counterproductive government regulations, debilitated public services and pervasive corruption, the underground economy employs, produces and sells. Without it, few things would work at all in Africa. The informal sector, therefore, constitutes a dynamic and enduring force that has shaped African cities (MacGaffey, 1988: 171–88; Green, 1981).

The second economy not only generates alternative economic opportunities for people; it also represents an alternative society, with parallel social and religious institutions alongside official ones. Squatter settlements, for example, represent not simply a shelter entity or a mere collection of shacks. They are sociopolitical entities, with their own rules, forms of organization and internal hierarchies, constituting a node of resistance and defiance against state domination. By offering new avenues to wealth creation and annulling government regulations, the second economy constitutes a potential political challenge to predatory rule itself (MacGaffey, 1983: 351–64). It undermines the capacity of the state to repress individual initiatives. The same applies to unregistered market and street vendors, backyard artisans, pirate taxis, and the entire arena of social reproduction for the majority of the urban population. Under the apparent chaos in this sector is a substantial degree of order.

What explains the resilience and dynamism of the voluntary sector? Research has demonstrated that it is maintained by the solidarity and organic nature of the institutional and organizational superstructure embedded within this sector. There is a high degree of participation, accountability and commitment, as well as a sense of obligation, in informal-sector activities (Bennetta, 1981). Over time, new types of voluntary association develop that often blossom into different kinds of political and social movements, whose importance spreads beyond the limits of the specific local shantytown or settlement. In short, a closer look at the informal sector in Africa provides a glimpse of what could be achieved if Africa's economies and financial policies were more attuned to the continent's everyday realities.

The human rights movement

Given the predominance until very recently of military governments in many parts of Africa, the human rights movement remained underdeveloped. In fact, Northern NGOs and church groups have conducted much of the human rights work regarding political prisoners and refugees. Since 1989, however, the continent has witnessed a proliferation of local human rights groups with agendas far beyond the traditional focus on political prisoners. While some groups focus on shelter or development as a human right, other deal primarily with the right of internally displaced persons, victims of forced evictions, street children, displaced pastoral communities that have lost their entitlement, and ethnic and religious minorities (Bediako, 1995: 205–14). In close collaboration with Northern NGOs and human rights organizations, African human rights organizations have been able to bring before international forums the complicity of national governments and donor agencies that support development strategies that often conflict with people's rights for development and self-management.

Grassroots ecology movements

Post-independence development has not only served to widen inequalities; it has also undermined the resource base that sustains life. The emphasis on export-led strategy, ranging from cattle ranching to timber exporting, has intensified the competition for essential resources. Peasants and pastoralists are dislocated by more powerful social coalitions to marginal lands to make way for export plantations (Rosenblum and Williamson, 1987; Timberlake, 1986). Rivers and water resources that have long sustained pastoralists and small farmers are rerouted considerable distances to serve agribusiness, leaving local people to fend for themselves. The case of the Ogoni people in the Niger Delta in Nigeria, who have been struggling against Shell oil company and the Nigerian government, is a sober reminder.

In the struggle for survival, ecology movements, peasant groups and women's organizations in Africa are at a political crossroads, challenging structures that have long kept them marginalized (Durning, 1989). An example is Wangari Maathai and the Green Belt Movement, which assists Kenyan women in planting trees on their homesteads. President Daniel Arap Moi was shocked to discover the muscle of the Green Belt Movement when foreign funding committed for the construction of a skyscraper in a popular Nairobi park was withdrawn after protests led by Maathai.

The overall consensus among popular organizations and environmental groups is that the process of poverty alleviation must go hand in hand with the institution of far-reaching political change. Even the World Bank, which tried for so long to separate economics from politics, now advocates democracy and the merits of popular participation in the development process. Ecology movements now think locally and act globally, for they see the usefulness of international support and publicity for their local struggles (McCormick, 1989). Furthermore, ecology movements have become more sophisticated in that they seek to understand the interrelatedness of issues previously handled as if they were separate, and they build coalitions around these issues. They now undertake to intervene in multifaceted issues, such as the relationships between debt and the environment, trade and sustainable development, and democracy and sustainable development.

Religious institutions

The challenge to the state from below is being further strengthened by the growing fundamentalist movements in largely Islamic countries and by indigenous Christian churches, whose appeal to a broader base of African society is growing. Church involvement in development activities has been contributing to the strengthening of the popular sector (Dalmalm, 1995: 127). Both Islam and Christianity are now at a political crossroads: do they seek change in the material conditions of their followers, or ignore political and economic conditions in expectation of a better life in the spiritual hereafter? Islamic fundamentalism and indigenous Christianity have developed into institutions that can offer viable opposition to government policy and have continued to do so despite government pressure and coercion (Mazrui, 1990: 26–9; Abdullahi, 1995: 129–35).

In Malawi, for example, in March 1992 the Catholic Church issued an open Pastoral Letter describing the oppressive policies of Banda's dictatorial regime. This sparked the movement for change. Within three months, major donors suspended non-humanitarian assistance, thereby pressuring the government into allowing the formation of political parties and holding a referendum to give people the choice between one-party rule and multiparty politics. On 14 June 1993 more than 60 per cent of Malawians voted to change to a multiparty system. Within a year a new constitution was drawn up, and on 12 May 1994 Malawians went to the polls to elect a president and 177 members of a new parliament by adult suffrage. The new constitution guarantees fundamental human rights and restricts the president to a maximum of two five-year terms. Human rights groups and NGOs that were never allowed under the Banda regime are now flourishing (UNDP–Malawi, 2000).

The trade-union movement

African trade unions are playing an important role not only in the promotion and protection of the rights of their members but also in the democratization process. Led by the Organization of African Trade Union Unity (OATUU) and the International Confederation of Free Trade Unions (ICFTU), trade unions in Africa are engaged in mass mobilization of workers for democratic change (Ihonvbere, 1997: 77–110). This involves advocacy and the development of workers' skills in democratic practices and processes. Zambia, Nigeria, South Africa and Zimbabwe are excellent examples of countries where trade-union activism was central to democratic change. In South Africa, the Congress of South African Trade Unions (COSATU), in collaboration with the African National Congress (ANC) and other mass organizations, played a prominent role in the liberation of the country (Bediako, 1995: 205). In Zambia, the backbone of the Movement for Multi-Party Democracy (MMD) was the Zambia Congress of Trade Unions (ZCTU), which spearheaded the restoration of multiparty politics and democracy in Zambia. In Zimbabwe, the spectacular success of the Movement for Democratic Change is partly credited to the prominent role played by the Zimbabwe Congress of Trade Unions, whose leader is now the chairperson of the opposition in parliament.

What distinguishes these progressive social movements from others is that they are inclusive and articulate the demands of the poor people and politically disenfranchised groups; they represent alternative forms of political organization; they are often at odds with their own governments; and they always seek to attain objectives that entail other paths to economic development, political control and social organization (Stavenhagen, 1997). These new dialogues have opened up along with new ways of thinking about how government relates to the society it seeks to govern.

What emerges from the above analysis is that ordinary Africans do not allow their frustration with state policies and programmes to get in the way of bettering themselves and maintaining their self-reliance and autonomy. In the process, citizens have become politically conscious and are educating themselves in organizational dynamics and self-government at the local level. In other words, social movements in Africa are redefining issues in terms that address more fundamental questions of resource distribution and access, and of political rights and processes. In democratic parlance, this is self-government.

The greatest challenge in the coming decades will be how to strengthen these internal forces which are best placed to defend the democratic project in their respective communities, to enable them to develop long-term transformative agendas and mobilize the necessary resources to fulfil these objectives. When people have overcome the local and national obstacles to their development, they are prepared to make the jump to global struggles.

At this point, a note of caution is in order. Despite the critical role that social movements are playing, they should not be romanticized, for they presently lack a coordinating mechanism. The emerging civil society in Africa is riven by deep cleavages and tensions, which may threaten both economic restructuring and political liberalization. The real danger is that pro- and anti-democratic forces will coexist. These forces may be elitist or populist, atavistic and divisive, or constructive and cohesive elements projecting a vision of an alternative order. How to identify potential agents of transformation in a diverse context will remain a problem, particularly in a situation of widespread poverty.

The Dilemma of Competing Agendas

Fundamental political change cannot come about in a country unless the relations of power between state and society are altered. Until this happens, the populace can only pressure government for policy changes and accumulate minor victories here and there. This implies that the populace must have another political agenda over and above its main business of disempowering centralized structures. In other words, it has to come up with a state agenda of its own. This is to enter the realm of the nation-state – that is, national politics. And herein lies the dilemma of non-governmental and people's organizations. Their main concern is social politics – in other words, self-governance whose success is measured mainly in terms of the circles or poles of popular power that they create at the base. In this context, state politics is of a different world. And yet civil society has to come up with an alternative agenda. It will have to find the appropriate combination of strategies to handle effectively the contradictory trajectories of state politics, which is integrative or centralizing, and social politics, which is horizontal or centrifugal. In their efforts to cope with this dilemma, the organizations of civil society are faced with problems that tend to confuse their identify and undermine their core values; these include issues such as autonomy, pluralism, diversity, volunteerism, and a grassroots, bottom-up perspective.

A related problem is parallelism. In their frustration with state policies, the organizations of civil society tend to go it alone, as though government does not exist. Because they have set up substitute structures, they become convinced of their ability to make an impact on the overall situation in spite of the government. It follows that self-appointed leaders representing that loosely defined entity NGO/CBO, along with bureaucrats, lay claim to jurisdiction over citizens and territories.

What Is To Be Done? Democratizing Democracy and the Market

Despite unfounded assertions by certain Western commentators that Africans are strangers to democracy, its ethos and practices are ingrained in Africa at the subnational level, the level that means the most to individual Africans (Kaplan, 1994). Indeed, many pre-colonial African societies included democratic elements. However, since the colonial era and the advent of the modern nation-state, Africans have been deprived of the opportunity for self-government. Given the history of authoritarianism and culture of state-sponsored violence, fear and mistrust of central authorities have been widespread; this has made it difficult to sustain democratic values and commitment.

The way out of the current political impasse in Africa lies in the strengthening of democratic governance. Democratic government helps to guarantee political rights, protect economic freedom and foster an environment where peace and development can flourish. In the absence of genuinely democratic institutions, contending interests are likely to seek to settle their differences through conflict rather than through accommodation. Democratization gives people a stake in society. Only when ordinary Africans have a political voice will their needs be properly addressed by governments. The task of strengthening democratic governance must include the following enabling mechanisms: the rule of law and constitutional legitimacy; a functioning and active civil society; recognition of and respect for the rights of different nationalities; a climate of political reconciliation; and commitment to an open and equitable economic regime of growth. These mechanisms will be briefly considered in turn.

Establishing the rule of law through constitutional innovation

The building of a democratic political base for development requires the creation of structures and the definition of relations between state and society. Therefore the process of adopting a constitution is as important as its substance: it must be legitimate and inclusive, taking into account the interests of all the people in a country, who must feel that they have control over the process. The constitution itself should integrate ideas from all the major stakeholders in a country. The entire process must be transparent, undertaken in full view of the country and the international community.

A constitution perceived as being imposed from above or having been adopted through the manipulation of the process by one of the stakeholders is unlikely to gain sufficient popularity or legitimacy to endure the test of time. To avoid this problem, the constitution should clearly elaborate the following:

Decentralization and de-bureaucratization

Solutions to widespread ethnic conflicts and to the crisis of state building will not be achieved without some sort of consensual and decentralized power-sharing arrangement. Popular democracy demands the institutionalization of a culture of consultation and reciprocal control with regard to law making and the use of power and privileges. An open, transparent and accountable system encourages the organization of people around common goals and their articulation in the political system. The devolution of authority to local levels makes this easier, as it brings policymakers closer to the targeted population, and allows for a better identification and ranking of local needs and priorities. Decentralization also serves as a means to effective planning of social spending, improving the efficiency of service delivery, and increasing the involvement of civil society in the planning and monitoring of government activities.

In Malawi, for example, the 1998 National Decentralization Policy mandated the decentralization of public services and decision-making powers to the districts. The policy was subsequently enshrined in the Local Government Act (no. 42) of 1998, which details the responsibilities assigned to each level of government. The Act devolves administrative and political authority to the district level. Moreover, the policy integrates governmental agencies at the district level into one administrative unit, through the process of institutional integration, manpower absorption, composite budgeting, and provision of funds for the decentralized agencies (Government of Malawi, 1998: 2). Both the policy and the Act promote people's participation in the governance and development of districts, consistent with the basic principles of democratic elections, participatory decision-making and social inclusion enshrined in the 1995 Malawi constitution.

For decentralization to be effective, the transfer of responsibilities and resources to the districts should be accompanied by efforts to build technical, operational, and administrative capacity at the local level. Donor governments, the World Bank, and others are undertaking efforts to improve the capacity of local government in twenty of Uganda's forty-five districts. In Malawi, the World Bank, UNDP and Britain's Development Fund for International Development (DFID) are supporting the implementation of the decentralization Act, although the issue of fiscal decentralization is still not resolved.

In African countries where traditional systems coexist with modern forms of administration, a re-examination of devolution of power must include a debate over the future of traditional institutions of governance. There is a consensus among Africans that traditional leaders should have a role in governance of the state, but the exact role remains largely undefined. There is a need to accommodate traditional leaders in constitutional arrangements. For example, they could be incorporated into the local government system and form its nucleus. This could enhance the effectiveness of local government in rural areas. If colonial powers were shrewd enough to use them in administering the colonial state, why should modern African political systems not involve them in efforts to reach out to small communities and build national consensus and cohesion?

Finally, decentralization is meaningless unless the credibility of public institutions is restored. There is particularly a need for a non-partisan, ethnically diverse and professional civil service to assist in the running of a country. To achieve this, the security of tenure of civil servants and competitive salaries should be guaranteed. An independent civil service can act as a hedge against anarchy when there are clashes among political leaders.

Freedom of expression and association

There should be no hindrance to alternative ideas, institutions and leaders competing for public support. The unfettered rights to organize and to dissent must be recognized by a clear constitutional stipulation. Laws which deny people freedom of association and peaceful dissent should be repealed. The constitution must safeguard not only the rights of individuals but also the independence of the judiciary.

A free press – the eyes and ears of the public – is one of the most significant ingredients of democracy and pluralism. The electronic and print media should contribute to enhancing democratic values of fair play and respect for individual rights. As custodian of civil liberties, the media should highlight abuses and violations. The media should provide forums for the diverse opinions, analysis and free debate that are necessary for ensuring that people are governed fairly, while keeping those who govern accountable to them.

The press can be said to be free to the extent that the society it serves is free of ignorance. The press and other media, in coordination with relevant professionals, will therefore have to engage in effective political and civil programmes. They must interpret the meaning of events as well as report the events themselves, and also play the role of watchdog to promote a culture of transparency and accountability.

Promoting transparency and accountability in public administration

Democracy is meaningless if transparency in decision-making and accountability of public officials are lacking. Corruption is a worldwide phenomenon. It has critically skewed Africa's development. Addressing the problem requires targeting both payer and recipient. African governments must get tough, and make the fight against corruption a genuine priority. A critical first step is to guarantee the autonomy of the offices of the auditor-general or the anti-corruption bureau, and strengthen their capacity to function effectively. A second and important step is to make the judiciary an effective institution and a true guardian of civil liberties and other rights. Ordinary citizens must be convinced that the government sincerely believes in, and is willing to use its executive powers and prerogatives to uphold the rule of law, the principle of equality before the law, and its due process. The costs of not doing so are very high – in lost resources and foreign investment, distorted decision-making, and failing public confidence.

Regular free and fair elections

Regular elections are the obvious and traditional way to ensure accountability. They must be organized in a manner that ensures maximum participation of all stakeholders in the political system. The design of the electoral system is increasingly being recognized as a key lever to promote political accommodation and stability in ethnically divided societies. The experiences of Namibia and South Africa suggest that ethnically divided societies need a system of proportional representation in one form or another. If minorities are to accept parliament, they must be adequately represented. Elections have proved unable to address this issue.

Moreover, the relationship between Parliament and the people can only endure when it is accepted that the people are supreme. Therefore, in matters of great national importance, parliament must consult and defer to the wishes of the people, who are the source of popular sovereignty. Popular consultation in the form of referenda should be entrenched in constitutional practice as a mechanism for obtaining the mandate of the people on constitutional matters and as a deterrent to amendment.

Respect for human rights and the rule of law

Respect for human rights and the rule of law are the cornerstones of good governance. By signalling its commitment to respect human rights, a government can demonstrate its resolve to build a society in which all can live freely. One way forward might be the development of a national plan of action for human rights aimed, for example, at advancing the ratification of human rights treaties, reviewing and amending legislation to ensure that human rights are adequately protected, or promoting the training of judges, police officers, lawyers and prison officials in human rights. The establishment of credible, independent and impartial national human rights institutions can serve as a significant confidence-building measure (UNHCHR, 1993). Civic education by government and non-governmental organizations, the media and others is important in order to inform people about their civic rights and legal protections while also explaining civic responsibilities.

A second step would be to guarantee fair and impartial enforcement of the law. This requires respecting the autonomy, integrity and independence of the courts, and ensuring fair and impartial enforcement of the law by the police and state security services.

Mobilizing civil society

The only way to ensure democracy in Africa is to allow rural people to build on the 'indigenous'. According to Ake, the indigenous refers to whatever the people consider important in their lives; whatever they regard as an authentic expression of themselves (Ake, 1988: 19–23). For the peasant, the conditions for democratic participation are very much present at the community level. This should determine the form and content of development strategy and the social institutions which are important in people's lives. People at all levels must be given the right to establish and manage their own organizations, such as cooperatives, organizations of women and youth, workers and consumers. These local-level organizations must be given greater control over the allocation of resources, the disbursement of funds intended to benefit them, and the appointment and control of officials meant to serve them.

Fostering civil society requires a gendered perspective. It is particularly important to recognize the role of women in the struggle for democracy since women constitute an important component of civil society (Hirschmann, 1995: 1291–1302). For democracy to succeed, there must be a firm commitment to full constitutional guarantees for women to have the right of access to land and control of resources, as well as to providing opportunities for leadership training. This is the only way to end the abuse and manipulation, as well as the anonymity, of their production.

Conscientization is the first step towards liberation

Introducing democracy before empowering excluded sectors is like attempting a space flight into orbit in the absence of combustion. Meaningful political participation requires grassroots education to create more active, self-confident and competent citizens. Only by expanding their visions and raising their consciousness can poor people and peasants undermine the vicious circle of mass exclusion and marginalization. While peasants, by and large, are aware of their situation at the local level, they have neither the capacity nor the resources to influence events in the world beyond their respective villages. Only heightened consciousness will give them awareness of the range of available value choices, and the social and political implications. Effecting such change is a slow and time-consuming job. As Hollnsteiner observed, in the case of the Philippines, it takes a long time for peasants living on the margin to move from simple, concrete and short-term personal issues to more complex, abstract, long-term and systemic issues (Hollnsteiner, 1979: 383–4).

Some of the education and capacity-building programmes funded by Western donors and executed by such institutions as the National Demo-

Box 2.1 USAID support for civic education in Zambia

USAID's five-year Democratic Governance Project (DGP) in Zambia, which was managed by the Southern University of Louisiana, extended grants to sixty-one organizations involved in civic and human rights initiatives. The grants were very effective in mobilizing an array of civic activities to inform the grassroots population about basic elements of democracy. The activities included workshops and discussion groups and a variety of innovative theatre productions, as well as a revision of the junior secondary school civic curriculum that should have a major impact in terms of schoolchildren being exposed to an explanation of democratic values (Braxton, 1998: 4–5). In addition, the project supported the efforts of the Foundation for Democratic Progress (FODEP) to change its status from that of an election-monitoring body to a civic education organization. FODEP's capacity has been strengthened; its activities range from the instruction of trainers to civic education workshops at national, district and community levels. It also supported the Zambia Institute for Mass Communication (ZAMCOM), a multimedia training facility for communications professionals. The main purpose of the support is the promotion of media independence.

cratic Institute (NDI) and AFL–CIO have been extremely useful in creating public awareness. Specifically, these include programmes in Zambia to foster the establishment of independent professional journalism, and civic education programmes in Mozambique designed to equip citizens for effective participation. In Mozambique, NDI conducted a series of seminars for national organizations on advocacy, coalition building, effective use of the media, and the right to petition. NDI also assisted the Mozambican Association for the Development of Democracy (AMODE) to build its capacity and become a viable civic education organization for developing the skills to conduct civic and voter education (Brophy, 1998: 4–5). During municipal elections, for example, AMODE organized candidate forums where mayoral candidates were given the opportunity to answer questions about their policies. Such forums provide citizens with the opportunity to listen to candidates and make informed choices on election day.

Building the capacity of civil society organizations

There is no point in talking about the importance of people's participation if the basic elements required for the instrumentalization of participation are not present at the village level. Capacity building entails leadership training for both men and women, developing locally based research skills, dissemination of information, networking and lobbying skills. Institution building would also involve improving communication flows between communities and different sets of rural institutions, thus helping peasants and poor people become the catalyst for change. Democracy cannot work without a high level of information and knowledge. Strong popular organizations, therefore, enable different sectors of society to assert and fight for their particular social right. These local organizations must also find ways to organize for the purpose of gaining influence at the national level, opening channels of communication and representing peasant interests at the top.

Recognizing the rights of nationalities

Politicized ethnic sentiments remain the most meaningful force in Africa today; hence the challenge of building democratic societies will constantly reflect this tug-of-war. Many of the new political forces opposed to one-party rule in African countries derive their strength from their appeal to ethnic identity or religious affiliation. Given a history of colonial and post-colonial authoritarian rule, in a context of scarcity and ethnic strife, democratic values and commitment are difficult to sustain. Ethnic nationalism cannot, therefore, be swept under the carpet. African states must come to terms with the issue. Regionalism and decentralization of power to the local level can go a long way in addressing this issue (Mengisteab, 1997: 111–32).

Ethiopia is one country in Africa where the call for political freedom has become intermixed with calls for regional freedom. The government of Prime Minister Melese Zenawi has been experimenting with ethnic-based federalism since 1991 as a way to end centuries of ethnic hostility. Although many commentators characterize this experiment with ethnic democracy as a contradiction in terms, warning that it may lead to further disintegration and conflict, the government is determined to push through its policies since it sees no other alternative to perpetual bloodshed in the country (Crummey, 1994; Ottaway, 1994). The 1994 constitution endorses the unconditional right of every nation (ethnic group) in the country to self-determination, including the right to self-governance, cultural autonomy, as well as secession. Furthermore, the constitution guarantees special representation for minority nations in the federal parliament.

The experiment in ethnic federalism has indeed brought relative peace to Ethiopia, a country accustomed to bloodshed and perpetual conflict. At the same time, rebuilding Ethiopia's war-torn economy and implementing radical economic reform programmes while simultaneously experimenting in state building have been very difficult tasks. Weak institutions and a lack of trained Ethiopians are hampering efforts at economic reform and consolidation of democracy. Moreover, while the bold experiment with ethnic federalism is a step in the right direction, it is meaningless unless accompanied by significant democratization and an improvement in the living standards of the people by creating the conditions for rapid economic expansion. Whether the government will be able to achieve economic recovery and consolidate democracy unaffected by the remote forces of globalization remains to be seen. As Ethiopia is one of the poorest countries in the world, the prospects for success are exceedingly dim.

Finally, any attempt to resolve ethnic hostilities through constitutional means and state-building experiments will not be sustainable if real efforts are not made through education and other means to change people's prejudices, which are socially constructed. The scrapping of apartheid laws in South Africa and Jim Crow laws in the United States has not ended white racism towards blacks. Similarly, ethnic federalism has not changed the attitudes of the various Ethiopian ethnic groups towards one another. This will take time. The media, religious institutions, sports clubs, schools, trade unions, and every other social and public institution in the country must play a critical role in promoting and respecting cultural, religious and linguistic diversity and coexistence.

Promoting political reconciliation

Promoting democratization can be a complex business, particularly in societies that have been torn apart by internal conflict. Effective governance requires political stability. National reconciliation is a prerequisite for sustainable peace and the development of civil society. Furthermore, efforts to resolve conflicts and promote peace must address the structural causes of conflict. Conflict is almost by definition associated with major human rights violations, and it is often difficult to strike a balance between justice and reconciliation (see Chapter 7).

One of the characteristics of political underdevelopment is that, in the face of conflict, people tend to fight out their differences with weapons of mass destruction instead of learning to fight with convincing words and ideas. Democracy is based on tolerance, peaceful persuasion and respect for the principle of the rule of the majority. We need to work very hard to find ways of resolving differences peacefully. We must develop different types of public education programmes to promote public dialogue and deepen the process of cultural tolerance and problem-solving.

Creating equitable economic growth with justice

The cause of economic renewal and social justice cannot be divorced from the crucial task of building a democratic society. It is difficult to escape the reality that a central element of the contemporary challenge of building democracy is tied to the task of eradicating poverty and related social injustices. While poverty on its own may not be sufficient to wreck a democratic project, its persistence or even intensification certainly does contribute to the creation of conditions that could stultify the basis for democratic politics. Tackling poverty and related social injustices is, therefore, simultaneously an investment in democratic governance and in the prospects for its consolidation.

It is accepted that the issue of Africa's economic renewal is very complex and multifaceted. The missing ingredients so far have been the absence of coherent policy and an enabling domestic political environment designed to harness the energies and entrepreneurship of ordinary Africans and the indigenous private sector. African governments must, therefore, create and maintain an enabling environment for economic growth that will allow individuals and businesses to save, invest and produce. Greater flexibility in policy can be afforded by providing viable alternative solutions to state policy and incentives for communities that have mobilized resources, and by encouraging greater NGO and private-sector involvement in service provision. The importance of investment in small and medium-sized businesses should be emphasized, as such enterprises are an important source of employment in Africa and contribute significantly to the continent's GDP. To create greater synergy, planning must become a more broadly based activity, involving different constituencies with different ideologies.

Moreover, if Africa is to participate fully in the global economy, political and economic reform must be carried out. It must include predictable policies, economic deregulation, openness to trade, rationalized tax structures, adequate infrastructure, transparency and accountability, and protection of property rights. To fail to redress the conditions of the poor through enabling policies is to undermine the empowering potential of democracy for the populace at large.

Conclusions

Democracy in Africa will not take root unless it is anchored in strong and effective local and national government institutions and strong legal foundations. Public officials will not be able to carry out their mandate if they are vested with very weak government institutions and courts. It is therefore difficult to conceive of development and democratization without a viable, accountable and active state (Mengisteab, 1997: 126). The crucial question is, how can African statehood be enhanced and development accelerated in a parallel fashion?

For democracy to take root in Africa, strong and independent social movements and civil society groups must be encouraged to check the excesses of state power. Until opposition leaders and urban elites respect the knowledge of ordinary Africans and accept that democracy does not flow down from the top, their efforts at building a democratic society will be futile. The participation of citizens cannot simply be ordered from above; it has to be demanded and carried out from below. This is the cardinal rule of democracy. Up to now, elite-led opposition parties have put the cart before the horse. It is not too late to go back to basics and put the horse in front of the cart.

Finally, democracy is less a formalistic system than an attitude. It is a way of approaching the business of government, a way of settling rules for government, a way of creating enough checks and balances so that the government is dependent less on individuals and their personal whims, and more on systems and processes. There is probably no strong connection between democracy and the existence of a written constitution. Britain and New Zealand stand out as strong democracies and yet neither has a written constitution. Where citizens of a country have no sense of democracy and are unwilling or unable to insist that their leaders deliver it, a written constitution, however eloquently it proclaims democracy, will be insufficient to guarantee it. Democracy depends on certain core values such as tolerance, trust and honesty, which cannot be secured by a constitution.

Notes

1. As Teodoro Obiang Nguema Mbasongo did in Equatorial Guinea in February 1996. Or consider the re-election of Togo's President Gnasingbe Eyadema in June 1998, when the vote count was simply halted when early returns showed Eyadema in danger of losing to his main opponent Gilchrist Olympio.

2. These important principles are incorporated in UNECA's *African Alternative Framework to Structural Adjustment* (UNECA, 1990).

3. Contribution by authors to International Policies, African Realities: An Electronic Roundtable, hosted by Africa Policy Information Center, Session 2: Democracy and Human Rights (www.africapolicy.org).

4. 'Farmers' boycott', *Nation*, 20 February 1993, p. 5.

CHAPTER 3

Reforming African Education for the Twenty-first Century

Education is the cornerstone of human development in every society. A sound development strategy aimed at promoting economic development, democracy and social justice must be fully cognizant of human resource development. For, when all is said and done, development is about people: their physical health, moral integrity and intellectual awareness. Through education, people become aware of their environment and of the social and economic options available to them. The mobilization and management of the necessary human and material resources to ensure that children receive appropriate and good quality education is a complex challenge, and one which requires the collaboration of many partners – teachers, parents, administrators and community leaders.

Despite the tremendous gains made by African governments over the past forty years in increasing access to education, greater challenges lie ahead if the global goal of 'Education For All' is to be achieved. The current state of education in sub-Saharan Africa is lamentable. Although enrolment in primary schools has increased since colonial times – from 25 per cent of all children in 1960 to about 60 per cent in 1999 – the numbers of those uneducated are also growing. According to UNESCO, around 40 million primary-school-age children in sub-Saharan Africa receive no basic education (UNESCO, 1993). Perhaps the most daunting challenge is that of promoting female education (Odanga and Heneveld, 1995). Current spending on each child is half what it was twenty years ago, and in sharp contrast to spending in the developed countries. The United States, for example, spends about $5,000 per student per annum at the primary-school level, while Zambia spends $27 and India $12 (Oxfam, 1999). Fiscal crisis, low student participation, high dropout and repetition levels, and poor academic achievement are widespread destructive trends throughout the system.

Moreover, the dynamic growth in quantity since independence has been achieved at the expense of quality and relevance. Education systems are not keeping pace with changes in the economy and technology that have enormous impacts on the type of skills and the critical thinking required in the emerging world economy. Today's low-quality education has serious implications for tomorrow's development tasks. The dreadful state of African education was well captured in a recent issue of the *Economist:*

> All over Africa every day children walk or run for miles to reach decrepit buildings, which often do little more than keep off the sun and rain. There may be no water or electricity and not enough benches or desks. Books and equipment, if any, are shared in classes of up to 100. Sport is kicking a ball of wrapped-up rags around a stony field. In some areas schools have to take one set of pupils in the morning, another set in the afternoon. And many children do not get there at all. (*Economist*, 27 March 1999: 45–6)

The root cause of the crisis in African education dates back to the colonial period. The problem has been aggravated by the ambitious but misguided policies of post-independence governments anxious to correct the legacies of colonialism. In its most recent manifestations, the educational crisis in Africa has been exacerbated by the regressive macroeconomic policies that African governments have implemented since the 1980s at the behest of the IMF and the World Bank. While the purported goal of these economic reform programmes was to bring efficiency in the economy and in the use of public resources, the outcome has been detrimental to three main components: education, health and nutrition. Many governments have been prompted to reduce their educational budgets, at the cost of lower standards. Teacher salaries have fallen to desperately low levels, and the acquisition of books and instructional materials has been severely disrupted (Kelly, 1991: 8). The cuts, combined with economic crises, have contributed to low educational standards. Sub-Saharan Africa is the only region in the developing world where total educational expenditures have been declining over the past two decades. These disinvestments in human capital development have come precisely at a time when the continent should have been doing the opposite: investing more in order to minimize the gap between Africa and the rest of the world and to build a foundation for lasting human development.

It follows from the decline in investment that, notwithstanding the new educational requirements being dictated by the current techno-economic paradigm, sub-Saharan Africa faces an altogether different set of problems. These problems range from difficulties in providing minimum basic education for a rapidly growing primary-school population to the development of skills adequate for improving standards of living in both rural and urban areas. Countries that do not keep up with global technology often collapse, unable to maintain their standard of living, much less to increase it (Sawyerr, 1998: 20–25). The educational system, therefore, requires fundamental reform and an infusion of funds, qualified managers and policy analysts to make it effective and consistent with the overall development needs of the continent. This must be followed by a plan to transform curricula and educational content to improve the link between graduating students (the outputs) and the needs of the economy.

The Scale of the Educational Crisis

Despite the evident strides made in expanding educational opportunities in post-independence Africa, a number of problems have emerged. These include high dropout rates at almost every level of the educational system; growing unemployment among graduates; regional and gender disparities in access to education; poor quality education; and unsustainable levels of educational budgeting (Psacharopoulos, 1990: 5). Expansionary pressure has left little time for qualitative changes. It is impossible to enumerate every aspect of the educational crisis in Africa in this short chapter. Nevertheless, the following stand out as the most critical problems facing the African educational system today.

Limited access

Demand for education remains high (partly due to the expanding population) and parents still want their children to attend primary, and in many cases also secondary, school. This is understandable since education was the primary qualification for access to well-paying jobs in the first few years after independence. For example, in Kenya rewards for individuals with a secondary-school certificate in 1970 far exceeded the returns that accrued to the most successful entrepreneurs or subsistence farmers (Marris and Somerset, 1971; ILO, 1981: 11). The policy of guaranteed employment for university graduates followed by many African governments, until the economic crisis of the 1980s, helped further to fuel the competition for higher education. This led to a tremendous increase in school enrolments in the face of a scramble for attractive white-collar jobs.

Table 3.1 Gross educational enrolment ratios in Africa (% of eligible students)

Level/Year	1960	1970	1980	1990	1995
Primary	44	57	78	76	78
Secondary	5	11	21	29	31
Tertiary	1	2	3	5	6

Source: UNESCO, 1996; UNESCO, 1998.

The forty-five African country reports prepared for the recent Education For All (EFA 2000) Assessment show that in the past three decades governments have primarily focused on expanding access to education. While some 40 million African primary-school-age children are out of school, at least 20 million more school-age children are in school today compared to 1990. On the other hand, despite greater demand, there are fewer resources available to finance education and other types of development. The aim of achieving universal primary education (UPE) within the first twenty years of independence has been abandoned (UNESCO, 1961: 10).

Current demographic projections point to the problems that lie ahead. Sub-Saharan Africa has a school-age population growing twice as fast as that of North Africa or the Middle East. Africa's primary-school-age population is projected to increase by 59 million between 1990 and 2010. Yet Africa is the only region in the developing world with a decreasing primary-school enrolment ratio due to limited resources for expansion (World Bank, 1995b: 40). Female enrolment rates in particular remain low despite improvements over the past three decades. In 1990 only 46 per cent of primary-school-age girls were in school.

Higher drop-out rates

Despite the good news of increased enrolment, drop-out and repetition rates are very high at all levels of the educational system. Moreover, the number of pupils dropping out before grade 5 has been on the increase in almost half of the countries for which data are available. In Malawi, for example, only a third of children starting school in 1995 were expected to reach grade 5. Approximate proportions of the school-age population entering grade 1 are 70 per cent for sub-Saharan Africa, 95 per cent for South Asia, 98 per cent for South America. However, the proportion reaching grade five for all three areas is approximately only 47 per cent (World Bank, 1994b). An estimated 25 per cent of those in school repeat the same class before they move forward to the next stage.

With increased demand for education, African governments were soon forced to limit the influx by introducing a pyramid structure into the system, which allowed a large number of pupils to enter primary schools and then progressively restricted opportunities as the students climbed the educational ladder through secondary school to university. The examination system is thus used not to measure progress in learning but, rather, as a tool for rationing limited spaces. This situation leads in turn to high repetition rates at primary- and secondary-school levels as students repeat the final year in the hope of improving their examination grade to gain entrance to the next level.

Low quality education

Rapid enrolment growth, coupled with declining resources, has significantly lowered educational quality. The problem has been exacerbated by a severe lack of tools, technology, instructional materials and textbooks; poorly trained and unqualified teachers; and curricula and syllabi not closely linked to performance standards and measures of outcome. Until recently, efforts at improving quality have focused primarily on teacher training and reducing student-to-teacher ratios. However, the system has fallen short in realizing these objectives due to a shortage of trained teachers and low retention ratios because of low salaries (Psacharopoulos, 1990).

While investing in education is clearly a necessity, increased expenditure does not necessarily boost equity or improve quality. A considerable degree of improvement can be achieved through more efficient use of existing resources. In addition to the bias in favour of the tertiary sector, a significant proportion of public expenditure on education goes towards salaries, pensions and infrastructure. Teacher costs typically account for about two-thirds of total spending on education (UNESCO, 1993). Improvement in quality will require the setting of standards; providing basic instructional material such as textbooks, graphic materials and computers; increased professionalism among teachers; in-service training to upgrade teachers' skills; and paying teachers a living wage.

Education costs at an unsustainable level

A consequence of rapid expansion of school enrolments has been ever burgeoning educational budgets in most African countries. These can no longer be sustained. Notwithstanding severe cuts since the 1980s as a result of structural adjustment programmes, education continues to claim the biggest single share of the public budget in most African states – an average of about 20 per cent. The rationale for higher public expenditure on education was based on the assumption that education will lead to equitable distribution of income and increased social mobility.

According to UNESCO and the World Bank, sub-Saharan Africa is misallocating its resources, since a disproportionate amount of public funding goes to tertiary education, rather than to primary education, which benefits the poor. Public spending per student in higher education in Africa is about fourty-four times the spending per student in primary education (World Bank, 1995b: 58). The share of public spending in tertiary education in sub-Saharan Africa is at the same level as in OECD countries.

While the need for efficiency in the allocation of educational resources is critical and long overdue, donor governments who advocated investment in favour of primary education have failed to understand the complexity of the problem. Despite growing demographic trends and limited options for those who come out of the secondary-school system, university education remains inadequate throughout Africa. The need to expand the system is self-evident to anyone who has lived and worked in the continent. Currently, barely 4 per cent of university-age people enter tertiary education. Moreover, existing university capacity has been effectively destroyed by the misguided policies of the World Bank and the IMF throughout the 1980s, and by the looting of the public treasury, and hence of the resources destined for education, by corrupt African elites. The recent Partnership for African Universities initiative launched by the Carnegie Corporation and the Rockefeller, Ford and MacArthur Foundations to spend $100 million over the next five years to upgrade the capacities of African universities in research and teaching is clear recognition of the damage that has been done to the continent's institutions of higher learning.[1]

High unemployment among graduates

Graduate unemployment, which in the early 1970s was limited to primary- and secondary-school graduates, has now become a permanent reality for a growing number of university students. The increasing imbalance between jobseekers, on the one hand, and widespread misperception about well-paying jobs in the modern sector, on the other, has merely intensified the demand for education. In Zimbabwe, for example, 250,000 school-leavers each year chase 40,000 available jobs in the formal sector (Mandebvu,

1994: 4). This phenomenon is found in almost every African country. Linking education and the economy remains one of the greatest challenges.

Rural–urban and gender disparities

The effort to achieve a wider distribution of educational opportunities by accelerating the rate of expansion in the post-independence period has, in fact, accentuated the disparities inherited from the colonial past. The inequalities are further aggravated by differences in the quality of teachers, educational facilities, and other inputs among schools serving different geographical areas and income groups. Educational access in rural areas is far more limited than in urban areas. Widespread disparities are also found in the educational opportunities available to boys and girls. As Oxfam's *Education Now* report notes, 'At the heart of the education systems of the developing world is a pattern of gender apartheid which distributes opportunity not on the basis of inherited rights, but on the basis of inherited chromosomes' (Oxfam, 1999).

Educational Policy after Independence

Throughout the 1960s, the main problem in the educational sector of developing countries, as perceived by planners, politicians and theorists, related primarily to the challenge of producing large numbers of educated people to promote rapid economic growth and the Africanization of the economy and public administration (Harbison and Meyers, 1964; Schultz, 1961: 1–17). Thus a consistent theme reverberated throughout the literature on human capital: accelerated development depends upon enlargement of the supply of educated manpower, which in turn depends on broadening access to formal education.

Proponents of the human capital approach argued that the rapid recovery of Western Europe with American capital through the Marshall Plan could be largely attributed to the existence of a ready pool of qualified manpower. Hence, less developed countries, lacking in the 'knowledge and superior technique of production', should be provided with aid and technical assistance to increase the quality of their human capital. This would result in the achievement of self-sustained growth (Karabel and Halsey, 1977). In sum, what American capital had done in Western Europe could be replicated in Africa if Africans invested more in the development of their human resources and if additional foreign capital was channelled into these countries for educational purposes. Subsequently, international organizations (World Bank, ILO, UNESCO) and foundations (Ford and Rockefeller) duly responded to this perceived need by funding educational and training programmes in Africa (Kinyanjui, 1980).

This approach to development was echoed in the years immediately after independence and, to a large extent, accounts for the rapid expansion of educational opportunities in the 1960s (Ginzberg, 1971; Jolly, 1969). The predominant themes of education policies were that education must foster (1) a sense of nationhood and national unity; and (2) the skills and knowledge required for national development. Thus, money and resources were directed into a tremendous expansion of a system still largely cast in a colonial mould. Fundamental changes in structure, curriculum and examination were not undertaken, however. Moreover, the whole style and approach of the educational system was never transformed to make it consistent with the post-independence reality.

To appreciate better the reasons why newly independent governments devoted too much attention to expanding access to education, it is important to understand the policies of colonial governments with regard to the education of Africans.[2] For example, in 1909 the British government commissioned a study of Education in British African territories. The Frazer Report recommended the establishment of education in British territories on a racial basis. The reason for this segregationist policy was summed up in the Beecher Report of 1949, which stated that

> African education cannot be compared with education in European or Asian society. The particular nature of African education, with its limited achievements, is such that long-term planning alone is appropriate. We are only (with African education) at the state of establishing standards, while European and Asian educational systems are concerned with maintaining long and well-established standards. (Kenya Colony and Protectorate, 1949)

The material reason for segregation was that the various racial groups, as in the case of Kenya, Zimbabwe and South Africa, were being trained to maintain their respective social status in the colonial economic and social order. The Europeans were being trained to be the masters, the supervisors, the leaders; the Africans to be the servants, the labourers. Each had to be educated to take his place in society, not according to his ability but according to his race (Mutua, 1975). A more recent incarnation of such a system was the Bantu Education system that functioned in South Africa until the early 1990s. Thus, the allocation of colonial state revenue, the ideological outlook and the skills imparted in colonial educational institutions all reflected the expected positions Africans and non-Africans would occupy in the colonial hierarchy (Kinyanjui, 1974).

Table 3.2 Post-Independence educational enrolment growth in Africa (thousands)

Level/year	1960	1970	1980	1990	1995
Primary	19,312	33,372	61,284	80,595	95,378
Secondary	1,885	5,353	13,738	24,345	30,378
Tertiary	185	479	1,316	2,856	3,795
Total	21,832	39,204	76,448	107,796	129,551

Source: UNESCO, 1997.

In settler colonies such as Kenya and Zimbabwe, the provision of elementary and secondary education on the eve of independence reflected a racial pattern that was characteristic of the colonial mode of development. In Kenya in 1963, for example, about 30 per cent of all secondary schools were located in the urban areas, mainly catering to the European and Asian communities, which formed about 3 per cent of the total Kenyan population. While 75 per cent of the European school-age population in Kenya was in school in 1963, the corresponding figure for Africans was only 35 per cent (Kinyanjui, 1974). Inequality was thus deeply embedded within the economy and the educational system. It was obvious that something had to be done in the immediate post-independence period.

The lack of sufficient numbers of qualified Africans to modernize the economy and run the affairs of the new states at the time of independence was, therefore, the result of deliberate colonial policy which restricted educational access. For example, in 1964, a Kenyan survey on high-level manpower revealed how few Africans there were in the prestigious professions: 36 doctors, 20 electrical engineers, 17 university professors and 7 economists (Republic of Kenya, 1972).

Newly independent African governments responded to the inherited educational disparities in two ways: (1) by Africanizing school enrolments, and (2) by rapidly expanding the educational system from primary school to university. Education was to serve as a vehicle for 'nation building' as well as in the Africanization of the economy (Samoff, 1987: 334). Rapid expansion of enrolments was also justified in order to achieve a rapid rate of economic progress. In the Gambia, Ghana, Kenya, Zambia, Sierra Leone and Botswana enrolments more than doubled between 1960 and 1970. This development suggests not only a general rise in the level of literacy but also substantial increases in access to educational opportunities for Africans. Table 3.2 shows the consequential post-independence enrolment explosion in Africa.

The Missed Opportunities: Africa's Experience with Educational Reform

Fundamental reform in each of the problem areas described above poses important challenges to African governments. Education is a contested terrain and involves economic, political and pedagogical dimensions. Educational reform is further compounded by a weak and inadequate planning and management capacity throughout the continent, the absence of data, weakness in policy analysis, an inability to mobilize resources, a lack of political will, and the failure to involve citizens in educational policy-making (Craig, 1990). In this section, the efforts of government to institute reform in two specific periods are examined: 1970–80 and the post-1980 period.

Emphasis on education and employment: 1970–80

The impetus for educational reform by African governments since the early 1970s has, more often than not, been driven by political considerations rather than by a conscious decision to improve the quality of education, streamline educational management, and contain costs. The driving force for government intervention in the educational sector has been the explosive problem of graduate unemployment and high drop-out rates. Measures to deal with the problem of graduate unemployment in Africa have concentrated on curriculum changes and the expansion of institutions to provide technical and agricultural education.

Curricular reform

Making education relevant to needs and situations in Africa meant that curricula and textbooks had to be reformed to take into account the African environment and cultural heritage, and the needs of the African economy. To this end, many governments shifted to technical, agricultural and vocational training under the erroneous belief that the inherited educational system fostered a 'white-collar mentality'. This mentality, it was believed, made youngsters set their sights on the limited number of civil-service jobs in urban areas, and caused them to reject agricultural or manual work. This 'white-collar' attitude, it was concluded, was the major cause of graduate unemployment and the high drop-out rate. According to an editorial in the Kenyan *Daily Nation*:

> The trouble with our educational system is that it just isn't suited to our development program. In its original form, the system was designed to produce a small group of clerical 'yes men' that would help perpetuate colonialism in Kenya. And the disheartening thing is that this sorry state of affairs has been allowed to continue in the post-independence period. So, each year, we are producing school leavers whose most important qualification is the ability to speak English with an Oxford accent. Because they have no skills, they start loitering in urban areas with imponderable consequences. *The solution to this problem lies in reforming the educational system to give it a rural orientation.* (19 January 1982: 6, emphasis added)

Reforming the educational system in this way involved promoting vocational and practical-oriented training. One solution proposed was the establishment of a village polytechnic to equip primary-school leavers with simple, practical skills which could be utilized locally in a self-employed capacity. The most common of these courses, some of which are still in existence today, were offered by the village polytechnic and non-formal educational entities run and operated by churches and non-governmental organizations, such as 4–H Clubs, YMCA and Young Farmers Clubs. These include carpentry and masonry for boys and tailoring/dress-making and home economics for girls. Other courses involved book-keeping, accounting and typing, leather tanning and shoe making, metal work, welding and fitting, motor mechanics, animal husbandry, horticulture, and beekeeping. It was believed at the time that investment in the village polytechnic would result in increased output for smallholder agriculture through the adoption of appropriate technology and promotion of rural trading activities. This would in turn increase rural income and lower the rate of rural-to-urban migration (Sheffield, 1967).

Instead of fostering aspirations to pass examinations and gain white-collar jobs, these programmes sought to impart the skills necessary for gaining local craft employment. While the new orthodoxy sought to reform the colonial educational system by making changes in the different components of the school system, in the end it simply consolidated it. By placing new ceilings and limitations on students' choice, it served to relegate African students to a lower status, thus maintaining intact the main elements of the colonial educational and economic structures: academic education for the rich and vocational education for the poor (Cheru, 1987).

Vocationalizing secondary education

A similar approach was taken to deal with the problems of secondary-school graduates. At first, it was suggested that secondary technical school graduates would have a better chance of obtaining employment than students with academic secondary training. Because of Africa's drive towards industrialization, it seemed certain that the expanding manufacturing sector would absorb the graduates of technical colleges (Cheru, 1987). But as these jobs in the manufacturing sector became increasingly scarce, partly due to capital intensity, governments began to emphasize the importance of technical and vocational education for self-employment in the informal sector. However, studies in Kenya, Tanzania, Botswana, Uganda and Ethiopia have shown that vocationalizing the curriculum had little direct bearing on the employment prospects of graduates.

A recurrent theme in all the reforms discussed above is the view that education and production ought to be closely linked. The integration of education and production was expected to discourage students from seeking employment in the urban economy and lead them into rural areas where agricultural employment was considered plentiful. In Kenya, this thinking was originally spawned by the National Christian Council of Kenya (NCCK) in the mid-1960s. One of its pioneering reports, entitled *After School What?*, focused attention on the hundreds of thousands of primary-school leavers (67,000 in 1964) who had little hope of finding well-paid employment or further education, yet who were unprepared in terms of knowledge, skills or expectations for the rural environment with which they were left (National Christian Council of Kenya, 1966). The skills they acquired had little in common with the skills needed to become successful in farming.

Combining education with production

Virtually every African state has taken initiatives to link the world of school with the world of work. These have taken four forms. First, most states introduced vocational subjects into the curriculum, while some, for example Zimbabwe, made them obligatory for all pupils. A second type of initiative was the introduction of polytechnic education, whereby pupils spent part of the school day on farms or in workshops; this was introduced in Mali and Zimbabwe. A more extreme form was the turning of schools into production units, such as in Benin in 1971, in Tanzania's Education for Self-reliance of 1967, or the Brigades, a private initiative in Botswana. Finally, National Youth Community Services schemes were introduced in countries such as Malawi, Ghana, Botswana, Nigeria and the 'Zemecha' project in previously Marxist Ethiopia.

Many of these vocational-oriented school reforms are to be welcomed on strictly educational grounds. Nevertheless, their overall impact on the employment prospects of graduates, and on reducing the pressure for expansion of upper secondary and higher education, has been negligible. Many of the schemes were not very successful, as they were difficult to implement. Some were mandatory and imposed by government from the top; students usually resisted them. The vocational training emphasis is rarely accompanied by other government support services, such as credit or land, to help the graduates succeed in the labour market (Middleton and Demsky, 1989). This point illustrates the difficulty of getting started in self-employment regardless of one's technical skills. Moreover, not everyone can enter vocational schools since access is severely restricted due to limited availability of space. This is partly explained by the relatively high cost per student in technical schools in comparison to that in ordinary primary and secondary schools.

The challenge of education for rural development cannot be met by good intentions alone. While a reassessment of the value of formal education for an essentially rural Africa is badly needed, advocates of vocational and technical education have missed the point. The provision of vocational training must be accompanied by other formal assistance. Rapid transformation of the rural economy will be critical to the functioning of village polytechnics. Graduates must have access to credit, further advice on how to set up a business, product development and quality control, and marketing techniques if they are to succeed in self-employment.

Moreover, advocating an expansion of vocational and technical education without addressing the existing disparities in educational resources and opportunities seems contradictory. Any vocational educational programme that leads to an essentially dual system will ultimately work to reinforce the status quo and thus will neither provide mobility for the school leavers nor promote the interests of society at large. The majority of African students resented vocational schooling since they perceived it as a continuation of the much-hated colonial educational policy, and as an attempt by elite-dominated governments to keep them on the farm, thus denying them the possibility of upward mobility into white-collar jobs. For example, in spite of the early emphasis on vocational secondary schools in Ethiopia, many more students went to academic secondary schools since more opportunities were offered in these (Kiros, 1990). Zambia and Tanzania experienced a similar outcome (Achola, 1990; Cooksey, 1986: 183–202). The lesson from this and from similar examples is clear: any system which contains dual educational institutions will be seen as prejudicial to the groups whose access is limited to the lower status level.

Finally, changes in the educational structure alone are insufficient to bring about employment in the labour market. Although education does effect major changes in society in the long run, schools are in the short run largely dependent variables of the society that surrounds them. Any attempt to formalize and ritualize vocational education without significant change in the existing structure of economic and social relationships, and particularly in the incentive structure that directly links the educational sector to the labour market, will be futile. It would be foolish to expect of schools that which they cannot alone provide. Rapid transformation of the rural economy will be critical to the functioning of rural polytechnics, even at the limited level at which they are now operating in most African countries. Moreover, vocational schooling must be complemented with more academic education to ensure sustained development and to strengthen Africa's ability to compete in the globalized marketplace.

Post-1980 reform: the efficiency approach

The widespread economic deterioration of the 1980s forced many African governments to sign up to structural adjustment programmes with the International Monetary Fund and the World Bank. These reform initiatives aimed at containing costs and improving efficiency involved the curtailment of state and particularly public expenditure. The downsizing of educational spending has had serious consequences for African education.

While improved efficiency in resource allocation to the education sector is long overdue, indiscriminate reductions in state expenditure on public goods and services and the introduction of user fees have done more to undermine African education than the exclusionary policy practised by colonial powers. The model of economic reform that the IMF and the World Bank practised in Africa in the 1980s was in stark contrast to the policies followed by the newly industrializing countries of East Asia, which the international financial institutions hold up as models to be emulated.

The 'efficiency' approach narrowly focused much of its proposal for education reform on the issue of whether national governments should spend less on tertiary education and redirect the bulk of their educational budgets towards the primary sector in order to improve access for the masses. Although there is clear evidence that the social rates of return on investment in primary education usually exceed those of higher education, it is extremely misguided to concentrate resources at the primary-school level and ignore higher and tertiary education. This strategy neither brings equity nor improves the contribution of education to national development (World Bank, 1994b). The real issue is not whether resources should go to primary or tertiary education, but that it should be a priority of African governments to invest in human capital across the board. The main concern of educational planners in Africa should be whether investment in education is being used efficiently. What Africa needs is well-conceived and well-managed educational projects that are designed to raise the analytical and skills levels of its citizens, so that they in turn can raise productivity and improve the welfare of the people. It is not primary-school diploma holders who are destined to shape Africa in the new century. Expansion and improvement of university education and investment in research and development are the best approach.

Priorities and Strategies for Education: Enhancing Human Capacities in an Era of Globalization

The increasing tendency towards the global assimilation of scientific knowledge and the diffusion of technology has resulted in a qualitative shift towards knowledge-intensive production. In the last fifteen years, the role of education has become even more important in economic growth and social transformation as the unprecedented pace of scientific and technological advances transforms the global economy. These developments have important social and economic implications for employment generation, standards of living, the capacity to achieve industrial transformation, and the enhancement of competitive advantage. As knowledge becomes the crucial factor in building global competitive strategies, it has significantly altered the educational and skills requirements of work and the workplace. An essential prerequisite for the success of this objective is the need to build broad-based networks or linkages between firms involved in domestic production, the educational system, and existing technological and physical infrastructures.

At the same time, the benefits of technological revolution are not evenly distributed across the globe. The pace of technological diffusion is now accompanied by a knowledge and skills gap both within and among nations. This technological/information divide is becoming more apparent in the specific case of sub-Saharan Africa (Sachs, 2000a: 81–3). The present situation makes it imperative that technological progress is incorporated into existing national human resource development strategies in sub-Saharan Africa. A new strategy of technological promotion must be based on the interplay of academia, government and industry. With this in mind, African countries will need to enhance their capacity to produce and trade in technology-intensive goods before they can break the core–periphery pattern of international trade. Only then will Africa experience an economic revival. Nevertheless, knowledge and technology cannot be produced and national systems of innovation fostered if governments do not invest in them.

Technological diffusion now involves more than the acquisition of machinery, product designs and related know-how. It requires continuous incremental technical changes in order to improve productivity and efficiency. The capacity of African countries to understand, access, apply, adapt and manipulate technology for development production essentially depends on the existing scientific, technological and educational infrastructure. Fundamental reform in African education is the starting point for technological progress. As Castells argues, 'every country's educational system has become fundamental to its national production and its role in the global economy' (Castells, 1993). Educational reform should, therefore, focus on the following.

Improvement in educational planning and administration

The challenge of improving educational planning and administration is very complex, requiring the collaboration of many partners, including teachers, parents, administrators and community leaders. At the minimum, reforming African education for the twenty-first century should include the following: (1) establishing better regulatory frameworks and administrative mechanisms; (2) delineating more sharply responsibilities among different levels of government; (3) ensuring that decentralization does not lead to inequitable distribution of resources; (4) making more efficient use of existing human and financial resources; (5) improving capacities for managing diversity, disparity and change; (6) integrating programmes within education and strengthening their convergence with those of other sectors, especially health, labour and social welfare; and (7) providing training for school leaders and other educational personnel; (8) ensuring gender equality.

Prioritizing investment decisions

Boosting Africa's capacity to control its own processes of change and improve welfare for the majority of the people necessitates committing a higher proportion of public spending to education. This spending should be cost-effective, reaching broadly across the population while targeting needy groups. Enhancing the quality of education and ensuring its relevance must also be an aim. The latter will specifically entail investing in areas of high return: basic education, technical and vocational training, science and technology, and agricultural research and development.

Investment decisions should go hand in hand with a strategy of resource mobilization for education. Fees, loans, taxes and other means should be used to finance upper secondary and higher education. In addition, incentives for public institutions should be provided which seek to diversify sources of funding, including cost sharing with students.

Emphasize quality and set high standards

Experience over the last decade has shown that efforts to expand enrolment must be accompanied by attempts to enhance educational quality if children are to be attracted to school, stay there, and achieve meaningful learning outcomes. Scarce resources have frequently been used to expand systems, with insufficient attention paid to quality improvement in areas such as teacher training and materials development. All aspects of the quality of education must be improved, and a high degree of excellence sought. Achievement standards must be set, and outcomes monitored. Measurable outcomes must be sought in all areas, particularly in literacy, numeracy and essential life skills. The linking of government funding to performance is fundamental (World Bank, 1995a: 89–120).

Quality is at the heart of education, and what takes place in classrooms and other learning environments is fundamentally important to the future wellbeing of children, young people and adults. A quality education is one that satisfies basic learning needs and enriches the lives of learners and their overall experience of living.

A 'new space' for communities and civil society

Education became a centralized service at independence. The powers for planning and direction were vested in a Ministry of Education to ensure the establishment and development of a unified service. One of the strongest reasons for this was the need to dismantle the racially based structure of education established during the colonial years. This approach has backfired in many ways.

Effective educational strategy will depend on active civic engagement in the formulation, implementation and monitoring of strategies for educational development. Learners, teachers, parents, communities, non-governmental organizations and other bodies representing civil society must be granted new and expanded political and social scope, at all levels of society, in order to engage governments in dialogue, decision-making and innovation around the goals for basic education (World Bank, 1995a: 126). Such participation, especially at the local level through partnerships between schools and communities, should not only be limited to endorsing decisions of, or financing programmes designed by, the state. Rather, at all levels of decision-making, governments must put in place mechanisms for regular dialogue, to enable citizens and civil society organizations to contribute to the planning, implementation, monitoring and evaluation of education. This is essential in order to foster the development of accountable, comprehensive and flexible educational management frameworks. While the ministry of education should continually evaluate educational development and stimulate the most appropriate changes, a more meaningful delegation of functions to local authorities and communities is essential.

Decentralization of decision powers to local jurisdiction

The experience of the last decade has underscored the need for better governance of education systems so that they can respond more effectively to the diverse and continuously changing needs of learners. This entails the need to delineate responsibilities among different levels of government – federal, provincial and local. Reform of educational management is urgently needed in order to move from highly centralized, standardized and command-driven forms of management to more decentralized and participatory decision-making, implementation and monitoring at lower levels of accountability. However, decentralization must not lead to an inequitable distribution of resources.

Harnessing new technologies

The process of decentralization of decision-making to local authorities must be buttressed by a management information system that benefits from both new technologies and community participation to produce relevant and accurate information. Swiftly changing information and communications technologies must be harnessed to meet basic learning needs as well as to reduce, not exacerbate, economic disparities related to geographical location and other causes. Each country should implement periodic re-evaluation of the availability and utility of these technologies for all aspects of basic learning.

Higher education reform in Africa

Higher education, particularly university education, in Africa is of paramount importance for economic and social development. However, the sector is in crisis. Shrinking budgets since the early 1980s further compounded the problem as governments across the continent were forced to squeeze expenditure. In sub-Saharan Africa, average expenditure on each student declined from $6,300 in 1980 to $1,500 in 1988 (World Bank, 1994b: 2).

Compounding the problem of declining resources per student is their inefficient use. A very large portion of the budget allocated to university education in Africa is devoted to non-educational expenditures, such as subsidized student housing, food and other services. As a result, non-salary expenditures for items such as textbooks, educational materials, laboratory equipment and supplies have dried up. The World Bank, in particular, has taken the position that high public subsidies to university students are not only an inefficient educational investment, but also represent regressive social spending; the focus should be on primary education in the many countries that have not yet achieved adequate access, equity and quality at the primary- and secondary-school levels.

While the debate on the merits of investing in primary or tertiary education is an important one, effective investments are needed at all levels of education and training in order to exploit the opportunities now being generated by the information technology revolution. The opportunity to exploit the new developments in process innovation will be determined by the levels of investment in new kinds of scientific programmes, information technology and technology management programmes, as well as the successful incorporation of these in new curricula.

Emphasizing science and technology

University education in post-independence Africa has largely focused on meeting the demands of the state for effective running of public institutions, and less on deepening capacity in science and technology. The existing programmes in science and technology suffer from underfunding and a shortage of trained African scientists. It has been estimated that up to 23,000 qualified academics emigrate from Africa each year (World Bank, 1995b: 1). The use of expatriate technical assistance remains at quite a high level, and this is partly to blame for the neglect of investment in science and technology (Moss, 1984). The scale of this neglect is astounding when one compares Africa with the rest of the world (see Table 3.3).

The number of African post-secondary students enrolled in natural sciences, engineering and medical science disciplines is extremenly low when compared with South America and the OECD countries. These figures are a clear warning that a lot more has to be done by African governments if the dream of the 'African Renaissance' is to become a reality.

Due to the central role of research and development in technological progress, the traditional goals of African universities must be revised in order to reflect the new requirements for global competitiveness. Development policies must identify the proper role of university research and training, and effective ways of linking them to domestic commercial applications, particularly in the industrial and agricultural sectors. University

Table 3.3 Scientists per 100,000 population, by discipline

Region	Natural sciences	Engineering	Medical sciences
Africa	13	9	7
South America	75	231	152
OECD countries	214	369	261

Source: Calculated from World Bank 1990: 27.

research must also facilitate the development of core technologies with a wide range of applications.

Narrowing the gender gap

Although the potential contribution of women's higher education to economic growth is great, a 'gender gap' in enrolment at the tertiary level is pervasive in sub-Saharan Africa. While the multiple and interrelated school, socioeconomic, sociocultural, political and institutional factors that constrain female education are increasingly well documented, much remains to be done to design and implement programmes to accelerate female education in Africa (Hyde, 1989).

Once enrolled at the university, young women are more likely to drop out than young men. Their academic achievement is below that of boys, and few young women opt for mathematics and science-related fields of study. A lack of role models and negative attitudes on the part of teachers further compound their problems. Gender streaming is pervasive in many African universities, with women being overrepresented in humanities and vocational schools (commercial/secretarial training). Proactive policies are therefore needed both at the secondary-school level (to induce girls to opt for sciences and mathematics) and at the university level (Raney et al., 1994). The institution of an affirmative-action programme for college admission must be explored as a way forward.

Knowledge production through sharing

Higher-education reform should also incorporate innovative approaches that promote cost-effective knowledge production through sharing of faculties and facilities. Considering the current stage of development of many African countries, very few governments can afford to establish additional universities and research centres. One way of overcoming this problem is through a regional approach to knowledge production. The African Economic Research Consortium and the African Regional Postgraduate Programme in Insect Sciences are excellent examples of how to carry out a regional approach to knowledge production.

The African Regional Postgraduate Programme in Insect Sciences (ARPPIS) was launched in 1985 by the Nairobi-based International Centre for Insect Physiology and Ecology (ICIPE). In an effort to reduce insect damage and increase Africa's agricultural output, ICIPE negotiated an agreement with twenty-four participating African universities aimed at increasing the number of insect scientists. The agreement ensured that doctoral students would enrol at a home institution while conducting course work and dissertation research within the context of ICIPE's research programme and under the supervision of an ICIPE scientist. Provision is made for the student by his or her local university.

Fifteen years later, the working relationship developed through ARPPIS is providing the basis for several collaborative training initiatives at the Master's level. Following an appraisal of university capacities for insect science instruction and research, three universities in East, West and Southern Africa have been selected to sponsor the M.Sc. programme in entomology on a sub-regional basis. These programmes will then play a 'feeder' role in furnishing more qualified candidates to the ICIPE doctoral programme. The African Economic Research Consortium (see Box 3.1) is organized along the same lines.

Box 3.1 The African Economic Research Consortium

The African Economic Research Consortium (AERC) is one of the most successful projects supported by the African Capacity Building Foundation, an initiative launched in February 1991 by UNDP, the World Bank and the African Development Bank. The AERC was established in 1988 with the principal objective of strengthening local capacity for economic policy research in sub-Saharan Africa. Its mission rests on two basic premisses. First, development is more likely to occur where there is sustained management of the economy. Second, such management is more likely to happen where there exists an active, well-informed group of locally based professional economists to conduct policy-relevant research. Hence, AERC's limited intervention is targeted at enhancing the capacity of locally based researchers to conduct policy-relevant economic inquiry, promote retention of such capacity, and encourage its application in the policy context. As an executing agency, AERC is responsible for all grant-making and contractual arrangements among collaborators. Its operations are based on the following principles:

- *A network approach to capacity building* AERC's capacity development strategy is based on the networking concept, which is considered to be cost-effective. The Consortium currently brings fifteen funders to support a commonly agreed programme of research activities, its dissemination and the training of future potential researchers. This enables achievement of a critical mass of support for a set of coordinated activities with shared overheads.
- *A regional approach to training* A major part of the AERC training programme is the execution of the Anglophone Collaborative M.A. programme in economics. This programme currently involves nineteen universities from fourteen countries, which collaborate to offer a high-quality Master's degree in economics. The collaboration features joint enforcement of standards through annual evaluation and assessment by external examiners, common curriculum and its development, joint facility for teaching electives, development of teaching materials, and student and teacher movements among the collaborating institutions. An Academic Board with membership drawn from the participating universities is responsible for the substance of the programme. Currently six of these universities (Category B universities) are deemed to have adequate capacity to offer core courses that meet jointly, and determine and enforce standards. The rest (Category A schools) send their students to these Category B universities. Provisions for expanding or contracting the number of departments qualified to offer the degree based on performance and evaluation are in place. The universities collaborate also in offering electives at a joint facility in Nairobi.
- *A team approach to research* The research programme involves individual researchers in the region, supported by resource persons, carrying out research on selected themes designed by the AERC's advisory committee to be most pertinent to policy needs. This cost-effective approach allows the programme to attain a critical mass of professional activity in the region, alleviates professional isolation, encourages exchange of experiences and creates peer pressure to enhance quality.
- *Establishing a link between research and policy* The research programme emphasizes quality and relevance of research to policy so as to ensure credibility and encourage utilization of its results. As the AERC has become well known in the region, national governments and regional organizations have continued to seek the services of AERC researchers and collaborating institutions to undertake relevant policy research and analysis, and to utilize research outputs to inform policy decisions. Extensive use of local researchers and institutions has in turn promoted the

retention of high quality African researchers who would otherwise leave the continent.

- *Focused on a limited thematic agenda* The programme has adopted a flexible but cautious approach to expanding its own themes in research. The current themes are External Balance and Macroeconomic Management; Trade Policy and Regional Integration; External and Internal Debt Management; Financial Management and Domestic Resource Mobilization. Long-term sustainable development issues are currently gaining ground in terms of research interest within the network. This is aimed at a better understanding of how markets function in the African context, of institutional structures affecting economic behaviour and performance, and of the link between policy and growth. The advisory committee considers new themes in line with the priorities laid down by policymakers and researchers.
- *Strong links to other non-African research institutions* The Consortium is linked to several other resource centres worldwide. Resource personnel drawn from these centres enrich the technical base and the variety of relevant experiences. Local researchers regularly team up with counterparts in other parts of the world within mutually agreed subject areas. This has helped to sustain interest in African research outside the region, to build competence through interaction, and to create self-sustaining arrangements for financing research outside of the AERC. Attachments to better research environments outside of the region have been arranged (e.g. the AERC/IMF visiting scholars programme) in conjunction with the implementation of AERC-supported research.
- *Sustainability through staff development* Staff development schemes intended to strengthen Ph.D. programmes in African universities are geared towards increasing the supply of trained teachers, as well as enhancing their competence to carry out rigorous research. The AERC continues to provide support for Ph.D. research, and for fellowships to augment teaching capacity and the pool of competent researchers.

Support for research

Higher-education reform should give priority to developing a basic capacity for research and development in key areas to pave the way for independent knowledge development, analysis and debate. According to the UNESCO 1996 *World Science Report*, African governments spent 0.4 per cent of GDP on research and development (UNESCO, 1996). This compared unfavourably to the 2.8 per cent of GDP spent by the governments of Japan and the USA, and even to the Indian government's 0.8 per cent of GDP. Knowledge and technology cannot be produced and national systems of innovation fostered if governments do not invest in them.

For the African economic renaissance to move beyond excited rhetoric and academic interest, the continent and its leaders must face the reality of its technological needs and do more than just measure and bemoan the science and technology gap that exists between the developed and developing countries. African institutions must train more engineers and scientists (and not lose them to the developed world) in order to prepare Africa's capacity to absorb technology flows. These trained Africans must build national systems of innovation that are appropriate to African needs.

Related to the urgent need to strengthen research and development is the requirement on the part of African governments to provide appropriate incentives and a conducive working environment to induce large numbers of African scientists and professors working in the developed world to return to their home countries. While African governments continue to complain about the lack of trained people, very little effort has been made by the OAU and member states to reverse the brain drain from the continent. Financial incentives alone are unlikely to redress this complex problem. Democratization of the political system and freedom of speech and of movement are equally important factors.

Conclusions

On its educational trek since independence, Africa has embarked upon a quantitative expansion of inherited educational systems, while seeking to Africanize curricula and enhance teacher training. Governments have also sought to invoke community participation in the supply of schools while linking the educational systems to economic development.

Despite such efforts, however, the African educational system is in serious crisis. For Africa to compete in the global economy, fundamental reform of education is an absolute necessity. Efforts to reorient African education should include international standards such as student outcome, system outcome, and labour market outcome. Performance indicators such as tests and examinations, as well as indicators for evaluating institutional achievements, can be used to monitor progress towards national educational goals. In addition to providing a mechanism for evaluating the effectiveness and efficiency of specific policies and programmes, such indicators can hold schools accountable for the performance of students, select and certify students, and provide feedback to teachers about individual students' learning needs. They can also be linked with incentives to drive a system towards higher achievement (World Bank, 1995a: 101). Transforming the African education system thus constitutes the second and most important pillar of the renaissance.

Notes

1. Cited in the July 2000 issue of *African Recovery*, p.17
2. See, for this, Great Britain, Colonial Office Advisory Committee for Education in the Colonies (1948); also Kenya Colony and Protectorate (1948).

CHAPTER 4

Agriculture and Rural Development

The disappointing economic performance of sub-Saharan Africa over the past three decades has been caused by two interrelated factors: a world trading system that rewards farmers who produce for export at the expense of those who produce for subsistence; and the failure of African governments to create the proper conditions for an agricultural revolution, which would propel the process of industrialization and social development. Africa is the only continent where per capita food self-sufficiency has declined significantly. Per capita food production in Africa actually dropped by 12 per cent between 1961 and 1995, whereas it advanced by leaps and bounds in developing countries in Asia (Table 4.1). Despite the negative trend, however, agriculture continues to dominate many African economies, accounting for about 35 per cent of the region's GDP, 70 per cent of employment, and 40 per cent of exports (World Bank, 1997). Sluggish growth in agriculture has had a direct bearing on the rest of the economy and on the welfare of the vast majority of the population who eke out a living from agriculture.

By contrast, agrarian reform was the major means of redistributing wealth and income in the newly industrialized countries (NICs) of East Asia, thereby increasing purchasing power and generating high levels of economic growth. The absence of agrarian reform to create conditions for a dynamic agricultural sector to emerge has been one of the major obstacles to industrialization in Africa. Although commercial farming, other than the traditional estate sector, is making inroads in a number of African countries, it remains as undercapitalized as the subsistence sector. Inappropriate government policies continue to hamper the productivity of agriculture. If Africa is to feed itself, reduce poverty, and become

Table 4.1 Agricultural production per capita by region (Index: 1961–64 = 100)

Year	Africa	Asia	Latin America
1965–69	100	103	102
1975–79	92	110	106
1985–89	84	135	112
1995–98	87	169	120

Source: Compiled from World Bank, 2000, Table 6.1.

competitive in world markets, government policies must undergo fundamental change. In addition to creating an enabling policy environment, governments must urgently tackle the pervasive effects of underinvestment. Few low-income countries have achieved rapid non-agricultural growth without sustained growth in agriculture.

Explaining the Decline: Contending Perspectives

The persistent decline in agricultural output in Africa cannot be understood in isolation from the strategies of development pursued by colonial and post-independence governments in the world economy. While persistent drought and protracted conflicts are partly to blame for the decline in many countries, structural factors, both internal and external, have also contributed to the continent's endemic agrarian crisis.

The basic philosophy of the now widespread 'internalist' explanation, which usually blames the victims, is the one expounded by the World Bank in its 1980 report *Accelerated Development in Sub-Saharan Africa: An Agenda for Action*, commonly referred to as the Berg Report (World Bank, 1981). Its fundamental thesis is that Africa's economic crisis has much to do with misguided policies pursued by national governments: insufficient price incentives, excessive taxation on export crops, insufficient and often corrupt marketing boards, low priority given to agricultural research, inadequate extension service and input supply system. The Bank argues that the maintenance of a trade and exchange rate system (overvalued currencies, import controls, export taxes and fertilizer subsidies) biases the incentive system against agriculture in many ways and stifles production.

To correct these distortions, the World Bank advocates the adoption of 'structural adjustment programmes,' the withdrawal of the state from economic management and its replacement by market forces.

African governments and their supporters countered by offering an 'externalist' explanation, putting the blame squarely on the industrialized countries and their trade and aid policies towards Africa. In its *Lagos Plan of Action for Economic Development of Africa*, the Organization of African Unity argues that the crisis and economic collapse came about as a result of overwhelming external shocks: soaring interest rates, declining commodity prices, Western protectionism against African exports, and unsustainable levels of debt service payments to creditor countries and institutions (OAU, 1979). African governments pointed out that the developed countries remain protectionist against agricultural exports, a sector in which African countries offer competitive products at attractive prices. The periodic dumping of surplus agricultural products on African markets further ruins prices for local farmers. A decade later, the UN Economic Commission for Africa echoed these sentiments when it criticized the structural adjustment programmes that African countries were forced to implement by Western donors (UNECA, 1989).

Time and space do not permit further consideration of this debate. Suffice it to say that both perspectives have validity and overlap to a considerable degree. The World Bank perspective, which points the finger at poor domestic policies and institutional failures, is now widely accepted by African policymakers in the face of the crisis of the state in Africa and the growing demand for democracy by the population. At the same time, though, the World Bank and the majority of Western donors have shifted their positions and now acknowledge the influence of exogenous factors, such as terms of trade and debt structures, on the performance of African economies (World Bank, 1989c; World Bank, 2000). This is not to suggest, however, that a consensus is emerging on an alternative development route for Africa.

Agricultural Reform under Structural Adjustment: The Post-1980 Experience

In the fall of 1984, Western television audiences were shocked to witness images of emaciated faces of the victims of famine in Ethiopia and the Horn of Africa. A massive outpouring of medical and food assistance to the countries affected was followed by a call from the donor community to convene a UN special session on Africa in order to address the root causes of Africa's economic crisis. Armed with the argument presented in the Berg Report, Western governments pressured African governments to accept responsibility for the continent's economic disaster and to resume fundamental reform if they expected to receive substantial sums of money from the West (United Nations, 1987a).

The pressure from the donor community could not have come at a worse time for African governments. The fiscal crisis of the state, peasant flight from official markets, growth of illegal cross-border trade in food and livestock, erosion of government credibility, and sporadic peasant rebellion in some countries left African governments with very little room for manoeuvre. The need for policy reform, and agricultural reform in particular, became the centre of national and international attention. African governments, given their precarious political position, grudgingly agreed to implement far-reaching structural adjustment programmes in exchange for financial assistance from the donor countries and institutions.

Since the early 1980s, most countries in sub-Saharan Africa have initiated and carried out substantial economic policy reforms under the watchful eyes of the World Bank and the IMF. The goal of these reforms has been to reduce or eliminate the bias against agriculture and to open the sector to market forces by reducing or eliminating state intervention in agricultural marketing and production (World Bank, 1981). To these ends, the reforms have emphasized rationalization and liberalization of input and output prices, especially exchange rates; food price structures and interest rates; prioritization of public expenditures towards human investment and infrastructure; and support for research and extension services. They also include programmes to increase the resilience of small farmers to adverse economic circumstances (United Nations, 1987b; United Nations, 1991a). The expectation was that by 'getting the price right', the supply response by farmers would dramatically improve and set the foundations for a well-functioning market.

On balance, the combined effect of these actions on the agricultural sector has been positive, but inadequate. State intervention in food markets has been sharply reduced and market forces now determine prices in many African countries. Whether the pace and extent of these reforms, which have varied widely across countries and crop subsectors, will be sustained remains a question. A recent survey by the International Food Policy Research Institute (IFPRI) points out that reforms were not fully implemented (Kherallah et al., 2000: 9–10). State-owned enterprises remain active in several commodity subsectors, notably cotton in West Africa and maize in Kenya, Malawi and Zimbabwe. In Benin, Côte d'Ivoire and Senegal, parastatals continue to handle the majority of marketing and distribution for export crops. In Mali, for example, two state enterprises account for 95 per cent of fertilizer distribution.

In some cases, countries reversed reforms as a consequence of external shocks or changing economic conditions. For example, Zambia reversed maize market liberalization under pressure from urban consumers who faced higher prices. Similarly, Malawi reinstated fertilization subsidies because devaluation of the currency raised fertilizer prices. In other instances, governments liberalized internal trade but maintained a state monopoly over external trade, as is the case with the marketing of groundnut in Senegal.

Despite these discrepancies, however, the role of the state in agricultural development in sub-Saharan Africa has been curtailed and market forces set in place in many countries. Agricultural market liberalization has encouraged private trade, even in cases where parastatals are still active. Increased private-sector participation in trading has, in turn, fostered the efficient transmission of information and prices among markets, particularly in countries like Benin and Ghana where the private sector controlled food marketing before liberalization.

By and large, though, agricultural reforms have failed to eliminate structural production bottlenecks, low rates of revenue generation, and weak state capacity in policy analysis and management. Despite market reforms, the average growth of agricultural production per capita has been negligible in sub-Saharan Africa since the 1970s. While production of export crops has increased, food production for local consumption has stagnated as a result of structural and institutional factors (Mamingi, 1997: 17–34; Chhibber, 1989). Constraints include the following: inadequate technical knowledge; inefficient research and extension; falling world prices; inadequate access to inputs, agricultural services and markets; poor infrastructure and storage facilities; inadequate financial resource availability at both national and farm-household levels; and high-cost public- and private-sector marketing systems (Cheru and Mathu, 1989). For subsistence farmers in particular, reform has meant the elimination of government input and credit subsidies – a loss that has stagnated or reduced yields. And where producers have benefited, the bulk of the gains have gone to export and cash-crop farmers with access to credit and modern inputs.

The Roots of Food Insecurity and Rural Poverty

In evaluating the literature on agriculture and rural development in sub-Saharan Africa, one is struck by the almost unanimous conclusion that rural development has frequently fallen victim to a 'lack of political will'.

The need to take action is freely conceded by African governments, but somehow the decision to take that action is still withheld (Delgado et al., 1998). One reason for this is that rural development, whose time frame is long (a generation or more), has often been crowded out of the national agenda by other problems – national security, import-substitution industrialization, foreign exchange shortage, and so on – considered by the central government authorities to be more pressing.

While the role of agriculture in national development is widely recognized, post-colonial African states have continued to play a central role in the production and marketing of agriculture, often to the detriment of the very subsistence farmers whom they claim to protect and support. Instead, elite bureaucrats and party loyalists, far removed from the reality of rural life, continue to dictate what peasants can and cannot produce, to whom they can sell and at what price. What the peasants know and what they might need is of no concern (Bates, 1981; World Bank, 1989c; Chambers, 1983; Rahmato, 1985). Central authorities naively believe that they are better placed to make key decisions on agricultural policy than illiterate peasants. As a result, poor policies and institutional failures have undermined the productivity of peasant farmers. The onset of subsequent droughts simply push the peasantry to the brink of starvation. The peasants can demand neither better prices for their goods nor a fair distribution of land or other productive resources since they are effectively shut out from the decision-making process.

Production failures caused by drought do not translate into famine unless other socioeconomic conditions are prevalent. Such conditions are the result of deficiencies in public policy, which limit the capacity of rural households to escape the poverty trap. These deficiencies in policies are explored in the following sections.

Inappropriate macroeconomic and trade policies

Excessive state interference and the maintenance of inappropriate macroeconomic and trade policies have exacerbated inherent food insecurity in many African countries (Ahmed and Rustagi, 1987). Overvalued national currencies, restrictive exchange rate regulations, and high export taxes have historically adversely affected rural economies, undermining productivity at the farm level. For example, a macroeconomic framework that allows importation of food could have the undesirable effect of discouraging local farmers from producing more food since they tend to be crowded out by cheap food imports. Similarly, overvalued currencies make export products less attractive and less competitive in world markets. Price controls on basic food items to subsidize urban workers act against the interest of rural producers.

Excessive rent seeking by the state further compounds the problem, as transaction costs for farmers rise far in excess of their investments. Peasants are expected to provide the bulk of the resources required for national development through increased taxes and by engaging in primary resource production, just as they had during the colonial period. At the centre of this process are the marketing boards that are considered symbols of oppression. Prices paid to farmers for food crops are kept artificially low, thus providing cheap food to people in the cities (Bates, 1981; World Bank, 1981). For example, in Côte d'Ivoire, Ghana and Zambia, from the 1960s to the early 1980s average direct taxation was 23 per cent, indirect taxation was 29 per cent, and total taxation was 52 per cent. The indirect component includes the effects of overvalued exchange rates (39 per cent) and tariffs (26 per cent) (Schiff and Valdes, 1992). The low prices granted to farmers fuel the downward spiral in agricultural output as the farmers switch to other more lucrative activities outside of the formal market. Insecure tenure systems, inadequate marketing, storage facilities and weak extension services compound this.

The most extreme cases of state interference in the agricultural sector took place in a handful of African countries that experimented with socialist planning. Ethiopia and Mozambique illustrate this situation (see Box 4.1). In Mozambique, the FRELIMO (Mozambique Liberation Front) government under President Samora Michael implemented an ambitious plan to reorient the Mozambican economy towards a socialist path. Since 95 per cent of Mozambicans are rural peasants, the agricultural sector was singled out for fundamental reform. Peasants were organized to live and work in cooperatives patterned after Tanzania's ujamaa or villagization scheme (Harris, 1980). Some two thousand abandoned Portuguese plantations were either subdivided or turned into state farms to prevent total paralysis of the cash-crop sector and to stem growing despair among the large unemployed workforce. This move is best understood in light of the orientation – under the colonial administration – of the Mozambican economy towards white-ruled South Africa and Rhodesia and the total absence of internal development, particularly peasant agriculture (Hodges, 1983: 64).

FRELIMO's ambitious plan for rural construction ran into a problem soon after it got off the ground, for both external and internal reasons. Despite the rhetoric regarding the role of small farmers in the development process, the government's agricultural policy concentrated on establishing large-scale mechanized farming. Between 1977 and 1981, Mozambique imported over $100 million in agricultural machinery, including 3,000 tractors, 300 combines and several hundred trucks (Hanlon, 1978). With an estimated 350,000 acres already committed to state farms, the Ten-Year Plan announced in 1981 called for 2.5 million acres to be developed by 1990 at a cost of $1 billion. Three years later, the agricultural sector came to a grinding halt and FRELIMO admitted that the emphasis on state farms was a strategic error. Production decline was further aggravated by a ravaging war that lasted until 1994.

The new government of Ethiopia that came into power in 1991 after the overthrow of the Marxist regime of Colonel Mengistu Haile Mariam proclaimed that land was to remain under state control, albeit in modified form. While many with the memory of the failed experiment of agrarian socialism of the Mengistu regime called upon the government to institute Western-style property rights, the government of Prime Minister Melese Zenawi felt that the commodification of land would turn the clock back to the feudal days and derail its policy of 'agricultural-led' development. The new policy grants legal rights to farmers and the right to pass the land to their offspring. The peasants cannot sell land in the case of bad harvest or to pay other debts.

Inadequate support services and infrastructure

One of the major impediments to improved agricultural production in many African countries is the lack of support services and infrastructure. Inadequate training, lack of improved seeds, fertilizers and other inputs, and inadequate marketing outlets due to poor roads and transportation facilities have all had a negative impact on agricultural production.

As land becomes scarce due to population pressure, many experts and donor institutions have been in favour of intensive application of inputs to enhance land productivity. Nevertheless, the available evidence indicates that 'modernizing' agriculture in Africa has been highly selective in that it has focused on high-potential areas with higher and more reliable rainfall as opposed to lower-potential and marginal areas; and on farmers with more resources, the so-called 'progressive' farmers, who are mostly men. Consequently, the small farmers, who are usually poor and have very few political connections, are excluded (Bates, 1981: 55; Bernstein, 1992: 9).

While the need to intensify technological applications in African agriculture is an urgent matter, field implementation must resume only after exhaustive research and testing. At the moment, many of the traditional varieties, such as maize and sorghum, that are grown by the vast majority of smallholders in rural Africa do not respond well to chemical fertilizer.

Further investment in research and development is required to increase yields from traditional varieties. In addition, modern inputs are expensive and beyond the reach of most subsistence farmers. Fertilizer application in kilograms per hectare of arable land for the period 1993–96 was as follows: 15 in Africa; 180 in Asia; 75 in Latin America (World Bank, 2000: 172). On the other hand, increased access to information by farmers through an effective extension network and access to credits are more important for improving yields than having access to chemical fertilizers. Yields can also be increased significantly with compost and more efficient use of plant residues. Therefore, research must be reoriented towards finding solutions based on local resources and knowledge.

Productivity decline is also attributed to the absence of efficient research, extension and training opportunities. Although the importance of agricultural research is well recognized in official circles, there is no connection between basic research and adaptive research. This is the result of a system that encourages researchers to write scientific articles instead of spending time in the field talking to farmers. Demonstration plots are non-existent or located far from the peasants. To reverse the situation, incentives have to be established for increasing adaptive research and on-farm research/demonstration plots, and a dialogue opened up between farmers and researchers. In this way, researchers can get a realistic picture of the problems subsistence farmers face.

Similarly, with regard to extension services, remote areas are less likely to be served by extension than communities closer to a major road. Training opportunities in agricultural production and soil and water conservation measures are often inadequate. Opportunities to visit demonstration centres do not exist. When remote areas are assigned extension agents, the staff are poorly trained, cut off from scientific information or any face-to-face contact with researchers, and are overburdened with other tasks, such as collecting taxes and the administration of central government directives that have nothing to do with agriculture (Cheru and Mathu, 1989).

Inadequate marketing, storage and transport services

Experience from other countries shows that, for peasants to increase agricultural production, there must be in place an efficient marketing, storage and transport system. If these important services are absent, peasants will not be compelled to raise their productivity. The lack of infrastructure makes a market-oriented response to food scarcity very difficult (Hayami and Platteau, 1996). The isolation of African farmers from major global markets retards agricultural development by increasing transportation costs, inhibiting technology adoption, raising the costs of agricultural and social services, and suppressing competitive product, factor and credit markets.

Transport bottlenecks remain a major problem throughout sub-Saharan Africa. Without roads, farmers cannot market their goods or access basic supplies in the major cities. The density of rural roads in Africa is very low, particularly when compared with Asia. Moreover, many of the roads are in a poor state of repair due to a lack of proper maintenance. Motorized transport services are often in short supply and expensive. In the early 1990s, for example, a group of eighteen countries in the humid and subhumid tropics had only 63 kilometres of rural roads per 1,000 square kilometres. Taking into account population density differences, this was less than one-sixth of the level in India in 1950 (Spencer, 1994).

In many African countries, the marketing of agricultural output is controlled by the state, which impairs incentives for farmers. Private agents are excluded, which increases the transaction cost for farmers. The problem is further compounded by poor roads and inadequate transportation facilities. As a result, the majority of farmers are unable to take their goods to the big urban centres where they can fetch better prices (Webb, Von Braun and Yohannes, 1991b). Instead, they must market only a portion of their goods at the village level or at the nearest market centres at below market prices in order to purchase necessary items such as matches, salt and oil. In many countries, surplus crops rot in the field due to transport bottlenecks, while only a few hundred miles away people go hungry.

Another factor that constrains agricultural marketing is a lack of proper storage facilities suitable for each ecological region. Although the situation varies from region to region, small farmers end up losing a significant amount of harvested crops to pests and insects. It is estimated that up to 40 per cent of African crops are lost to poor transport and storage. For example, a farmer in Niger could double his earnings if he could keep his harvest of rice for an additional three months. He could do this if he had access to a small amount of credit to build a structure for storage. The traditional method of storing grain in a hole underground has proved to be detrimental since the grain is either destroyed by humidity or eaten up by ants. Research and demonstration in alternative and cost-effective methods of storage are in short supply.

Land scarcity, insecure tenure, and landlessness

Perhaps the most important non-technical issue constraining agriculture in much of Africa is access to land and security of tenure. Although agrarian reform has now become a dirty word in international circles (because it is equated with leftism or revolution), African countries cannot hope to establish real democracy, increase agricultural output, or reduce poverty without fundamental land redistribution and a reorientation of agricultural policy. The ownership structure determines the extent to which peasants will cultivate land in a sustainable way. No rational peasant will grow trees and build check dams unless he or she is guaranteed to reap the benefits from such investments in both the short and the long term. Empirical studies have shown, for example, that land tenants have a lesser tendency to adopt new technologies than landowners (Jibowo and Allen, 1980: 47).

Historically, land in many parts of Africa has been communal property, and in many cases still is. Land changes hands largely through inheritance. It is distributed in accordance with the size of family groups within the same clan (Bruce, 1988: 23–52; Berry, 1988: 53–75). Land belonging to the clan is inalienable and is administered by the head of the clan. Although this arrangement has worked well for several generations, the system is now in a state of anarchy as population pressure grows and corruption has become endemic. Communal land tenure also has several disadvantages in the context of today: (1) it leads to greater and greater fragmentation of land through subdivision as land is bequeathed from generation to generation; (2) it prevents consolidation of land to achieve economies of scale; (3) it forfeits the advantages of rapid innovation diffusion associated with increases in farm size; and (4) it is associated with frequent boundary and ownership disputes, which discourage long-term investment. As a result, agricultural land is exhausted, as the scope for the traditional fallow system, where land is taken out of production for a year or more, becomes more and more limited (Migot-Adholla et al., 1991: 155–7).

The alternative approach advocated for years by donor institutions, private ownership of land, has run into similar problems. Over the past several years, there has been a very clear shift to individual ownership of land in most African countries. Land survey departments have come into the picture and the registration of land on an individual basis is spreading. With this new trend, however, it has become clear that some social groups, women in particular, are being limited in their access to or ownership of land. In some cases, this has led to the concentration of land in a few hands, resulting in the dispossession of poor peasants.

Kenya is an example of an African country that has attempted to break with tradition by shifting from communal to individual land ownership. The shift has been justified, persuasively, on the grounds that individual land ownership enables even small farmers to mortgage their titles to land against loans from lending institutions, thereby granting small farmers access to credit. But in practice this arrangement has not always been permitted to run its full course. In a country where basic democratic rule does not exist, the shift to private tenure has simply empowered a new wealthy indigenous class to engage in grabbing hitherto communal land. These wealthy groups, using their hold over the state, have pushed the policy of private tenure towards a de facto privatization of tenure. This has not only resulted in mass forced evictions but has also led to deterioration in the natural resource base (Apiyo, 1998: 18–19).

Moreover, both public and private lending agencies have remained wary of small farmers, whom they continue to regard as 'bad risks' because of difficulties in supervising loan repayments and in exercising powers of foreclosure, sale or receivership in cases of default (Okoth-Ogendo, 1976: 175). In effect, therefore, the relevant authorities have laid down policies, which practical considerations have obliged them almost simultaneously to rescind. The commodification of land, in the absence of effective financial institutions, has made small farmers the object of exploitation by local loan sharks, forcing many to become tenant farmers or agricultural labourers.

A handful of African countries experimented with socialist planning. State control of land was a response to the concentration of land in the hands of a few under capitalist farming. Unfortunately, it resulted in excessive bureaucratic control and discouraged peasants from cultivating land in a sustainable fashion. The Ethiopian case illustrates this point very well. According to the 1975 Land Proclamation, each peasant was entitled to 10 hectares of land for his own use. However, the lack of clear-cut rules relating to ownership of land hampered investment (Provisional Government of Ethiopia, 1975). Since land ownership was, and still is, vested in the state, peasants felt insecure about their long-term use of the land.

A third example is drawn from Tanzania, a country that has made a conscious decision to retain communal land ownership, albeit in modified form. Tanzania's famous ujamaa programme brought rural inhabitants together in communal villages. Village communities were registered as cooperatives and then granted legal status – designed, among other things, to qualify them for loans (Hyden, 1981). After a decade and a half of implementing liberalization policy, however, Tanzania adopted a new Land Act in 1998, which confirms that all land in Tanzania 'shall continue to be public land and remain vested in the President as trustee for and on behalf of all the citizens of Tanzania' (Havnevik and Harsmar, 1999). The Act was designed to prevent the incidence of 'land grabbing' by persons in positions of power during the liberalization period. Both the Ethiopian and the Tanzanian approaches are mere compromises in the face of the real danger of peasants losing their land under a system of private ownership. Once a country's economy has been diversified, opening up extensive economic opportunities outside of agriculture for a significant proportion of the peasantry, tenure relations must be revised to allow individual ownership.

Cash crops versus food crops

Like the colonial system, rural development policy in post-independence Africa has, by and large, been geared towards the production of primary commodities for the export market. This has been promoted to finance state-led import-substitution industrialization policy. Agriculture has historically been relegated to the role of supplier of labour, raw material, and cheap food to industry. Since export agriculture is highly mechanized and often requires high recurrent costs, scarce land, water, inputs, technical expertise, technology and credit are regularly directed towards the growing of luxury crops in large-scale irrigation projects. In some African countries, the forced removal of peasants and graziers from fertile areas to marginal lands in order to make way for export plantations and game parks has been justified on the grounds of advancing the 'national interest' (Rosenblum and Williamson, 1987; Timberlake, 1986).

On the other hand, subsistence agriculture has never been accorded the same level of support, as it was seen as inherently inefficient because uneducated farmers were unwilling to apply modern techniques such as mechanization. As a result of this misperception, the demands of subsistence farmers for government support in the areas of soil conservation, agricultural research, extension, credit and access to markets and transportation are conveniently ignored. Because of these views, state enterprises, often inherited from colonial powers, were given the responsibility of organizing food markets and fixing nationwide prices for farmers and consumers. State enterprises also managed export crop production by providing inputs on credit, fixing crop prices, and monopolizing the processing and export of the crop and the distribution of fertilizers (World Bank, 1981; Bates, 1981). The abuses poor peasants sustained from state marketing boards are well documented and need not be recounted here. The overall effect on peasant productivity has been negative.

Box 4.1 Agricultural decline and state–peasantry relations: the case of Ethiopia

Ethiopia is one country in Africa that has made little progress in raising agricultural productivity in more than fifty years. Throughout the feudal rule of Emperor Haile Selassie, peasant agriculture stagnated, partly due to the parasitic nature of the feudal lords and the land tenure system, but more because of the regime's bad economic policies. The imperial regime starved peasant agriculture of capital investment, technical services and extension support until the early 1970s, when an experimental green revolution package called the Minimum Package Programme was introduced in easily accessible parts of high-potential areas to help improve the performance of peasant production. This minimal programme was initiated following prodding by donors, not in response to the needs of the peasantry (Aredo, 1990: 45–57).

The condition of the peasantry deteriorated further in the absence of any channel of communication by which they could air their grievances to the highest authorities. The emperor had ruled that no major mass organization be formed without his approval. The Office of Association in the Ministry of Interior was granted broad authority to judge whether a registration application was 'unlawful or immoral' or 'against the national unity or interest' (Clapham, 1969). In practice, the ministry used its authority under the Association's Registration Regulation of 1966 to outlaw all organizations it deemed a potential threat to the interests of the regime.

The 1974 revolution, which ousted the emperor from power, brought a fundamental break with the past in Ethiopian agriculture. The feudal land tenure system was cited as the major cause of agricultural stagnation and ecological degradation (Hoben, 1975; Weintraub, 1975). It was obvious that some form of land reform was necessary to eliminate the ill effects of the pre-revolutionary agricultural system. Fundamental change was brought about in Ethiopian agriculture through enactment of the Public Ownership of Rural Lands Proclamation of 29 April 1975, which outlawed private ownership of land and tenancy. All the land was to be held by Peasant Associations, which were to grant peasants user rights based on family size (Rahmato, 1985; Ottaway, 1975).

The demise of Imperial rule and the abolition of feudalism, however, did little to change peasants' perceptions about central government-directed development initiatives. Forced villagization after 1979, excessive taxation through the Agricultural Marketing Corporation (AMC), forced conscription of peasants into the army, lack of tenure security, and inadequate support for farmers were the major impediments to agricultural production and resource conservation (Pausewang et al., 1990; Dejene, 1987). Although the Marxist regime introduced piecemeal reforms to revive agricultural production in the country, both before and after the attempted coup of May 1989, the reforms were too little and too late to reverse the general resignation among the peasantry (Government of Ethiopia, 1987; Government of Ethiopia, 1990).

Until the mid-1980s, the socialist government concentrated its investment policy on establishing large-scale mechanized state farms patterned after the Eastern European model, and operated on strict production schedules that required accurate planning. Between 1976 and 1980, the Marxist regime imported thousands of tractors costing millions of dollars from Eastern Europe. The underlying assumption was that large-scale, capital-intensive production would enable the country to increase its food and foreign exchange requirements in the shortest amount of time. This unquestioned assumption that modernization and mechanization were synonymous was a critical mistake (Rahmato, 1990: 100–110). A high degree of dependency on imported inputs and technology soaked up virtually all government investment in agriculture, while small peasants were left to fend for themselves.

Long before the Ethiopian famine of 1983, there was ample evidence that state intervention had contributed to the agrarian crisis. Yet the government of Ethiopia pushed for more, not less, emphasis on state intervention in the agriculture sector. In the early 1980s, it introduced two new collectivization programmes: villagization and resettlement. While the former envisioned the movement of peasants to large villages with the aim of providing each village with schools and other social services, the latter was intended to resettle peasants from ecologically degraded zones to high-potential areas. Both programmes were mandatory and helped alienate the majority of peasants (Lirenso, 1990: 135–43; Pankhurst, 1990).

The number of peasants who suffered relocation and marginalization is unknown. According to Dessalegn Rahmato, a leading expert on the Ethiopian peasantry, some 3.5 million people may have been affected altogether, of whom 6 to 8 per cent may have perished due to disease, malnutrition and food shortages. More than 400,000 households (over 1.8 million people) suffered eviction (Rahmato, 1993). The resettlement programme, which was often carried out by force, affected as many as 750,000 households, some 600,000 during 1984–85 alone (Rahmato, 1989). Peasants were resettled in distant provinces far from their place of origin and often in areas of low agricultural potential and high health risk.

Finally, the impoverishment of the peasantry was accelerated by excessive taxation to fund the government's war with Eritrea and its failed socialist experiment. Peasants were burdened with an unfavourable pricing structure, and a variety of state taxes. On average, peasants paid up to one-third of their annual disposable income in the form of taxes and other contributions. In some cases, peasants sold their assets, such as cattle, to pay for these contributions or to meet grain delivery quotas (Cohen and Isaksson, 1987: 435–64; Lirenso, 1990: 135–43). Peasants who engaged in trade or other endeavours to supplement their income were condemned as petty capitalists and threatened with punishment. The inter-rural movement of goods and people was highly restricted for a greater part of the 1980s.

On the whole, peasant society was shattered as a consequence; families were torn apart, communities were dislocated, and property wantonly destroyed. Agrarian socialism eventually came to be associated in the peasants' minds with the ideology of impoverishment – a determination on the part of the authorities to level everyone in a state of destitution. In response, peasants began to sabotage government projects, feed and protect armed groups bent on overthrowing the socialist government, and join in the liberation movements. The settlement programme was plagued throughout by high rates of desertion (Pankhurst, 1990). The peasantry in other parts of Africa consistently took similar actions against the colonial powers.

Source: Cheru, 1997: 153–70.

Despite the overwhelming bias of agricultural policy towards export agriculture, the economic returns from cash crops have fluctuated, often to the detriment of African countries. Since 1970, Africa has suffered losses in its world market share of agricultural exports, though recent trends have been more favourable. The export shares of five of the region's nine main exports (bananas, cotton, sugar, tea, tobacco) rose in the period 1990–97, compared to 1980–89, though some increases were small.

Some countries, such as Kenya, Zimbabwe and Tanzania, have successfully developed a niche market in the export of non-traditional crops, such as horticulture and floriculture, in an effort to break away from dependence on the traditional export of coffee and tea. Kenya in particular has been successful in its new venture because it has a good marketing chain linking growers to agents, exporters and freight companies, as well as a national airline with ample cargo space on frequent international flights. On the other hand, working conditions for farm workers on horticulture farms remain extremely poor. These farms operate under the same conditions as the export processing zones in Asia and Latin America, where labour organizing is prohibited and governments often exempt farm owners from adhering to national labour codes and minimum wage requirements.

Lack of rural diversification and the shortage of non-farm employment

Access to agricultural land is a necessary condition for making an agricultural livelihood, but it is not a sufficient condition. A recurrent theme emerging in studies of patterns of poverty in rural Africa is that the poorest groups are those without access to remunerative off-farm income. This pattern of rural poverty is not confined to landless labourers. Even those peasants with abundant land and reasonable soil fertility can experience some degree of destitution (Hill, 1972: 191). Access to remunerative off-farm income has been identified as a key factor in upward mobility in rural areas (Kitching, 1980; Iliffe, 1987; Coousins, Weiner and Amin, 1992: 5–24). Research has shown that rural poverty in Senegal has been linked to lack of access to non-farm income, while in Tanzania the accumulation strategies of better-off rural households are based on income diversification and the simultaneous exploitation of both rural and urban resources (Baker, 1995: 117–32).

Public works projects that are labour intensive can play a vital role in supporting the purchasing power of the poor. Such projects, which involve the building of infrastructure, such as roads and bridges, upon which development depends, prevent migration away from the area to camps or cities. Such projects, largely funded by the World Food Programme and Christian aid agencies, have been used as a tool for food and/or income relief in both Ethiopia and Sudan (Webb, von Braun and Yohannes, 1991b). The long-term solution for employment generation and poverty reduction in rural areas, however, lies in the development of a coherent rural industrialization strategy, involving a network of agro-processing industries, service centres, and marketing and transportation services that directly support rural productivity.

Land degradation and productivity

Land degradation is becoming a major mechanism through which poor peasants in Africa are being pushed off the land (Salih, 1994). Land degradation from both natural and man-made sources takes an average of 25,000 square miles of African land out of agricultural production each year, an area about the size of Ireland. As the productivity of the land has been reduced, crop yield potential is lowered and harvests become less reliable. According to Oldeman, degraded soils have caused a 25 per cent drop in Africa's cropland productivity since World War II (Oldeman, 1998).

Degradation also leads to a reduction in the supply of wood for domestic fuel. In addition, the biomass (the vegetative cover) available for grazing and animal feed diminishes, livestock production declines, and therefore one of the main sources of cash income for farmers disappears. In an environment of diminishing yields and loss of cash income, seasonal labour migration, mostly by men, increases to make up for the cash deficit, exacerbating the burden on the women who remain at home.

It is, therefore, a great mistake to assume that the peasantry alone is responsible for the ecological crisis in Africa, as many governments and aid agencies would like us to believe. While drought and regional wars are partly to blame, much of the poverty and ecological destruction are caused by a complex web of factors: inadequate focus on adaptive research, lack of investment in infrastructure, lack of proper extension and demonstration services, inappropriate pricing and marketing policies, and the exclusion of peasants from access to productive inputs and key policy decisions that directly affect their well-being and productivity (Cheru and Mathu, 1989).

Even in situations where extension personnel are available, they are not supported by the necessary facilities and inputs (implements, polytene bags, seed of good quality, nursery tools and equipment, and bicycles for transportation) (Dejene, 1987; Rahmato, 1987). Opportunities for training extension agents in new farming and conservation techniques rarely exist, and this hampers their ability to offer proper advice to farmers. Film and video technology to show farmers 'best practice' farm trials from other countries is a novelty in most African countries.

Box 4.2 The International Fund for Agricultural Development (IFAD) programme for combating land degradation in Africa

Under its Special Programme for African Countries Affected by Drought and Desertification (SPA), IFAD directs its assistance to poor farmers in dry areas. The SPA promotes simple technologies, builds grassroots institutions, and provides small-scale credit and better agricultural training. The programme gives a lot of emphasis to indigenous technology and farmers' intimate knowledge of their own environment. Some of the most useful methods of water and soil conservation are:

- *Earth mounds* made between plants during weeding. The cut weeds are heaped into piles and covered with soil. The resultant mounds help to slow runoff, and also become mini-compost heaps.
- *Stone bunds* are rock walls about one foot high, built along contour lines across a field in areas where there is a good supply of loose stone. The bunds both prevent runoff and keep water on the field, where it sinks into the soil. They also trap silt and other organic matter, retaining them on the fields.
- *Half-moon ditches* are shallow, semi-circular pits with a 3–4 foot radius dug into barren soil near desert areas, with a separation between each ditch of about the same size. A layer of manure is put in each half-moon ditch. The shallow ditches, because of their half-moon shape, catch water whenever it rains. The combination of rain, fertilizer and nutrients in the soil enable perennial grass to grow rapidly; the grasses are excellent feed for cattle.
- *Hillside terraces* are constructed on steep slopes. These drastically reduce water runoff and improve water infiltration. The development of such terraces is being promoted as part of a holistic approach in watershed management.

- *Conservation-based farming systems* are ones in which farmers, in addition to planting grass to help stabilize terrace banks, also plant a mixture of crops that are grown continuously by using the relay technique to spread the harvest throughout the year.

These techniques have allowed people to grow more food and fatten their cattle. The techniques work well because they are low cost, relatively simple to teach and learn, easy to replicate, and require minimal amounts of labour. The techniques are often built on indigenous practices.

Source: IFAD, 1994.

Gender disparities in rural development policies

Rural women play a significant role in agricultural production in Africa. They provide the bulk of hoe farming, planting, weeding, winnowing, storage and marketing. In addition, women are responsible for looking after the cattle, and for collecting water and firewood. Yet they remain all but invisible to policy-makers and extension advisors. Their dual role in society is rarely recognized. The competing demand of household responsibility reduces the time available for women to participate in organizations or to engage in other productive employment. The lack of significant advancement in women's economic position is rooted in traditional values, which determine the position of women in society. Women's position in society is regarded as secondary to their status in the family under the male-headed household (Kebede, 1990; Pankhurst and Jacobs, 1991: 202–27). Policy-makers continue to hold the view that the real problem is 'poverty' not 'gender' – the implication being that if you improve the general welfare of the society, it will result in improved economic resources for women. In reality, this is not true.

Women's economic advancement in rural areas is further hampered by lack of access to productive assets, particularly land. Both the customary law and the body of common law derived from the relevant colonial power, as modified by statute or decree since independence, adversely affect women's access to and use of property. The customary systems typically prohibit women's direct access to land, either by ownership or inheritance. Statutory systems affect property rights in other ways, often limiting women to the status of legal minors, hence rendering them incapable of owning property (Davidson, 1991).

Efforts to reform these laws have been made at the margin, leaving untouched the customary prohibitions (Butegwa, 1991: 45–57; Himonga,

1991: 59–73). For example, despite statutory laws, which in theory provide for a woman's right to own property, 'only 5 per cent of Kenyan women own land in their own names in the areas under individual tenure' (Mackenzie, 1993). In short, the right to inherit property is still governed by customary laws in many African countries. Direct purchase is almost impossible, since women do not have the money or access to credit to obtain a loan.

Even when women have access to land, much discrimination is observed in the provision of agricultural education, training and extension. Agricultural extension programmes generally are inherently male-oriented because men are supposed not only to be the heads of family but also the major producers in rural areas. Most educational programmes organized for women are biased in favour of home economics, while other agricultural courses, like crop production and protection, animal husbandry, and farm management, are offered only to men. In summary, women's access to economic resources, training, extension and credit is generally limited.

In the absence of aggressive government policy to remove the legal obstacles to women's equal participation in the rural economy, women continue to depend on informal associations such as labour groups, rotating credit associations and funeral associations to increase their economic and social welfare. Although these institutions existed in the past, they have assumed greater importance in recent years as modern government structures continue to alienate large numbers of women and increase their household and community responsibilities.

Finally, development policies generally do not consider the actual distribution of labour in the countryside and exclude the needs and interests of women, who account for the lion's share of agricultural production in Africa. Programmes to increase food production and preserve the natural resource base in Africa must, therefore, reach women if they are to succeed. Efforts must be made to improve women's access to productive resources, and to reorient agricultural training and other supportive services such as credit and appropriate technology (Knowles, 1991: 250–64).

Insufficient attention to technological modernization

The rate of technological change in agriculture depends ultimately on agricultural research. Although African farmers increasingly produce for local and world markets, they do so with outmoded and primitive tools. As an example, the number of tractors employed per 1,000 hectares of land in 1994 was very low in Africa when compared to other regions:

1,165 for Latin America; 804 for Asia, and only 290 for Africa (World Bank, 2000: 172). Whatever little technological modernization has taken place is exclusively limited to large commercial agricultural estates, and the technology used there is exclusively imported from outside. There has been no effort to link national industrialization strategies to increasing agricultural productivity by supplying intermediate technologies and basic inputs to the rural areas, as the Asian NICs did in the early phase of their development. Similarly, investment in research and development to raise the productivity of the agricultural sector has been neglected. Insufficient attempts are being made to create a multiplier effect by establishing agro-processing industries to increase the value-added on processed goods. Basic rural industrialization strategy is where the greatest opportunities for off-farm employment can be generated.

In the African countries that have had significant experience in mechanized farming, the farming operations that were first to be mechanized were those activities that fell to men in the sexual division of labour. There has been little mechanization of the farm work done by women. Mechanization is mainly confined to land clearing and ploughing. As a result, the workload of women is greatly increased because mechanized ploughing increases the cultivated area, whereas the work of hoeing, weeding, collection and harvesting are not mechanized.

Declining agricultural output in Africa is, therefore, part of a wider pattern whereby governments of all ideological persuasions have consistently failed to recognize the role of small farmers when setting their development priorities. Government investment policy across the continent has tended to favour projects in urban areas or on highly mechanized export agriculture. The needs of the majority of subsistence farmers are rarely addressed. Tenure insecurity, inadequate marketing and storage facilities, and weak extension services have further constrained agricultural production and proper management and utilization of natural resources. Thus, by their own misguided actions, African governments have succeeded in 'killing the goose that laid the golden egg'. The combined effect of these anti-peasant policies has had the undesirable consequence of forcing peasants to turn inwards – that is, to concentrate on satisfying their own needs instead of producing for the market.

The crucial lesson from the past forty years of rural development strategies in Africa has been that peasants will never be able to challenge the vicious circle of marginalization and mass exclusion until they organize themselves politically to gain sufficient influence at the national level. Yet, on the other hand, their precarious economic condition – the daily struggles around subsistence – makes the task of developing a counter-project exceptionally difficult and slow. While peasants are aware, by and large, of their situation at the local level, they have neither the capacity nor the resources to influence events in the world beyond their villages. The widely publicized 1992 peasant uprising in Mexico by the Zapatista movement is an exception. Africa is yet to experience a well-organized peasant movement ready to challenge autocratic regimes in a credible way.

The 'Revenge of the Poor': Peasants' Response to Anti-peasant Agricultural Policies

After many years of being treated like cattle, the peasants in Africa have become aware of their powerless situation and drawn the conclusion that it is better to avoid the state altogether and withdraw into their local communities on a subsistence basis by engaging in collective action to find solutions to common problems. Everyday forms of resistance are not spur-of-the-moment reactions by the marginalized to the problems they confront daily. Rather, the desire to resist is based on a rational calculation of both risks and gains by the participants. Such resistance requires little coordination, avoids direct confrontation with authorities, and is not subject to elite manipulation (Scott, 1993; Cheru, 1989).

Like the colonial system, the post-colonial state has lost its role as an instrument of development. Ordinary citizens do not expect anything from the state. Instead, they are determining their own development. Peasants now market their produce and livestock through their own channels, disregarding political boundaries and marketing boards. For example, in the Kaolack region of Senegal, peasants have formed a federation called the Peasant Association of Kaolack (ADAK), which established barter agreements with farmer groups. They exchange millet and salt for palm oil, dried fish, and honey, thereby avoiding the market, taxes and government boards (Pradervand, 1989). In eastern Senegal, the Federation of Sarakolle Village has successfully resisted efforts by the state agricultural agency and the United States Agency for International Development (USAID) to promote rice production via large-scale irrigation schemes and centralized control over production and marketing (Adams, 1981). The federation's persistence has forced changes in the state marketing board's approach in other areas where it operates.

In Burkina Faso, for example, thousands of innovative village development groups have been transforming their communities. The most visible institution has been the Naam, the traditional Burkinabé village co-operative. These groups grew spontaneously in the early 1970s in response to the rapid and far-reaching environmental and economic crisis facing their communities. Using the traditional concept of self-help, the Naam groups organized themselves at the village level and began constructing dams and dikes, reforesting, opening new roads, digging wells and undertaking soil conservation projects. The groups also introduced basic literacy, improved cooking stoves, and constructed cereal banks, grain mills and village pharmacies (Cheru and Bayili, 1991). Six S, another indigenous organization, provides the funding for local communities. Six S is organized so that it can respond to local needs without intimidation.

In Zimbabwe, the Organization of Rural Associations for Progress (ORAP) began as a series of women's clubs. It rapidly expanded to over six hundred affiliated groups of women and men engaged in a variety of village-based development actions. Among its activities are the propagation and use of indigenous seeds, rainwater catchments, inter-village food marketing and community grain stores. Its staff take the lead from a village-level analysis of problems and offer assistance in negotiation with external contributors, including pressuring the government for expanded land redistribution (Nyoni, 1995: 187–96).

There exist thousands of similar, locally initiated self-help experiments in villages all across Africa. The few examples cited above are indicative of the fact that, as people become more active in their own organizations, they build skills and self-confidence, and thus strengthen their capacity to participate in political life more broadly. In the long run, they will be able to challenge the vicious circle of mass exclusion and marginalization.

Changing Course: A New World Order for Peasants

The priority task of agricultural revolution for several decades to come is obviously complex and multifaceted. It is clear that huge investments will be required to accelerate agricultural growth and rural development. New inputs and innovative technologies have to be introduced on a massive scale to improve productivity, reduce poverty and raise Africa's competitiveness in world markets. Future agricultural policy reforms in Africa must, therefore, address the following critical factors:

- *Technological* What kind of equipment and inputs (water, fertilizer and so on) could bring an improvement in productivity per cultivator and per acre?
- *Macro-economic* What kinds of economic policies are needed to support this effort? (One option would be a price and income structure to encourage behaviour in accordance with the aims, industrial policies

and appropriate financing mechanisms). What would be their social and political implications?

- *Management/administration* What kinds of rural social administration (organization of property and its utilization, ground rents and agricultural wages, marketing, credit or producer cooperatives) can help movement in the desired direction, or, in contrast, obstruct it? How can the mode of social administration produced by historical social relations (particularly between the state and the peasantry) be an obstacle to change?
- *Public–private interface* What types of social administration beneficial to trade and industry may also be required for agricultural progress?
- *Ecological* Due to the interrelationship between deforestation, soil erosion and low agricultural productivity, these problems can only be tackled by integrating them into every aspect of the agricultural development strategy. A compartmentalized conservation approach is inadequate to solve such multidimensional and multi-sectoral problems.

Creating an 'enabling state' and deepening participation

A key precondition for achieving a successful agricultural revolution is the presence of a strong and effective 'enabling state', or what some analysts refer to as a 'developmental state', with the capacity to respond effectively to the demands of interest groups engaged in the agricultural sector. While the state in Africa has been part of the problem, it would be a serious error to underestimate its critical role in any effective rural development strategy. The crucial challenge is how to dismantle the 'disabling state' and replace it with 'a state, which is not only protector and supporter, but also enabler and liberator' (Chambers, 1991: 20).

If local initiatives are to succeed, it is clear that new power-sharing relationships must be worked out with important state actors. Decentralized processes and choice are central to the reversal of current paradigms. A political space must be opened up to allow local communities to establish new relationships between themselves and central government. Until African farmers are given the right to manage their own affairs, with support from the central administration, agricultural production will continue to stagnate and the resource base will continue to erode. These local-level organizations must be given greater control over the allocation of resources, the disbursement of funds intended to benefit them, and the appointment and control of officials meant to serve them (World Bank, 1989c; UNECA, 1990; UNECA/African NGOs, 1990).[1]

Democratization efforts must also address the special circumstances of women farmers. Even though political leaders are becoming more aware of the need to integrate women in development, that awareness is not tangibly reflected in the policies being pursued. It is important to improve women's access to productive resources by revising existing legislation that denies married women access to land. Other necessary actions include: upgrading the capacity of women's organizations, including self-help groups, through training; reorientation of agricultural training and services; and the introduction of measures designed to reduce the work burden of women, by improving social facilities such as water, mills and alternative cooking devices.

Finally, devolution of power is meaningless unless accompanied by a strategy to strengthen rural administration. Local officials will not be able to carry out their mandate if they have weak institutions and unqualified staff. It is difficult to conceive development and democratization without a viable, accountable and active state at both national and local levels.

Maintaining a sound macro-economic framework

Efforts to revitalize peasant agriculture will not succeed unless accompanied by a radical revision of macroeconomic policies with regard to government budget, pricing policy, liberalization of trade, an increase in the role of the private sector, and public-sector reform. More specifically, there must be a review of pricing policies to eliminate biases against small rural producers, such as price ceilings on agricultural products, overvalued exchange rates and the heavy taxation on farm produce (World Bank, 1981: ch. 5; World Bank, 2000: ch. 6). Expenditures should be directed away from non-productive to priority sectors, such as agricultural production, education, and infrastructure development and maintenance.

Apart from the tenure and ownership aspects of land, pricing and marketing have an influence in stimulating agricultural production and conservation of natural resources. In order that peasants have adequate incentive to take conservation measures and grow more food, the liberalization of marketing and pricing policies should be pursued vigorously. The provision of credit, increased access by farmers to consumer goods, and flexible pricing for farm produce should be emphasized.

Investment in agricultural research and infrastructure

Population density figures for rural Africa are growing, while the technological and organizational capacity of agricultural production remains static.

The predominant technology – single hoe cultivation – is completely outdated. Draft animals are in short supply since most people can barely afford to keep even one or two due to shortage of fodder. As land becomes scarce, production increases must come from raising yields per acre through the adoption of low-cost affordable intermediate technology. Multiple uses of animal power and selective mechanization by diesel-fuelled equipment must be tried.

Higher productivity and effective markets require investment in research and extension, access to market information, and efficient transportation and communication networks. Strengthening agricultural research hand in hand with an improved extension service is a key dimension of agricultural modernization (Lipton, 1988). Research should be reoriented towards solving the problems facing peasant agriculture by involving the peasants themselves in decision-making and tapping into their knowledge of the natural environment. Research on drought-resistant crops or yield-increasing agricultural innovations, genetically improved livestock, and improved animal traction can reduce the pressure on marginal lands. Improving traditional tilling techniques and adjusting them to soil conditions and the introduction of new and improved methods of soil and water conservation should be accorded priority.

For example, during the 1984–85 East African drought, Sudanese farmers participating in the Jebel Mara Rural Development Project in Darfur were able to cope better than non-participating villagers, since they had access to modern inputs through extension services offered by the project. Furthermore, within the participating villages, households that participated in the project had higher grain production per capita and sufficient intake to meet calorie needs, which meant that fewer household members were forced to migrate in search of food. This success highlights the key role that improved agricultural technology can play in famine prevention and mitigation (Teklu, von Braun and Zaki, 1991).

The rate of adoption of an innovation is dependent upon the availability of complementary inputs. Such inputs may be supplies (fertilizers in the case of a new seed, or spare parts in the case of farm machinery) or services (timely purchase of a perishable new cash crop, or prompt repairs of broken equipment). Reliable supplies of these inputs allay fears of a crop failing for lack of them. In addition, lack of credit significantly limits adoption of new technologies. Since smallholders rarely have capital in either form, the observed non-adoption of new technologies on small farms is partly attributable to this lack of capital, and not exclusively an effect of farm size per se.

Finally, if food production in Africa is to improve significantly, scientific research will have to be developed at the same time as extension services are expanded. Important in this connection is the necessity of increasing the number of students in technical and scientific disciplines. In addition to developing human capital, rural roads constitute perhaps the most important infrastructure needed to assure distribution of those inputs.

Improved education and extension

One important constraint on agricultural production identified by peasants is the lack of adequate extension services. Many studies have examined the relationship of education to the rate of adoption of new technologies, taking the 'marginal product' of education to be the effect of education on output, with all physical inputs held constant. The results indicate that farmers with better education are earlier adopters of modern technologies and apply modern inputs more efficiently throughout the adoption process (Feder, Just and Zilberman, 1985).

In many African countries, the overemphasis by governments on both extension and other resources in high-potential areas has left subsistence farmers to fend for themselves. Even in such areas, agricultural extension programmes are inherently male-oriented. There is therefore an urgent need by African governments to improve the outreach capacity of the ministry responsible for this sector, by strengthening extension networks in the field, developing communication systems, extension manuals and audio-visual materials for the dissemination of information to peasants. Farmers must be shown, on their own farm or nearby, how to put improved techniques into use. Organizing farmers' field days is an excellent way of spreading new agricultural innovations. For this to happen, extension agents must have a basic understanding of agricultural sciences as well as the ability to translate technical jargon into a language understandable to rural people.

Land reform and security of tenure

The most significant disincentive to conservation-based agricultural transformation in Africa remains a lack of the security that accompanies ownership of trees and forests. Empirical studies have shown, for example, that tenants have a lower tendency to adopt new technologies than landowners. Since farmers have no long-term guarantee on the use or control of the land they farm, there is little incentive to make long-term investment in the land. Governments need to clarify, through legislation, the legal rights and duties of individual farmers with regard to the use of land, trees and water.

Linking conservation and agricultural productivity

Concern with land degradation and water depletion in Africa is not new. It has to be recognized, however, that previous efforts to reverse it have failed (Cleaver and Schreiber, 1994; Oldeman, 1998). The conventional approach suffered from three problems in relation to the poor: (1) resource conservation was carried out at their expense; (2) resource management excluded their participation; (3) resource conservation and management used technologies that were inaccessible by them. In effect, conservation activities were alien impositions.

Land degradation in sub-Saharan Africa can be halted and in many cases even reversed. To achieve this goal, reclamation projects based on simple techniques must be initiated in close cooperation with the farmers themselves. Conservation begins with those who use the land, not with the land they are using. The most meaningful index of success is the extent to which the resource users – farmers, herders, smallholders and gatherers – adopt more sustainable agricultural practices. Success depends on the use of resources, which should be financially profitable to the farmers. Kenya's Machakos district is a well-documented example where farmers, with favourable policies and institutions, protect natural resources in a sustainable way (Monitimore and Tiffen, quoted in World Bank, 2000: 196).

Assistance to farmers in the form of material, technical and organizational know-how can go a long way in strengthening community efforts at land conservation. Special emphasis must be given to indigenous technology and farmers' intimate knowledge of their environment. Research has shown that measures undertaken at national, regional and international levels will be futile unless farmers are involved in all phases of the programme. Only when the right conditions are created will farmers be willing and able to embark on sustained conservation efforts. In addition, action in the following areas must be taken:

- *Policies on population growth* Although population is a very sensitive topic, African governments have confronted the problem. Population growth and a shortage of arable land have compounded the environmental crisis in Africa. Even if the policies outlined above were put in place, the need would still exist to strengthen existing family planning activities. In addition, urgent steps need to be taken to improve access to productive employment and to raise the educational status of women.

- *Easing fuel wood shortages* Wood is still the main source of energy for domestic consumption in almost all African countries. And in rural areas, where three-quarters of the the continent's population live, wood is the only fuel used. Wanton felling of trees and the consequent destruction of a fragile ecosystem are the main factors behind the higher risk of desertification that Africa runs compared to that of other continents. In order to cope with the problem of land degradation, reforestation programmes and environmental protection should be accorded high priority, especially in those areas with a fragile ecosystem. Efforts must be made to introduce efficient stoves and solar technology, supported by strong extension, demonstration and promotional activities. The technology introduced must be simple and easy to reproduce using local materials, and must be affordable for poor people. This step will drastically reduce the amount of fuel wood used for cooking purposes. Legal clarification of land tenure relations will go a long way in encouraging peasants to grow trees on their farms.

Box 4.3 Alternatives to slash-and-burn agriculture

The problems of slash-and-burn agriculture and rural poverty in the tropics are enormous and complex. They not only threaten tropical farmers and forests; ultimately they affect every person on the planet. Approximately 15 million hectares of the world's primary rainforests are destroyed each year; some 60 per cent of this destruction is caused by slash-and-burn agriculture. With support from UNDP and GEF, Alternatives to Slash-and-Burn (ASB) is working to reduce deforestation caused by slash-and-burn by providing technological alternatives and policy options that eliminate the need to clear additional land and encourage the reclamation of degraded and abandoned lands. It is evident that the option to link environment-oriented strategies with economic ones provides a practical, realistic approach.
What contributes to the success of this project?

- *A multidisciplinary perspective* The ASB programme addresses both policy and technology dimensions in a multidisciplinary manner, by linking environmental and socioeconomic policies that encourage the adoption of technologies that discourage deforestation, and develops guidelines for policies that address macroeconomic issues such as subsidies, agricultural marketing strategies, import tariffs and credit.
- *Building on lessons learned* ASB recognizes that small-scale farmers who practise shifting cultivation are the victims of complex socioeconomic

and political factors such as inappropriate policies governing land use and tenure (attention to women's land rights), migration schemes and access to markets. Consequently, policies that try to contain deforestation by establishing forest reserves, which neglect the human dimension, are unsustainable in the long term.

- *Consultation and involvement* During the design of the project, there were sufficient consultations with potential partners and stakeholders (farmer-producer organizations, national research centres, NGOs). Every attempt has been made to mesh project goals with national and/or institutional objectives. This has instilled a sense of ownership on the part of partner institutions and governments.
- *Emphasis on global/local institutional collaboration* The project explicitly recognizes that progress depends on the collaboration of international, regional, national and local organizations as partners in the governance, financing and implementation of project goals. Therefore a key feature of the project is synergism between global, regional and national perspectives.
- *Indigenous resources for local needs* Bottom-up research is driven by the farmers' needs. By making the most of indigenous knowledge, the project applies modern technologies to domesticate wild plants for the production of food, fodder, fuel wood, timber, poles, medicines and fibre.
- *Capacity development and information sharing* This is accomplished by developing training and information programmes that ensure technologies are transferred to those who need them most. Equipment, vehicles and other support services are made available within national research systems, thereby facilitating national scientists' participation at international seminars.
- *Highly participatory governance structure* The ASB programme is designed to ensure the full participation of partners in programme planning and implementation, but with a clear definition of roles and responsibilities. It involves a total of fifteen national programmes, international research centres (CGIAR) and NGOs. These form the ASB Consortium, members of which are represented on the Global Steering Committee (GSG) that meets annually to set general policy guidelines. Regional Steering Groups, led by CGIAR research centres, ensure regional coordination and set priorities and institutional responsibilities. IRRI coordinates work in Southeast Asia, CIAT in Latin America and IITA in West Africa. ICRAF is the ASB's coordinating institution.

National Steering Groups, chaired by the heads of National Research Institutions (NARs) for each country, maintain government support and the active participation of government research and extension institutions, indigenous NGOs and universities. The Local Steering Groups, chaired by the NARs–ASB representatives, are concerned with collaboration among farmer-producer organizations, NGOs, community leaders and governments. They are responsible for the implementation of project goals at the local level.

This project has contributed to a paradigm shift in natural resource management by emphasizing the links between complex socioeconomic and political factors and resource degradation in the tropics. It tries to tackle the problems resulting from slash-and-burn agriculture from the farmer's perspective. This entails spending a lot of time with farmers, conducting on-farm trials and demonstrations. It encourages household and institutional participation in designing and implementing policies to conserve forests and land resources. In short, information and knowledge flow both upstream and downstream.

Source: Cheru, 1996.

Expanding non-farm employment

In sub-Saharan Africa, notwithstanding the unwarranted assumption that the continent's destiny is necessarily rooted in peasant agriculture, the population is becoming less agrarian in nature (Bryceson and Jamal, 1997). Environmental degradation is a major driving force in this process. Decreasing agricultural productivity, in conjunction with population growth and land subdivision, makes it difficult for large numbers of farmers to rely solely on agricultural production for their survival (Bryceson, 1997: 237–56). Non-agricultural rural employment is therefore an essential component of any poverty reduction strategy.

In addition to increasing the productivity of agriculture, attention must be given to generating and expanding employment in non-agricultural sectors through diversification of the rural economy. This is arguably an even greater challenge for development than the biological/technical rehabilitation of agriculture itself. At the centre of rural diversification is rural industrialization, designed not only to increase the productivity of the agricultural sector but also to serve the needs of urban centres. Public policy should be reoriented to provide incentives for the establishment of small- and medium-scale rural industries to serve the needs of rural people for services, capital goods, agricultural inputs and agricultural processing, as well as basic consumer goods.

Both forward linkages between non-agricultural and agricultural activities, such as processing and other manufacturing of agricultural raw materials, and backward linkages, such as the manufacturing of agricultural equipment, tools and inputs, as well as tourism in many areas, are the basis of the most profitable types of non-farm rural employment. Rural productivity increases can also be achieved through the intensification of public works, such as secondary roads, reforestation and soil conservation, clean water supplies, rural electrification, health clinics, schools and agro-service centres. These activities, while providing gainful employment, would strengthen the internal working of the national economy by stimulating production and consumption of local goods and services.

Ensuring gender equality in access to productive assets and services

African women play a significant role in agricultural production, performing 90 per cent of the work of processing food crops and providing household water and fuel wood, 80 per cent of the work of food storage and transportation from farm to village, 90 per cent of the work of hoeing and weeding, and 60 per cent of the work of harvesting and marketing (Quisumbing et al., 1995). Despite their importance in agricultural production, women face disadvantages in accessing both land and financial, research, extension, education and health services. This lack of access has inhibited opportunities for agricultural investment, growth and income.

Evidence from Kenya shows that when women do gain access to these services they increase yields by more than 20 per cent (Saito, Mekonnen and Spurling, 1994). Thus more must be done to ensure gender equality in access to productive assets and services. Efforts could include provision of clean, accessible water to reduce the time burden of domestic work, investing in girls' education, ensuring gender-neutral land policy and legislation, and building women's skills and capabilities to reduce their political deficit.

Conclusion

Africa's persistent agricultural crisis does not appear insurmountable in the light of the above analysis. To remedy the situation, however, national governments must play an active and supporting role by investing in agricultural research, storage facilities, transport and communication, which are essential factors for raising productivity and increasing farmers' incomes. Government-guaranteed prices and security of tenure are the most effective incentives to shift peasant farmers from subsistence to production for the market.

Finally, agricultural growth in Africa requires more than just reforming policies and institutions and increasing rural public investment. It also requires developing open political systems in which organizations of the poor can thrive, and creating political coalitions that help improve policies and consolidate the gains already achieved.

Note

1. This important principle is incorporated in three important documents: The World Bank (1989c), *Sub-Saharan Africa: From Crisis to Sustainable Growth*; UNECA (1990), *African Alternative Framework to Structural Adjustment*, and the joint UNECA/African NGOs (1990), *African Charter for Popular Participation in Development and Transformation*.

CHAPTER 5

Rethinking Regional Economic Integration: From Rhetoric to Reality

It is meaningless to open markets when these economies do not produce anything to trade.

Jackie Selebi, Director-General,
South African Department of Foreign Affairs

Since the end of the Cold War, and with the emergence of powerful trading blocs, there has been renewed interest in Africa regarding the need to create strong regional economic integration mechanisms to promote economic growth in the continent.[1] Regional economic integration is not conceived as a counter-hegemonic project to deflect the ill effects of globalization on weak and vulnerable African economies, but as a necessary vehicle to accelerate Africa's integration into the new knowledge-driven global economy. The Abuja Treaty, signed at the OAU Summit in June 1991 with the aim of establishing an African Economic Community by the year 2025, is indicative of African resolve to become an important player in global economic relations. Whether this ambitious goal can be achieved is another matter. Establishment of the Community by 2025 will depend on the ability and willingness of African governments to create the appropriate conducive environment for economic cooperation to take root in the continent.

Interestingly, the World Bank, an institution well known for its opposition to similar ideas in previous decades, has welcomed the renewed interest in regional economic integration in Africa. The Bank now believes that global interdependence and economic liberalism is the only route for Africa to follow, and that such a strategy should be central in Africa's economic integration efforts (World Bank, 1989c). The Bank has, therefore, singled out the Common Market for Eastern and Southern Africa (COMESA) and the Southern Africa Development Community (SADC) for financial and technical support. The Bank argues that regional integration should not become a means of salvaging failed import-substitution industrialization programmes; rather, the strategy should focus on creating open markets harmonized with ongoing structural adjustment programmes at the national level.

This chapter examines the following questions: What are the challenges, both internal and external, that governments in the region will confront on their way to establishing viable economic integration? What are the major impediments to cooperative behaviour? What is to be done within African nations, as well as in subregional entities such as COMESA, SADC, and the Southern African Customs Union (SACU) to facilitate more unity in the future? What are the obstacles to translating the principles of the Abuja Treaty into deeds? More importantly, how can African countries encourage the growth of a much more production-oriented (rather than commerce- or landlord-oriented) private sector that is efficient as well as socially responsible? To answer these questions, we will review the various theoretical paradigms of regional integration that have influenced past approaches to regional integration in Africa.

Competing Paradigms on Regional Integration: What Lessons for Africa?

Economic integration and economic cooperation are concepts that are often, erroneously, used interchangeably. This can lead to flawed theorizing about the appropriate model that groups of countries should follow to expand economic exchange.

According to Davis, *economic integration* refers to a process in which the economies of individual states are merged (in whole or in part) into a single regional entity. *Economic cooperation*, on the other hand, is a much more open-ended concept referring to a range of situations in which individual states share or make available to each other resources, technology or expertise, collaborate in joint projects, or act together in external economic relations. Such cooperation may or may not be undertaken with the aim of promoting economic integration (Davis, 1992).

Neoclassical economists have conventionally approached the issue of integration through what is known as the theory of customs unions. This approach is also known as *trade or market integration* (Viner, 1950; Robson, 1980). Within this paradigm, integration is viewed as a process in which

Table 5.1 Stages in regional economic integration

Stage	Key elements
Preferential trade area	Member countries charge each other lower tariffs than those applicable to non-members, but customs duties are still levied on imports from other members and there is not yet free movement of goods within the area.
Free trade area	No duties are applied to goods from other members, but each member determines its own tariff policy in relation to goods imported from outside the area.
Customs union	Trade with non-members is governed by a common external tariff. Each member therefore gives up sovereignty to determine its own tariff policy.
Common market	There is free movement of capital and labour, as well as of goods. Some harmonization of fiscal and monetary policy also takes place.
Economic union or community	There is either a single currency or joint management of monetary policy.
Political union	The political institutions of member countries are unified or federated.

Source: Ojo, 1985.

tariff and non-tariff barriers between cooperating partners are progressively removed and external trade and eventually fiscal and monetary policies harmonized. Progress up what might be termed 'the ladder of integration' is conventionally seen as involving the creation in linear succession of the types of institutional arrangement shown in Table 5.1.

The neoclassical paradigm on integration puts great emphasis on the distinction between trade creation and trade diversion. Trade creation refers to a situation in which the production of particular goods is shifted from a high-cost producer to a a lower-cost regional producer. Trade diversion, on the other hand, takes place if a country turns from lower cost external supplier to a high-cost regional supplier, now enjoying an 'artificial' advantage because of a preferential tariff arrangement. Under the trade integration paradigm, economic integration is held to be economically desirable in cases where the trade-creation effects are greater than trade diversion.

The neoclassical approach, which is based on the theory of 'comparative advantage', has been widely criticized as presenting an unrealistic vision of mechanisms and power relations in contemporary international trade. The approach to the issue of 'trade creation' versus 'trade diversion' has been seen as static in that it refers to existing comparative advantages without considering the potentiality of regional cooperation to overcome obstacles and create new comparative advantages. Moreover, the neoclassical approach fails to address the real causes of African countries' inability to expand exports: supply capacity constraints and poor transport and communications networks. Critics also argue that, under conditions of underdevelopment, the neoclassical approach tends disproportionately to benefit stronger partners and could thus lead to polarization ultimately prejudicial to the whole integration effort. For this and other reasons, the neoclassical integration approach was rejected by developing countries. With globalization and the ascendancy of global neoliberalism, however, the neoclassical approach has emerged as the dominant model of integration today, and African countries are increasingly forced to abide by it.

It is in this context that the issue of regional economic integration and South–South cooperation became a dominant topic in the 1960s in Africa, Asia and Latin America. Regional integration was widely seen as potentially making a significant contribution to the efforts of Third World countries to recoup their declining share of world trade and close the gap with the advanced industrialized countries. By the end of the 1970s, however, with the collapse of most projects promoted in the 1960s (such as the East African Community and the Andean Pact), pessimism and cynicism about integration as a means of promoting growth and development reigned. This attitude was not to change until the late 1980s and early 1990s.

Notwithstanding these disappointments, Third World political leaders deliberately avoided experimenting with the 'trade integration' approach, for obvious reasons. It was widely held that the special conditions of underdeveloped countries required policy measures different from those applied in developed countries. According to Ostergaard, two approaches were widely held up as alternatives to the neoclassical model (Ostergaard, 1993: 27–47): the functional integration approach and the development integration approach.

The functional integration approach

This approach, also known as 'integration through project cooperation', is premissed on the view that underdeveloped production structures and infrastructural deficiencies constituted major barriers both to regional trade and to integration in 'Third World' regions. It therefore proposed co-operation in the formulation and execution of joint projects in infra-structure and production in order to remove immediate barriers to regional trade (SADC, 1980).

As the discussion of SADC will show, the assumption that project cooperation will lead to integration was wrong. Although project co-operation, as in the case of the Beirra Corridor, has tremendous impact on intra-regional trade, such a strategy can only become fruitful when enabling macroeconomic policies are in place, supported by strong government commitment to harmonize policies across frontiers. While co-operation in infrastructural projects is important in its own right, such initiatives need to reach beyond this and embrace trade issues, as well as the issue of currency convertibility. These are very difficult issues – 'thorny questions' that have taken fifty-three years for the European countries to settle on their way to forming the European Union. They will take even longer for poor, underdeveloped, and politically unstable Africa to settle.

The development integration approach

Unlike the functional integration approach, the development integration approach stressed the need for both macro- and micro-coordination in a multi-sectoral programme embracing production, infrastructure and trade. It stressed the need for close political cooperation at an early stage of the integration process, and, in contrast to the market integration approach, also stressed the need for an equitable balance of the benefits of integration. It also argued that trade liberalization measures should be oriented particularly towards the least developed member countries. It therefore saw a need for trade integration to be complemented by efforts to promote coordinated regional industrial development and for regional funds or banks to be established to give priority to the least developed members. It also granted less developed members greater preference in access to regional markets and facilities, a longer period to reduce tariffs, and some coordination of macro-policies to be achieved at an early stage, particularly in relation to fiscal incentives for investment.

The development integration approach has drawn criticism from a number of different perspectives. Supporters of laissez-faire approaches have criticized it for its emphasis on political cooperation and state-directed approach. Others have expressed scepticism on the grounds that the high level of political cooperation required is difficult to achieve in practice. Attempts to implement such programmes have been beset with practical problems of implementation (Ostergaard, 1993: 27–47).

In the case of Africa, and particularly Southern Africa, both trade integration and project coordination approaches have informed programmes and institutions. The trade integration approach can be recognized as broadly underlying the operations of SACU and of COMESA. On the other hand, the project cooperation approach informed the activities of the SADC in 1992; the SADC's operation is now informed by the trade integration approach. Needless to say, however, neither approach has tackled sufficiently the issue of how African countries can go about encouraging the growth of a much more productive-oriented, rather than commerce- or landlord-oriented, private sector that is efficient as well as socially responsible. Any regional trade strategy that gives too much emphasis to trade in commerce (mostly involving goods imported from the developed countries) is unlikely to add any value or promote sectoral integration at national or subregional levels. How countries can escape the pressure from global liberalization of trade and find ways to refocus their domestic and subregional trade on productive-oriented activities is the Achilles heel of regional economic integration.

Africa's Poor Track Record in Regional Integration

Economic cooperation and integration within and among groups of African countries has been difficult to achieve. The Southern Africa Development Community (SADC), the Economic Community of West African States (ECOWAS), the Common Market for Eastern and Southern Africa (COMESA), the Economic Community of Central African States (ECCAS), the Central African Customs and Economic Union (UDEAC), and the Economic Community of the Great Lakes Countries (CEPGL) are all subregional economic groups intended to serve as rallying pivots for the total economic integration of the African continent.

In addition to these subregional groupings, there are some two hundred ECA-sponsored intergovernmental organizations (IGOs) established as training or service centres in major fields including banking and finance, science and technology, industry, trade, natural resources, transport and communications, and economic planning and management (UNECA, 1997). In West Africa alone there are three subregional economic groups (ECOWAS, Mano River Union and CEAO) with multiple aims in the field of economic integration. Additionally, there are more than thirty-two other IGOs, some dating back to the colonial period, all purporting to promote cooperation in various fields.

Despite the multiplicity of subregional economic groups and IGOs, however, progress in regional economic cooperation and integration has been disappointing. The multiplicity of overlapping and largely similar arrangements, a notorious phenomenon in Africa, actually dissipates effort and energy. Not only do they make claims on the limited resources of their members but are also, in several cases, in competition with one another in terms of objectives and operations (Ezenwe, 1990: 27–33; Diouf, 1990: 21–6; Saangare, 1990: 111–12). One obvious reason is that most of the economic cooperation and integration schemes adopted in Africa to date have been replicas of the schemes designed to suit advanced market economies. For example, the very ambitious Abuja construction – a carbon copy of the institutional framework of the European Community – does not take sufficient account of the actual political, economic and cultural realities of the African continent. The common market approach (or the market integration approach) aiming at trade liberalization presupposes that economic structures are fully developed and that what is required is optimization along the production frontier. The assumption has been that once goals are set for regional integration, implementation will follow automatically. In reality, however, translating words into deeds in the African context has been consistently difficult.

Moreover, many economic integration schemes in Africa have largely confined their operations to intergovernmental institutions, leaving out non-governmental institutions, which are key actors in national economies (Barad, 1990: 102–8; Wangwe, 1990: 34–9). These latter might include the business community, bankers, consultants, researchers, mass media, associations of manufacturers, national farmers' unions and chambers of commerce. Specifically, African governments have ignored the importance of introducing policies and institutional requirements necessary for regional integration at the national level. These failures have been among the factors that have contributed to the divergence of policy responses and actions at the national level from those at the subregional level.

Finally, regionalism, whether in Africa or in the most advanced countries of the West, cannot get far unless the participating countries deal effectively with their own economic, political and social problems – problems such as fiscal discipline, human resource development, oversized bureaucracies, corruption in public life, and transparency and accountability of government. Simply put, regionalism cannot be a good substitute for poor national economic management.

Key Impediments to Effective Economic Integration

Space limitations do not allow for a full explanation of why many regional integration efforts in Africa have failed. An examination of the Southern Africa Development Community and the Common Market for Eastern and Southern Africa might shed some light on the critical problems African nations face as they try to lay durable foundations for workable regional integration arrangements.

The choice of Southern Africa as a case study is obvious. More than any other region in the continent, Southern Africa is the subregion with the greatest prospect for establishing a workable economic integration arrangement. Rich in mineral resources and well-developed railways, road networks and harbours, the subregion has always had a strong economic interdependence, particularly South Africa. With the end of apartheid in 1994, the new South Africa was expected to play a critical role in invigorating the region's economy. Increasingly, however, South Africa's neighbours have expressed scepticism about its role in the region.

Despite these reservations, however, some development initiatives in the region have taken place, particularly in the areas of transport, water and hydropower energy. The Maputo Corridor project, for example, linking South Africa's Mpumalanga province and Mozambique, will reduce the distance between the two countries, and thus stimulate development. Another initiative, the Lesotho Highlands Water Scheme, was conceived to provide a new water source for both Lesotho and South Africa. Other corridor projects are being constructed to facilitate trade across the Kalahari in Namibia, and from Zambia to the Indian Ocean at Nacala, Mozambique.

Notwithstanding these developments, the countries in the subregion face the economic and political challenges of structural reform and adjustment under unfavourable international economic conditions. Existing regional integration schemes, namely SADC and COMESA, have been unable to make significant progress in promoting regional trade and investment, for the following reasons.

The lack of political will to succeed

Efforts at economic cooperation have been hampered by a lack of effective leadership. The absence of a human rights culture and democratic practices have done more to kill the spirit of entrepreneurship and productivity than the perceived lack of resources in many parts of Africa. Many governments exhibit an excessive preoccupation with preserving their power base rather than creating the conditions for economic growth and social development.

An unfavourable legal environment, weak institutions and inadequate infrastructure

The majority of governments in Southern Africa are far from creating a policy environment conducive to greater intra-regional trade and investment. There exist too many unnecessary and bureaucratic barriers to trade within the SADC–COMESA region. Import controls and export licensing, customs hold-ups, restrictive exchange controls, and a complicated system of documentation are some of the factors hindering intra-regional trade. For example, Zimbabwe's import control system involves twenty-two different government bodies; this is very costly for the private sector. Entrepreneurs interested in cross-border trade are often frustrated by the shortage of foreign exchange and complicated visa requirements. The problem is further compounded by the underdeveloped monetary and banking system, inadequate transport and communication networks, and the high transaction costs involved in conducting business because of endemic corruption (Cheru, 1992b).

In the area of macroeconomic management, few countries have successfully completed the transition from command (dirigist) to market economy. Overvalued currencies, unrealistic minimum export prices, and high import duties are insisted upon, and there is a bewildering range of different systems of customs tariffs and procedures. This situation is unlikely to be resolved in the near future. Reform in the areas of pricing policy, exchange rates, privatization, containment of budget deficits, liberalization of trade, public sector reform and the like will be slow, particularly in the face of dwindling external assistance, an uncertain commodity environment, lack of rain and domestic political events.

A widespread shortage of skilled Africans

One obvious outcome of the economic crisis has been the dramatic growth in the brain drain involving middle- and high-level manpower vital to Africa's recovery and development. A joint ECA/ILO report estimated that 70,000 Africans had left the continent by mid-1987, up from 40,000 in 1985. This represents approximately 30 per cent of Africa's skilled human resources.

The unprecedented flight of highly skilled Africans is the result of hostile domestic economic and political environments. A decline in real earnings, the removal of subsidies on basic commodities, increases in the costs of medical, educational and other services, and massive retrenchments from the public sector have made life difficult for all Africans.

The end of apartheid has further compounded the shortage of skilled Africans in the subregion. This situation has created the conditions for new patterns of migration and 'intellectual pirating' to develop. Faced with its own human capital crisis, South Africa has taken a more liberal approach to the migration of skilled Africans to the country, while at the same time tightening its immigration policy for non-skilled Africans. The loss of skilled people elsewhere has an enormous impact on the functioning of institutions of higher learning, industry and enterprises. Reversing this trend is a precondition for a well-functioning national economy and regional integration.

Vulnerability due to high commodity dependence

No other region in the world depends on commodity export as much as sub-Saharan Africa. This is equally true for the countries of Southern Africa (see Table 5.2). These countries remain primarily exporters of raw materials while importing manufactured goods from the industrialized countries. Over the past decade, the export prices for African commodities have been subjected to very large fluctuations, and are currently at the lowest levels in thirty years. As a result, the purchasing power of Africa's exports have fallen sharply. Many of Africa's exports are also facing mounting competition from substitutes, such as synthetics for cotton and sugar beet and corn syrup for cane sugar.

In addition, market access for African exports has not improved in recent years. Non-tariff measures are being used as significant barriers to these markets. A feature of many of these barriers is that they are tied to the degree of processing. The greater the degree of processing (i.e. value-added to the exporting country), the higher the barrier. Other barriers include quotas, voluntary export restraints, and technical and sanitary regulations. The issue of quality and standards will affect the capacity of Southern African states to compete effectively in Europe. Since quality is dependent on technology, it will be difficult for SADC countries to compete on an equal footing with the NICs.

Finally, the Lomé Convention, which until recently provided all Southern African countries, with the exception of South Africa, duty-free access to the European Union, has been superseded by a new post-Lomé Africa–Europe arrangement that extends the same treatment to all developing countries. The new Africa–Europe partnership arrangement effectively

Table 5.2 Southern Africa: commodity dependence

Country	Main export	Share of total exports (%)
Angola	Oil	90
Botswana	Diamonds	78
Lesotho	Mohair	24
Malawi	Tobacco	55
Mozambique	Prawns	42
Swaziland	Sugar	42
Tanzania	Coffee	50
Zambia	Copper	85
Zimbabwe	Tobacco	20
South Africa	Gold	40

Source: SADCC, 1988.

brings the Lomé Convention in line with the general principles of the WTO by removing preferential treatment for African products. It remains to be seen whether the EU–ACP partnership agreement or the US government-driven Africa Growth Opportunity Act are going to improve the situation.

Unbreakable colonial trade links

Historical trade relations with Europe pose a serious constraint to viable regional economic integration in Africa. The direction of trade in sub-Saharan Africa has changed very little since independence, oriented largely to the markets of former colonial powers. This pattern of trade can be seen in Southern Africa, despite regional efforts by COMESA and SADC to reverse this trend. Almost 77 per cent of SADC's trade is still with countries outside the region, mainly with the former colonial powers. SADC–South Africa trade has largely remained unchanged despite SADC's efforts to reduce its dependence on South Africa.

There are many reasons why sub-Sahara's trade is heavily oriented towards Europe. First, the existing physical and financial infrastructure has been developed to facilitate trade with Europe rather than intra-regional trade. The Lomé Convention and other aid programmes have strengthened this historical relationship (Nabudere, 1991). Many of the purchases from overseas suppliers are tied directly to aid programmes, which tend to favour imports from the aid-giving countries. Nearly two-thirds of capital and commodity aid, and an even higher proportion of technical assistance, is tied in this manner. As a result, trade patterns become distorted in favour of overseas suppliers, as the recipient country is tied to the donor country for repeat orders and services. Through advertising, African consumers have become captives of goods produced in Europe, tending to look down on goods produced locally.

Poor and inadequate transport and communication networks

Establishing and maintaining a transportation network that can efficiently serve dozens of countries is no easy matter. Besides expanding the physical infrastructure, each country has its own cumbersome transport regulations, customs requirements, charges and levies. All this adds up to high transaction costs for exporters and importers. Clearly considerable coordination is required between various national port authorities, civil aviation bodies, customs and excise departments, and shipping agencies to simplify and facilitate regional transport.

Between 1982 and 1990, for example, the member states of COMESA spent approximately $1.2 billion rehabilitating and upgrading the tarred interstate roads. These funds, mobilized from bilateral and multilateral donors, made significant improvements possible in a number of Eastern and Southern African countries. But a lot more remains to be done.[2]

Neo-liberalism and the Changing Context of Integration

It was stated earlier that the World Bank has recently welcomed the renewed interest in regional integration in Africa, since the approach is consistent with that of the Washington Consensus. But the context in which this support is given is quite different. Two factors are of particular significance: the hegemony of neoliberalism in the current international order and the failure of an earlier generation of integration projects. These two factors have led to significant modifications in the major paradigms that are likely to influence future regional integration efforts. The EU–ACP partnership agreement, the EU–South Africa bilateral trade agreement, and the US–Africa trade agreement must all be understood in this context.

There is consensus among policymakers that international economic integration is the fastest and surest way of reducing poverty in poor countries. As countries reduce tariff and non-tariff barriers to trade and open up to international capital flows, the expectation is that growth will increase. This, in turn, will reduce poverty and improve the quality of life for most of the population of developing countries. To support this assertion, policymakers are quick to point to the successful economic development experience of the 'Asian Tigers'.

Does this glowing description of globalization and liberalization paint a true and complete picture? Is opening up to capital markets alone sufficient as a development strategy? Or does globalization – with all its potential benefits – need to be seen as only part of the picture? These questions need to be asked because strategy and priorities matter when administrative capacity, human resources and political capital are limited, as they are in small developing countries. The majority of African countries have characteristics and vulnerabilities that present them with special challenges over and above the normal challenges of development, as they adjust their economies and exploit the opportunities of closer integration into a rapidly changing global economy.[3] Moreover, in the specific case of Africa no trade can take place where production is non-existent. Therefore the obsession with trade expansion in the absence of coherent national and subregional policy to remove the main obstacles to productivity is unlikely to yield the desired results of expanded trade between member states.

From the point of view of the World Bank, regional integration in Africa should be consistent with an outward-oriented strategy that promotes incentives that are neutral (World Bank, 1989b). In other words, integration should be seen as a process of 'mutual regional liberalization' which would strengthen and extend ongoing adjustment efforts by adding another dimension. The ultimate objective should be to create conditions which would allow the private sector freely to work, trade and invest across African borders and with relatively low barriers against third parties. This approach assumes that what is good for business is good for the community as a whole. Its essential thrust is to accommodate the demands of capital without taking account of the interests of other social forces. The Cross-Border Initiative (CBI), which is supported by the World Bank, is the first experiment with this particular strategy (World Bank, 2000). The EU–ACP agreement and the US–Africa trade agreement simply expand on the CBI.

Despite the widespread belief that countries with lower policy-induced barriers to international trade grow faster than those who do not, there is a growing consensus among economists that integration into the world economy may not, by itself, be the best or only way for countries to grow. Dani Rodrik asserts that the empirical evidence on the links between trade policies and growth is ambiguous and that the proponents of openness 'conflate trade policy with other policies and variables, such as level of macroeconomic stability, quality of institutions, and geographic locations' (Rodrik, 2001). Even in the case of Korea, trade and industrial policy in the 1980s was characterized by marked subsidization, administrative guidance, and implicit guarantees for investors in favoured sectors. Yet the economy performed well.

It is therefore disingenuous to take the experiences of the 'Asian Tigers' as an example. Before the latest crisis they, like Korea, had been following models that did not adhere to the rules of free trade and open markets. While policymakers may want to incorporate some features of external models into their development strategies – especially those that will enhance a country's attractiveness to foreign investors – the choice of priorities and institutions should be home-grown. These should be tailored to domestic needs, aims and objectives and be based on a consensus drawn from all segments of the domestic population.

EU–Africa relations: post-Lomé IV ACP–EU trade agreement

In February 2000 the European Union and ministers of the seventy-one African, Caribbean and Pacific countries concluded a new twenty-year partnership agreement that replaced the Lomé IV Convention, which expired at the time of the signing of the new agreement. The new partnership agreement between ACP countries and the European Union is set to undermine decisively Africa's own continent-wide collaboration for economic development and the ability to reduce its dependency on Europe. In return, Europe stands to acquire even more enhanced and protected access for its industrial products in the more successful African economies. The partnership agreement is designed to be consistent with WTO rules, which stipulate that when a WTO member liberalizes its tariffs it must do so for imports of all members equally (Muriu, 2000: 5–7).

The original Lomé agreement was a set of technical aid and trade instruments between the European Union and the ACP countries, which grew haphazardly following its launch in 1975. It was hailed as an important breakthrough in North–South relations. Instead of imposing a trade regime on its former colonies, the European Community was prepared to negotiate a trade and development assistance package with them. Under the Lomé Convention, trade between the ACP and the EU was conducted on a non-reciprocal basis. All ACP-manufactured and some agricultural exports were allowed to enter European markets duty and quota free, while the ACP countries were allowed to maintain tariffs for European imports. Combined with targeted development assistance and schemes to reimburse ACP countries for the fluctuation of primary commodity prices on world markets, non-reciprocity did enable some ACP countries not only to protect and develop their own agriculture and manufacturing industries, but also their export industries.

The Lomé Convention also exempted ACP countries from the Multi-fibre Agreement, which places restrictions on the textile exports from developing countries to industrial markets. This assisted countries such as Lesotho and Mauritius, whose textile exports accounted for 48 per cent and 38 per cent respectively of total exports to the EU, to maintain and expand their textile industries. Special protocols, giving preferences to beef, banana, sugar and rum exports from ACP countries to European markets, have created sustainable livelihoods and led to economic growth in many Small Island or landlocked ACP countries. In Southern Africa, for example, Botswana, Namibia and Zimbabwe have benefited from the Beef Protocol, and Mauritius, Malawi, Swaziland and Tanzania from the Sugar Protocol. Their mutual ambition was to further development through partnership.

With the end of the Cold War and the ascendancy of neoliberalism, however, the EU's approach towards the ACP has undergone a radical change. The World Trade Organization Dispute Settlements Body ruled that the Lomé Convention provided unfair preferences to the banana exports of Caribbean countries, forcing the EU to apply for a waiver of the most-favoured-nation rule until the Lomé Convention expired in 2000. EU policy underwent a marked shift from aid to trade as the main instrument of cooperation – that is, the focus is now on commercial links that are mutually beneficial, and politically motivated agreements have been replaced by those driven by economic interest. An end to non-reciprocal treatment is the fundamental meaning of the new partnership agreement: the rebalancing of obligations and benefits, the subordination of Lomé and all regional trade and integration arrangements to the WTO. The introduction of reciprocity in trade between unequal economic partners – which the EU and African economies are – will undoubtedly impact adversely on the economies of most African countries (Lambrechts, 1999: 7).

The new EU–ACP partnership agreement creates a basis for organizing individual countries or groups of African countries into separate free-trade arrangements with the European Union. In essence, the agreement has facilitated the division of the ACP into regional groups and, more importantly, the establishment of a hub-and-spoke relationship between the EU and ACP regions. The effect will be to undermine the existing regional economic groupings, which African countries regard as the building blocks of their economic integration, thereby perpetuating the fragmentation of African economies. While the European countries will operate as a united solid group within the institutional framework of the EU, no similar role is envisaged for the OAU/AEC as Africa's continental economic organization. Rather, individual African countries and regional economic communities like SADC are expected to negotiate with the EU, independent of each other.

The outcome of the negotiations indicates the inherent inequality of the donor–recipient relationship, and the failure of the ACP to determine its own development path, take initiatives and assert sovereignty in national economic policy formulation. It is difficult to see the link between the stated objective of the agreement – poverty alleviation – and the instruments to be used to achieve the objective. By agreeing to free-trade arrangements with a stronger partner, the ACP has further endorsed the neoliberal approach to development, despite its serious shortcomings. The agreement serves as a vehicle for discipline by the WTO, at the same time locking World Bank and IMF economic reform programmes in Africa, undermining African regional integration, and promoting a spoke-and-hub relationship between African regions and Europe.[4]

The EU–South Africa trade, development and cooperation agreement

The multiplicity of trade regimes in Southern Africa is a major concern to the member states of SADC. The conclusion of the EU–South Africa bilateral free-trade agreement of March 1999 does not sit well with many SADC/COMESA governments, who are suspicious of South Africa's hegemonic impulse. The agreement, which took more than five years to negotiate, provides, *inter alia*, for a reciprocal process of removing tariffs on bilateral trade, governed by the rules of the WTO on free trade agreements (FTA). These require the removal of customs duties on 'substantially' all trade over a maximum of ten years (Mayer, 1999: 10–13). The EU will, within ten years of implementation, remove duties on imports from South Africa of approximately 95 per cent of its tariff lines. Restrictions on the entry of agricultural products, such as sherry and port, remain contentious issues. For its part, South Africa will be required to remove duties on approximately 86 per cent of its total imports from the European Union. The products subject to this removal of duties are divided into four categories, each with a different phase-out schedule (Mayer, 1999: 11).

The reciprocal obligations will require adjustment, particularly on the South African side, although it will be given more time to implement the agreement. The adjustment costs of an EU–South Africa free-trade area will, of course, be felt not just in South Africa, but also in the neighbouring Southern African countries. The partners in the South African Customs Union – Botswana, Lesotho, Namibia and Swaziland – will all be confronted with increased competition from EU goods, both in their own domestic markets and also in the case of industries that produce for the South African market. The removal of duties on a substantial part of total imports is likely to impact negatively on the revenue earned by customs duties (Davis, 2000: 5–16). Customs revenue accounts for a very important part of total state revenue in the four countries.

Given that the BLNS states (Botswana, Lesotho, Namibia and Swaziland) rely heavily on tariffs for revenue purposes, the EU has agreed to provide them with a structural fund and assistance in raising revenue from other sources during the transitional period. In addition, the BLNS countries can invoke the safeguard clause in the EU–South Africa trade deal if imports from the EU threaten to destroy local industries. This will enable them to raise tariffs in the affected industries in order to protect them.

In addition to the above two trade arrangements driven by the European Union, the implementation of the Africa Growth Opportunity Act (discussed in Chapter 1) will signify the consolidation of a uniform trade regime in Africa consistent with WTO rules, bringing to an end non-reciprocal trade relationships between Africa and the developed countries. These rules are increasingly being reflected in the rules governing intra-Africa trade and investment policies. Both SADC and COMESA are moving in this direction. While the trend towards openness is a necessity, the gains will only materialize if the structural bottlenecks hampering production and trade in Africa are removed. None of these new bilateral and multilateral trade agreements addresses Africa's weak capacity (human, financial, institutional) and endemic infrastructure problems.

Regional Integration in Southern Africa: Problems and Prospects

The four principal regional cooperation and integration organizations in Southern Africa are the Southern Africa Development Community (formerly the Southern Africa Development Coordination Committee), the

Common Market for Eastern and Southern Africa (formerly the Preferential Trade Area for Eastern and Southern Africa), the Rand Monetary Area (RMA) and the Southern Africa Customs Union, which dates back to 1910. The four members of the RMA are all members of SACU, and the five members of SACU take part in SADC, eight members of which join COMESA. The urgent question in this context is, how can these four overlapping arrangements be rationalized?

Although both SADC and COMESA have undergone changes since 1990 in response to the dramatic political events that took place in the region, their track record in promoting regional trade and development has been quite disappointing, for reasons discussed below. COMESA has followed the classical model of integration, using foreign trade as an engine of growth, and has failed to achieve integration of the member economies due to the absence of the relative prerequisites discussed above in detail. The SADC adopted regional projects, but, in turn, did not achieve striking success, for several reasons. These will be briefly considered.

Assessment of the Southern Africa Development Community

The Southern Africa Development Coordinating Committee (SADCC) was established in 1980 to promote southern African regional development and reduce dependence on South Africa. Its original members include Zambia, Zimbabwe, Angola, Mozambique, Tanzania, Malawi, Lesotho, Swaziland, Botswana and Namibia. Since 1994, the renamed Southern Africa Development Community (SADC) has admitted South Africa, Mauritius, Congo and Seychelles. All the members of SADC, except for Angola, Mozambique and Botswana, are members of COMESA. Of the fourteen SADC members, Botswana, Lesotho, Swaziland and Namibia are members of the Southern Africa Customs Union. With a GNP almost four times that of the other thirteen countries combined, South Africa's presence unavoidably adds an altogether new dimension to the entire regional situation.

In its first decade of existence, SADC's strategy centred on the rehabilitation and creation of infrastructure, with the emphasis on transport, telecommunications, civil aviation, food security and energy. The rehabilitation of transport corridors has been the most notable achievement of SADC. It allocates responsibility for coordinating activities in different sectors to its member states. It lacks the elaborate bureaucracy of ECOWAS or COMESA. Member countries set up a sector coordination unit in a relevant ministry to manage the sectoral programme. The secretariat in

Gabarone, Botswana, oversees the activities of the sector-coordinating units and sectoral commissions.

One of the most glaring weaknesses of SADC had been its excessive dependence on external funds. By 1990, this dependence had reached a critical threshold with more than 90 per cent of financial requirements coming from foreign donors. The dependence on external assistance to finance its projects placed SADC at the mercy of donors and thereby rendered it unable to determine its own programmes (Cheru, 1988: 250–73). Since donor funding to SADC is tied to the purchase of goods from these same donors, trade patterns become distorted and restricted in favour of the overseas suppliers (Cheru, 1992b: 30; Nomvete, 1993: 50–59).

Furthermore, SADC's approach to coordination was never followed by a commitment to strengthen institutional capacity and managerial skills at the national level. Project initiation, preparation and implementation have been weak (Lee, 1989: 272). Although each member country is responsible for coordination of a specific sector (e.g. Angola for energy and Zimbabwe for food security), subregional programmes and projects have been poorly integrated with national plans and budgets. No effort has been made by member states to harmonize policies so as to encourage growing economic interaction between them.

Another factor inhibiting SADC's success has been the lack of grassroots support at the national level. Relative neglect of the wide diversity of non-governmental social and economics operators (private-sector associations, business groups, chambers of commerce, employers' associations, trade unions, women's organizations, etc.) is probably one of the major causes of the lack of progress in economic development and regional integration (Laporte, 1993: 60–62). These groups were completely excluded until the closing months of 1989. To the extent that cooperation arrangements become the private property of a few politicians and civil servants (and are forged without the full participation and knowledge of the population), their stability and the implementation of their programmes cannot be guaranteed.

SADC: from functional integration to trade integration

With the end of apartheid, SADCC underwent profound changes, including a name change to the Southern Africa Development Community (SADC). It moved from project integration to an emphasis on regional development and trade integration. The strategy for the second decade, as elaborated in the 1990 annual conference, gave priority to creating an enabling environment for the development of enterprise, skills and productivity. In place of the previous mission to isolate South Africa, African governments today present regional integration themselves as the first step towards global integration.

This shift in emphasis has brought not only praise from donors but also some needed cash. The World Bank has proposed a $30 million PTA/SADCC Intra-Regional Trade and Investment Project, centring on the financing of the foreign exchange component of cross-border investments resulting from the adoption of regional liberalization policies (World Bank, 1989b). According to the former World Bank vice-president for Southern Africa, Edward Jaycox,

> Successful economic integration will be contingent on the implementation of policies that elicit the correct response from markets and which will boost regional production and demand. Policy changes such as encouraging realistic exchange rate movements, liberalizing trade, designing price incentives for exports, improving public sector investment strategies, and increasing private sector activity must go hand in hand with specific investments in physical human resource development. (World Bank, 1989b)

In short, the basic role of donor support since the early 1990s has been towards overall collective economic liberalization of COMESA/SADC countries by improving conditions for a more active role by private agents across the frontiers of the region. The approach is designed to be consistent with and to promote liberalization efforts at the national level and not to set back programmes that any individual country may want to undertake on its own.

SADC's recent decision to embark on a more ambitious market integration approach similar to COMESA is a high-risk strategy. The SADC Trade Protocol has received more verbal support from governments than actual commitments. Few countries have ratified the Protocol, whose aim is to reduce all tariffs to zero by the time of full implementation in 2008. The reluctance by member states to ratify the treaty is explained in part by their fear of South Africa's hegemonic impulse, although South Africa has proposed to accelerate tariff reductions and allow 85 per cent of SADC imports into South Africa free of duties.[5] In its present form, SADC does not have the institutional capacity and the binding rules and regulations to promote economic integration on the basis of balance, equity and mutual benefit.

SADC member states' suspicions regarding South Africa's hegemonic motives were further strengthened when South Africa concluded a free-trade agreement with the European Union. Although the agreement – which has not been without contention – is viewed by SADC governments as detrimental to their development, certain safeguards have been put in place. The EU is committed to compensate Botswana, Lesotho, Namibia and Swaziland, through direct financial and other forms of assistance, for the potential loss of revenue from the SACU common revenue pool. In the case of SADC, safeguard clauses in the agreement would allow South Africa to introduce safeguard measures against EU imports should they displace SADC imports into South Africa. This would apply particularly to Europe's agricultural exports. In addition, SADC will get access to South Africa's market earlier and by a greater preference margin than the EU countries.

Assessment of the Common Market for Eastern and Southern Africa

The Common Market for Eastern and Southern Africa (COMESA) – previously known as the Preferential Trade Area for Eastern and Southern Africa (PTA) – was established in 1981 to promote the development of its member states by creating a single internal market, undertaking regional development projects and programmes, and encouraging cooperation in all fields of economic activity. In 1992, the PTA was transformed into a common market. The original members include Burundi, Comoros, Djibouti, Ethiopia, Kenya, Lesotho, Malawi, Mauritius, Mozambique, Rwanda, Somalia, Swaziland, Tanzania, Uganda, Zambia and Zimbabwe. The group has a GDP of $33 billion and a population of 146 million. In contrast, South Africa has a GDP of $79 billion and a population of only 34 million. Tanzania and Mozambique have withdrawn from the community in the past two years.

Broadly speaking, COMESA aims to intensify the economic integration and development of member countries by allowing the free movement of persons, goods, services and capital within the region. It also aims at increasing the production of competitive goods and improving transport and communications networks. This means fewer or no trade barriers, a smoother payments system, easier and simplified customs and transit procedures, improved transport and communications, and an increased role for the private sector.[6]

COMESA's trade activities are geared towards enhancing intra-regional trade through tariff and non-tariff concessions, market surveys, trade information dissemination (workshops and trade directories), trade promotional activities (trade fairs, buyers and sellers meetings), trade facilitation, and interaction of the business community of the subregion. The first phase of the Treaty (1975–92), aimed at promoting intra-regional trade, established the following objectives:

- a gradual reduction and eventual elimination of tariffs among member countries for selected commodities;
- to establish a common list of commodities that are eligible for preferential treatment;
- to determine a common Rule of Origin for products eligible for preferential treatment;
- to establish payment and clearing arrangements that encourage the use of national currencies for intra-regional transactions;
- to adopt common classification and valuation methods for customs purposes; and
- to simplify and harmonize customs procedures and documents.

Accomplishments to date include the following. First, the establishment in 1984 of a regional COMESA clearing house in Harare which houses local currencies for trade transactions, thus enabling trading partners to save valuable foreign exchange. Second, the establishment in 1985 of the COMESA Trade and Development Bank, located in Burundi, for financing regional projects. Third, the creation of the COMESA travellers' cheque, which can be purchased with local currency and can be converted in any PTA member bank. This allows business people to purchase goods anywhere in the region and meet their travel expenses without using any hard currency such as the dollar (Martin, 1989). Fourth, the formation of the Association of Commercial Banks, in 1987, to encourage correspondent relationships between banks and to provide information, ancillary services and credit facilities to businessmen. In addition to the above, trade fairs and buyers/sellers meetings have been held. In short, considerable progress has been made.

Despite having instituted these measures, however, COMESA has achieved limited success with regard to the promotion of intra-Africa trade (World Bank, 1989a: 45). The reasons for this lack of progress are many. The first is the lack of tradable goods of international quality within the community. Even when such goods are available, such as textiles from Kenya and Zimbabwe, the lack of trade financing and export credit guarantees has been a problem. The problem is further compounded by prohibitive transport costs, particularly for the landlocked countries. The smaller and weaker members complain about the lack of adequate mechanisms to enhance the equitable distribution of costs and benefits among member states (Mutharika, 1991: 45–6). Also, the tendency on the part of the most industrialized members, such as Kenya and Zimbabwe, to dominate the subregion has consistently been raised in COMESA annual meetings. Malawi, Mauritius and Djibouti in particular have been critical of the organization's inability to adopt compensatory and corrective measures.

Second, the Rules of Origin and local content requirements have been contentious. Most countries have challenged the Protocol on Rules of Origin, which stipulates that goods declared for trade must come from companies with at least a 51 per cent equity holding by nationals. Since most countries cannot meet this requirement, the rule has been relaxed. The concern now is more on where the good is being manufactured rather than the nationality of the manufacturer. Thus, the local content criterion now states that at least 40 per cent should be of local value, or alternatively not more than 60 per cent c.i.f. of the cost of the imported material. Where goods are in short supply, the local content can be relaxed to 30 per cent (Mbilima, 1989: 36–7).

Third, progress on trade liberalization has also been slow. The main focus of internal liberalization has been tariff preferences for a limited list of products (see Table 5.3). Here it is the lack of political will on the part of member states to create a conducive environment that has been the main problem. Restrictive exchange control policies, complicated customs regulations, tax systems that reward inefficient producers and traders at the expense of the more productive ones, and the underdeveloped monetary and banking systems have had a crippling effect on raising productivity and expanding trade. This policy environment reduced the incentives to invest, save and produce efficiently. Because of these factors, COMESA postponed a 1992 deadline for implementing various intra-union liberalization decisions to 1996, and this goal still had not been met. The problem is further complicated by the fact that individual governments hold loyalties either to SADC or to COMESA and thus are unable to put the interest of the entire region above that individual national interest.

Fourth, regional economic integration has been hampered by a lack of information regarding what other African countries can offer to substitute for the products presently being imported from the developed countries. Institutionalized access to and quick transmission of information on rules and regulations implemented in partner countries and on bureaucratic procedures and standardized statistical data may lay the groundwork for effective cooperation. Recognizing this fact, COMESA, with assistance from UNCTAD, established the Trade Information Network (TINET) in 1995. The programme is yielding good results (Cheru et al., 1997).

Finally, efforts to strengthen intra-Africa trade within COMESA have been complicated by the reintegration of South Africa into the Southern African community. South Africa's decision to join SADC in 1994 was the final blow to COMESA's confidence and credibility. Since then, SADC has admitted Mauritius, the Seychelles and the Democratic Republic of the Congo, bringing the total membership to fourteen. On the other hand, COMESA lost three of its long-standing members, Mozambique, Tanzania and Lesotho, when they decided to terminate their membership. Only three SADC members – Zambia, Malawi and Tanzania – have ratified the COMESA treaty. Many member countries have failed to adhere to the approved timetable for implementing treaty obligations.

Box 5.1 COMESA trade development and promotion programme

The objective of the programme is to accelerate the process of market integration through capacity building in private-sector institutions (e.g. chambers of commerce, trade associations); establishing a trade information network and database to ensure the regular flow of information on product development, tariff rates, and so on. It therefore concentrates its efforts on strengthening the management and networking capacities of Chambers of Commerce through training and provision of equipment. This includes supply-and-demand surveys, buyers and sellers meetings, and training in the use of computerized databases.

The programme has emphasized that regional integration is difficult to achieve if both governments and the private sector have no reliable data on product-related trade information on member states. The establishment of a computerized trade information network (TINET), linking the COMESA secretariat with designated 'national focal points' in the member states, has been the success story of the project. The national focal points are responsible for collecting national trade-related data and for disseminating information distributed by the central unit of TINET to the respective national organizations and private-sector operators.

Another important innovation has been the built-in emphasis on utilizing expertise and facilities available in the subregion, through the principles of 'networking' and subcontracting, and involving technical cooperation between TINET focal points and enterprises with differing levels of operational efficiency. The project has given the private sector centre stage, assisting it in building the capacity to become a catalyst for change.

Source: Cheru et al., 1997.

COMESA's new Free Trade Area: a promising project or another cliché?

On 30 October 2000, nine member states of COMESA launched a free-trade area with a total market size of $128 billion and a population of 170 million. This is part of COMESA's ambitious plan for full economic integration, including the free movement of skilled labour by 2004, the free

Table 5.3 Reductions in customs tariffs

Group	Commodity type	reductions (%)
I	Food	30
II	Raw materials:	
	agricultural	50
	non-agricultural	60
III	Intermediate goods	65
IV	Manufactured consumer goods:	
	durable	65
	non-durable	40
	of critical importance to economy	70
V	Capital goods	70
VI	Luxury goods	10

Source: COMESA, n.d.

movement of people by 2014, and a currency union by 2025. Initially, only nine of COMESA's twenty-member states will participate, removing all barriers on intra-regional trade immediately, though each country will retain tariffs on imports from non-COMESA sources. The countries participating in this fast-lane integration are Djibouti, Egypt, Kenya, Madagascar, Malawi, Mauritius, Sudan, Zambia and Zimbabwe. Another six countries are expected to join over the next year (Hawkins, 2000).

This ambitious and worthwhile initiative seems to ignore the political reality of the region. If one goes by the track record of African leaders since independence, the free-trade area initiative will remain a pipe dream – another lofty idea that will be relegated to the shelf. Six COMESA member states – Angola, Democratic Republic of the Congo, Zimbabwe, Rwanda and Uganda – are on opposing sides in the war in the Congo; two others – Eritrea and Ethiopia – fought a deadly war in 1998, which gave way to a peace agreement brokered by Algeria and the United States, with the UN sending a peacekeeping mission to ensure that the two sides honour the agreement. Furthermore, no investor in his right mind would put a dime into countries like Zimbabwe, Kenya and Sudan where corruption and internal political strife are hard to bury under the carpet.

In terms of competitiveness, three of the twenty-four COMESA member states – Madagascar, Zimbabwe and Kenya – filled the bottom spots in the Africa Competitiveness Report published in mid-year by the World Economic Forum.[7] Many COMESA member countries have tiny manufacturing sectors and most of these countries went through deindustrialization during the 1980s and 1990s. Of the $16.2 billion of manufactured goods exported in 1997 by sub-Saharan Africa plus Egypt, South Africa accounted for almost 60 per cent, and Egypt, Mauritius and Zimbabwe a further 20 per cent. Not surprisingly, given their embryonic industrial sectors, manufacturers in several COMESA countries have expressed alarm that free trade might accelerate rather than reverse deindustrialization. There are real concerns among businesspeople and politicians that tariff-free trade will exacerbate the polarization that favours the heavier hitters – most obviously Egypt, Mauritius, Zimbabwe and non-COMESA South Africa. For that reason, COMESA members such as Uganda have stayed on the sidelines to see how the free-trade agreement pans out. Others – Tanzania, Mozambique and Lesotho – have pulled out altogether.

Among the sceptics is the African Development Bank (ADB), which recently warned against overblown expectations of free-trade areas. The ADB argues that the volume of intra-regional trade has stagnated or even declined slightly due to structural factors such as low incomes and long distances between markets, as well as the failure to implement trade agreements. The ADB warns that trade-focused regional integration could actually be 'counterproductive', since both industrialization and economic growth would suffer should imports be diverted away from low-cost external sources, such as East Asia, to higher cost regional sources, such as South Africa, Egypt or Kenya.

Whether the balance between trade liberalization and overcoming infrastructural bottlenecks throughout Africa can be adequately struck is still an open question. But it is clear that the problems of African economies can only be effectively addressed by an approach that is oriented towards raising production by promoting efficient agricultural and industrial development, based on the exploitation of local comparative advantages and economic networking. The joint development of regional infrastructure is a potentially fruitful area where the benefits of regional cooperation should first be demonstrated. Success in achieving physical integration will create the necessary conditions for progress towards fuller economic integration at the level of markets and of enterprises. Once the existing production bottlenecks are removed and output has increased as a result, the pressure to find outlets for excess production capacity will grow, leading to eventual liberalization.

Conclusions and Recommendations

Clearly, sub-Saharan countries cannot easily jump into ambitious market integration schemes involving detailed blueprints, rigid time frames, and formal institutional structures. The administration involved would require technical and management capacities that are not present in sufficient quantity. Initial efforts must be focused on seeking all possible forms of coordination by setting up structures of consultation and information among the countries concerned to encourage the growth of a much more production-oriented private sector across the continent, with high value-added as a result of robust forward and backward linkages between agriculture and industry. Simply focusing on creating the conditions for a growth of commerce in foreign-produced goods creates very little in the way of multiplier effect, thus resulting in less income from taxation, limited employment, and minimal wealth creation across the continent.

One of the lessons of the past is that less ambitious, more flexible institutional regional economic cooperation initiatives may have more potential because of their responsiveness to member states' priorities and interests (Ravenhill, 1990: 81–5). This implies less binding, project-oriented and functional cooperation schemes involving action on certain aspects or in certain sectors that offer immediate benefits. Pragmatic institutional arrangements with realistic and well-defined objectives responding to specific short-term needs may offer better prospects. On the basis of the foregoing analysis, I offer the following pointers:

Cooperation instead of integration

Ambitious market integration approaches along the lines of the European Union do not yet seem ripe in Africa at the present time. Given Africa's endemic problem with economic management, inadequate transport and communications infrastructure, fragile institutions, and shortages of skilled people, a modest approach in economic cooperation is to be recommended. Cooperation should concentrate on achievable goals with tangible short-term benefits (Ravenhill, 1990: 81–5). This implies greater emphasis on the coordination of policies by member states and less on formal economic integration, thereby allowing countries to keep their autonomy in terms of economic policy, but at the same time to cooperate in areas where they perceive a need to do so. Limited functional schemes appear to offer far greater potential than more grandiose projects such as customs unions and a common market. A gradualist and pragmatic approach offers better prospects of reducing difficulties linked to distribution of costs and benefits since it concentrates on those areas that bring benefit to a majority of participating countries (Ezenwe, 1990: 27–33; Diouf, 1990: 21–6). The emphasis should be on a more efficient use of resources through sharing and paying greater attention to the facilitation of investment.

Addressing the capacity gap in policy analysis and management

The most neglected aspect of regional integration has been the failure to build strong institutions and managerial skills at the national level for the implementation of complex economic and trade treaties. National-level capacity in economic policy analysis and development management is extremely weak in most African countries. One way of addressing the weakness is through a regional network approach whereby existing expertise is shared among member countries. This is an effective instrument for counteracting the brain drain.

Proper integration with national plans

Regional integration should be viewed as a complement rather than a substitute for individual country self-reliance. Properly functioning national economies are certainly a necessary condition for effective integration arrangements. Yet, in his comparative analysis of the PTA and SADCC approaches, Wange discovered that subregional programmes and projects have been poorly integrated with national plans and budgets (Wangwe, 1990: 34–9). The implementation of structural adjustment programmes at the national level has been particularly insensitive to regional dimensions of economic reforms. Devaluations or exchange controls at a national level could have significant ramifications for regional trade.

In the absence of local budgetary contributions towards subregional programmes, it is very unlikely there will be a high degree of national ownership (Wangwe, 1990: 34–9). For example, trade between Ethiopia and other COMESA member states has been hampered for a long time by the failure of the Kenyan government to complete the resurfacing of the main road connecting Nairobi to Moyale at the Kenya–Ethiopia border. Not only does this hurt Kenyan and Ethiopian exporters; the spillover effects reach as far south as Zambia. Due to high transport costs, it makes more sense for Ethiopia to import toilet paper from Europe than to incur high airfreight charges for the same product imported from Kenya.

Greater involvement by the private sector, civil society and non-governmental organizations

Regional economic integration cannot be imposed from above; it must be a commonly felt necessity supported by public concern. Yet many economic integration schemes in Africa have largely confined their operations to intergovernmental institutions, leaving out non-governmental institutions, some of which are key actors in the national economies.

The shortcomings of this top-down approach have been quite obvious in Africa. Drawing largely from his study of cross-border trade flows in West Africa, Barad suggests that efforts toward regional economic integration will be more effective if they build from the realities of African economies and enlist the support of political constituencies (i.e. the private sector, NGOs, Chambers of Commerce) whose interests are directly served by the removal of barriers to trade and investment. In short, for regional economic cooperation to succeed, civil society should not be left out of the debate (Barad, 1990: 102–8).

The need for a strong intergovernmental coordinating body

Improved coordination among governments, regional organizations, and donor agencies ensures the most efficient use of financial and human resources that can be mobilized from sources both within and outside Africa. In the final analysis, however, regional integration and cooperation will not succeed unless the cumbersome and outdated procedures of customs and immigration, and the rules governing cross-border currency flows and other related regulations, are completely overhauled, and corruption is kept at a minimum so that traders can conduct business freely. Ease of entry and efficient customs and immigration clearance systems reduce transaction costs significantly.

The importance of macroeconomic coordination

The conduct of a country's macroeconomic policy is a crucial factor in economic integration. Monetary management is part of macroeconomic policy and is the means for releasing resources for currency convertibility. No integration is possible unless each member country has some minimum control over the main aspects of its economy. At the end of the day, regional integration cannot become a poor substitute for efficient national economic management.

It is important to note that recent regional and externally driven trade initiatives, such as the Africa Growth Opportunity Act of the US government and the EU–ACP partnership agreements, have focused on the expansion of trade between Africa and the developed countries and have, therefore, paid very little attention to the structural factors that constrain increased production and trade in the continent. Overemphasis by the developed countries on trade liberalization before tackling the rampant infrastructure and production bottlenecks in Africa is a serious mistake. Prohibitive transport costs, poor telecommunications networks, underdeveloped banking sectors, complicated visa and customs clearance requirements, bureaucratic delays and corruption have been the major impediments to intra-Africa trade, further increasing transaction costs for the private sector in the region (Saasa, 1993: ch. 6).

Liberalization of the trade regime in Africa has focused more on the expansion of domestic private sectors specializing in commerce in goods largely imported from the developed countries, with less emphasis being given to the development of a robust domestic private sector specializing in more production-oriented enterprises, with the potential to create linkages between agriculture, industry and the service sectors. Without a strengthening of the linkages between many sectors of African economies, petty commerce in goods is unlikely to shape the continent's future in the new global economy.

The reorienting of trade policies to strengthen production-based local enterprises and producers will inevitably entail the need for governments to manage the current global trade regime, rather than their being managed by it. This will require administrative guidance on the part of the state. It will entail protecting domestic producers, instituting capital controls when needed, providing subsidized credit to particular industries selected for competition, investing in research and development, and a commitment towards gradual as opposed to indiscriminate liberalization (Rodrik, 1999). Inevitably, such actions would put African countries on a collision course with the apologists of unrestricted liberalization, such as the WTO and the Bretton Woods institutions. Yet African governments could overcome these external pressures if they have the political will to work collectively to gain sufficient influence over the policy decisions of these institutions. After all, the 'Asian Tigers' followed a model that did not adhere to the rules of free trade and an open market. There is no reason why such a strategy should not work in Africa.

Finally, economic cooperation in Africa will not succeed in the absence of peace and stability at both national and subregional levels. Countries that engage in violent conflict over a long period of time risk being permanently underdeveloped. The socioeconomic destruction and misery evident in the Democratic Republic of the Congo, Sierra Leone, Angola, and even Mozambique until recently, are painful reminders of why Africa needs a regional consensus on collective security. Without peace, African countries cannot hope to build a durable foundation for long-term and sustainable development in the continent.

Notes

1. These include, the North American Free Trade Agreement (NAFTA), the European Union (EU), and the Asia-Pacific Economic Cooperation forum (APEC).

2. Interview with Dr. Bengu Wa Mutharika, Secretary-General of COMESA, in *Southern African Economist*, April/May 1991, p. 45

3. The Report of the Commonwealth Secretariat/World Bank Joint Task Force on Small States, www.worldbank.org/html/extdr/smallstates/.

4. 'Agreement threatens African Integration', interview with Ambassador Vijay S. Makhan, Assistant Secretary General of the OAU, in *African Agenda*, vol. 3, no. 3, May/June 2000, p. 15.

5. Interview with Alec Erwin, South African Minister of Trade and Industry, quoted in *Global Dialogue*, vol. 4, no. 1, April 1999, pp. 19–21.

6. COMESA, n.d.

7. World Economic Forum, 1998.

CHAPTER 6

The Urban–Rural Interface: Managing Fast-growing Cities in Africa

Sub-Saharan Africa, like many other regions in the world, is confronted with the challenge of rapid urbanization in a context of economic stagnation, poor governance, and fragile public institutions. It is estimated that by the year 2010 approximately 55 per cent of Africans will be residing in cities (UNDP, 1991a: 1). This urban growth has brought with it a host of problems, including unemployment and underemployment,[1] a burgeoning informal sector, deteriorating infrastructure and service-delivery capacity, overcrowding, environmental degradation, and an acute housing shortage. Moreover, this urban explosion coexists with an economic base that is inadequate to the task of providing either jobs or urban services to the population.

Despite these alarming trends, there is a persistent tendency by development planners to focus solely on rural poverty. Policymakers have tended to equate urban life with a small group of national elites who govern the country. In his persuasive book, *Why Poor People Stay Poor: Urban Bias in World Development,* Michael Lipton argued that to invest in urban areas is to undermine rural development, the mainstay of many developing countries (Lipton, 1977). This argument has helped shape the anti-urban bias in African development strategies, which continues today. The result has been a neglect of the particular problems of the majority of urban dwellers, especially the poor who live in squatter settlements or slums (Stren and Lee-Smith, 1991: 23–36).

The anti-urban bias goes against the prevailing view that sees urbanization as a progressive process and one of the key forces underlying technological innovation, economic development and sociopolitical change. Urbanization has been found to have positive impacts on fertility, mortality and other demographic trends. The current resurgence of interest in and attention to urban management, and the view that cities are the engines of national economic growth and development in general, is in part based on this pro-urban perspective. This is particularly true today in the knowledge-intensive gloabalizing economy, where cities have played a central role as agents of innovation diffusion and socioeconomic transformation.

It was argued in Chapter 3 that a radical transformation of peasant agriculture should remain the number one priority of African governments. However, the effort to reverse agricultural decline in Africa should be carried out with a clear strategy to strengthen the relationship between urban and rural economic production and exchange. This is because there exist visible and invisible flows and interconnections between rural and urban areas. Therefore an emphasis on reversing rural decay and stagnation alone is unlikely to stem rural-to-urban migration or the present unmanageable levels of urban poverty. Empirical evidence from sub-Saharan Africa has shown that the income gap between urban wage earners and the rural population has narrowed considerably in most African countries; real wages of urban workers have fallen dramatically and the distinctions between the formal and informal sectors are becoming blurred. At the same time, overall income distribution has worsened since the 1980s and the implementation of structural adjustment programmes. In fact, with the fall in formal sector employment, many former wage earners have moved into the informal sector to supplement their incomes.

Despite this evidence of a 'vanishing rural–urban gap' in Africa, rural-to-urban migration has not abated (Jamal and Weeks, 1988: 271–92). This migration is part of a much more complex and dynamic struggle to survive in the face of falling incomes for the poor, both urban and rural. The rapid expansion in urban population has occurred without the needed expansion in basic services and productive employment opportunities. The problem is compounded by weak urban government structures with very limited capacity to stimulate economic growth, mobilize resources and provide the most basic services. Needless to say, the now discredited anti-urban perspective continues to dominate current official African thinking in urban management, as well as in donor-mandated national economic reform programmes. The relevance of this approach needs to be examined carefully in light of the profound economic and political changes that have taken place throughout Africa in the post-1980 period.

The Colonial Roots of African Urbanization Management 1960–90

African countries enjoy rich demographic and political diversity – their differences in size, population, resource endowments, climates, and political cultures challenge general analysis and policy prescription. At the same time, however, there is a large degree of similarity in terms of critical development issues:

- High rates of urbanization, resulting in the exponential growth of informal settlements. Whereas the main component in the growth of the largest cities was rural-to-urban migration in the earlier post-independence period, natural increase or population growth is now the major element.
- Stagnating rural sectors, which spatially cover 90 per cent of the continent, accommodating about 60–70 per cent of the population.
- Increasing poverty, characterized by high rates of unemployment and a lack of adequate shelter, infrastructure and services. The majority of urban dwellers now live in slums and shantytowns.
- Overcentralization of service and administrative functions in capital cities.
- Inadequate institutional frameworks and human settlement development.

In spite of this obvious and glaring social neglect, the official approach to national development and urban management appears to be out of touch with the reality on the ground. Several clear indicators point to the inability of national and local governments to guide sustainable urban development. The most glaring failure has been the inability (or unwillingness) of governments to harness civil society efforts towards developing sustainable mechanisms for urban development. In many African countries, planning has been developed as a system of procedures imposed from above, almost exclusively concerned with limitations and regulations, and rarely submitted for approval by those it was meant to serve (Bubba and Lamba, 1991: 37–59).

The root causes of the present urban crisis can be traced to the colonial period. Colonialism gave to Africa many of the contemporary qualities of its urban areas. Such qualities vary according to the nationality of the colonial legacy, but certain patterns can be generally observed. Urban primacy, centre-versus-periphery administrative orientations, and urban elitism are general characteristics of formerly colonized areas. Cities such as Nairobi, Windhoek, Abidjan and Harare, among others, reflect colonial urban planning. Such patterns represent the unvarying colonial need to control (Obudho and El-Shaks, 1975).

After independence, many colonial institutional structures were retained by the new governments without any modification to suit the new political, economic and social reality (Poinsot et al., 1989: 11). These structures included zoning regulations, building codes and laws governing the use of urban space. At the same time, race-based residency requirements, which restricted the movement of Africans into the cities, were lifted. This further opened the way for large numbers of Africans to migrate to the capital cities. Reconciling these two historical phenomena has been a major challenge facing governments across the continent.

Many African countries sought to respond to this urban contradiction with a major exercise in 'master planning', and with large-scale government-sponsored construction of residential dwellings. Such activities, however, merely represented a continuation of colonial practices. One influential source of colonial legislation was the British Town and Country Planning Act of 1932 – the basis of urban planning legislation in Kenya, Tanzania and Nigeria (Cheery, 1974). The inherited structure has proved ineffective across the continent in managing urban change. A disproportionate share of infrastructure became concentrated in urban areas, which in turn unleashed powerful currents of rural-to-urban migration. In Kenya, for example, 52 per cent of waged employment and 49.5 per cent of manufacturing employment in 1985 were located in the capital Nairobi. Planned investment in main infrastructure in urban areas during the 1974–78 Development Plan was as follows: 51 per cent for Nairobi and 31 per cent for Mombassa (Government of Kenya, 1974).

Despite the attempt to manage urban development through 'master planning', urban growth continued unabated. The 'master plan' approach was unrealistic, expensive, and devoid of political and economic sense. Large-scale infrastructure projects were beyond the financial means of newly independent countries. Moreover, projects often catered only to a minority – mainly people in the civil service. Policymakers soon began to articulate an 'anti-urban' position in the hope of discouraging people from migrating to the cities. Planners saw the growth in urbanization as inimical to human development. They began to argue that the underdevelopment of rural areas, characterized by limited infrastructure, was the result of an urban bias in public policy (Lipton, 1977). Subsequently national governments and aid agencies began to pay greater attention to the countryside. In reality, however, official policy encouraged both urbanization and industrialization, considered to be important symbols of modernization.

Policies to reverse the urban–rural divide took three forms: migration control by reintroducion of colonial residency requirements; employment deconcentration through the establishment of 'growth poles'; and transformation of the rural economy. Programmes to control migration from rural to urban areas included the issuing of identification cards to dissuade migrants from coming to the cities, and the bussing of urban dwellers back to rural areas. In Mozambique and Ghana, for example, migrants were cleared out of cities under programmes such as 'Operation Feed Yourself'. None of these programmes succeeded in stemming the rural-to-urban tide. Where such a policy was effective, efficient authoritarian means were used to enforce it, as was the case in apartheid South Africa.

When migration-control policies failed, governments sought to deconcentrate employment by establishing secondary towns (or 'growth poles') along major transport corridors. Firms were given tax incentives to relocate to these towns and industrial estates were built and infrastructure provided. Such rural industrialization efforts seldom met with success. Few wanted to stay in artificially created settlements and business centres that made no economic sense.

In the early 1970s, it became obvious to policymakers that bulldozing squatter settlements and harassing hawkers in the informal sector had done little to discourage people from providing their own shelter or scratching out a living in cities. With the publication of the 1972 ILO mission report on Kenya, official policy shifted toward recognizing the importance of the 'informal sector' in employment generation and service delivery (ILO, 1972). Estimates made in the mid-1970s suggested that the informal sector employed 60 per cent of the urban labour force. Individual country estimates were as follows: the Congo, 55 per cent; Senegal, 50 per cent; Niger, 65 per cent; and Burkina Faso, 73 per cent. For individual cities, the figures were also high: Abidjan, 44 per cent; Nairobi, 44 per cent; Kumasi, 65 per cent; Lagos, 50 per cent; Lomé, 50 per cent and Banjul, 42 per cent (ILO, 1985: 13–15). Although reliable statistics are hard to come by, the proportion of the urban labour force employed in the informal sector since the economic crisis of the 1980s has increased dramatically.

Given the central role of the 'informal sector' in the urban economy, national governments reluctantly began to relax the rules controlling urban growth. In some cases, they even began channelling resources to support and strengthen the informal sector. In the shelter sector, for example, national governments tried to provide low-cost housing and basic services. Squatter upgrading and limited provision of public housing were the central feature of the new strategy. Given the limited financial base of municipal governments, attention soon shifted towards giving squatter and slum dwellers more responsibility for maintaining their settlements. This included tenure and credit opportunities, alongside efforts to encourage housing improvements and investment. Given the scope of the problem, however, the effect of these policies has been negligible. Harassment of informal-sector operators and eviction of slum dwellers have intensified, despite government pronouncements to the contrary.

By the early 1980s, it had become clear that the large-scale urban infrastructural development projects of the last two decades had failed to stem mass urban migration. Adequate shelter and basic services remained a major problem for those residing in squatter settlements (Keare and Parris, 1982; Bamberger et al., 1982). In general, donor-funded sites and service projects failed to reach the poor. The high level of subsidies involved in shelter projects and the high maintenance costs involved in large-scale urban infrastructure projects prompted donor institutions and national governments to search for viable solutions (Cohen, 1983).

In 1986, the World Bank along with UNDP, UNCHS and WHO launched the multi-donor Urban Management Programme (UMP), with the sole objective of strengthening the contribution that cities can make towards human development. Executed by the World Bank, Phase I of the UMP (1986–92) focused on the development of 'generic policy framework papers, discussion papers and tools with global validity and applicability'. Research was undertaken in six thematic areas: urban land management, urban infrastructure, municipal finance, municipal administration, urban environment, and poverty alleviation (UNDP, 1991a). Phase II (1992–95) aimed to translate the result of this synthesis of experiences into operational support for policy action planning at national, provincial and city levels (UNDP, 1992).

The results of the first phase of the research were presented in two important analytical documents: the World Bank's *Urban Policy and Economic Development: An Agenda for the 1990s* (World Bank, 1991) and the UNDP's strategy paper *Cities, People and Poverty: Urban Development Cooperation in the 1990s* (UNDP, 1991a). These documents provided the analytical framework for redirecting the UMP, with increasing attention placed on the need to decentralize decision-making powers from central government to local authorities and to strengthen local government institutions in urban management (Devas and Rakodi, 1993). Specifically, this latter entails the upgrading of the management capacities of urban institutions in ways that enable them to plan, manage and finance urban programmes. It also calls for the improvement of systems for land management, information and community participation. Needless to say, the goal of anchoring this new perspective at the local level remains problematic (Cheru, 1996).

Dimensions of the Urban Crisis in Africa

Rapid urbanization in Africa has led to economic, social and physical problems that command the attention of policymakers. Some of the key problems will be briefly considered.

Urban–rural imbalance

Sharp disparities exist between urban and rural areas. The rural areas have become marginalized from the mainstream of national development. Low levels of agricultural production, a lack of non-farm-employment opportunities, and the absence of vibrant small and medium-sized urban centres facilitating interaction between rural areas and major cities are factors that collectively accentuate the rural exodus to primary cities (Gilbert and Gugler, 1982: 49–65).

It is estimated that by the year 2020, over 55 per cent of Africans will live in urban areas. The existing economic base is inadequate to provide either jobs or urban services. High rates of rural–urban migration compound the already high birth rates of the urban population, further burdening an already inadequate municipal infrastructure and services (UNCHS, 1996). Yet Africans continue to be drawn to cities because they hope for better job opportunities, education and improved health care. Once migrants reach the city, they confront the same conditions of low productivity, joblessness and poor income that they encountered in rural areas, now compounded by overcrowding, pollution, and other urban problems.

One of the critical ingredients missing from the development equation in Africa is small towns and city centres with the transport and communication infrastructure and the political–administrative apparatus necessary to stimulate, facilitate and normalize economic exchange with rural areas (Baker, 1992). Consequently, the engine of agricultural production is not sufficiently powerful to increase growth. Low agricultural productivity in turn leads to poor conditions of life in rural areas, further compelling people to migrate to the cities.

Therefore, a sustainable approach to Africa's development must address all aspects of human settlements irrespective of the spatial population distribution (Jamal and Weeks, 1988: 271–92). The key is to foster a balanced national development strategy capable of improving living conditions for both urban and rural areas. Clearly, the state must play a central role in initiating and supporting initiatives at all levels. Justification for this view lies in the visible and invisible flows and linkages between rural and urban areas. These linkages have traditionally been categorized into economic, service, demographic, environmental and infrastructure, even though these categories are not mutually exclusive (Mtizwa-Mangiza, 1999: 1–5).

Unmanageable levels of poverty

In Africa, a large proportion of the population today live in absolute poverty. Increasingly, however, poverty is becoming an urban phenomenon as those in the rural areas migrate to cities. Recent analyses have shown that urban poverty is not only growing rapidly but has tended to be underestimated (Satterthwaite, 1995: 3–10; Sparr, 1994). As a result, specific policy attention to issues of urban poverty has lagged behind the research.

Urban poverty is unique. The valuable policy and programme lessons generated by decades of work in rural Africa may not be directly applicable to cities, for several reasons. First, urban life has a different effect on the major determinants of nutritional status to that of rural life, including the capacity of households to provide adequate nutrition for all members. Second, vulnerable groups in cities often have fewer informal safety nets (e.g. kinship and community networks). Formal safety nets for urban populations have largely collapsed or been dismantled. Third, the structural adjustment programmes which most African states have implemented since the 1980s are widely believed to have had a deleterious effect on wage-dependent urban workers. These policies have created a new class of vulnerable people (Becker et al., 1994; Moser, 1995: 159–71).

In the 1980s, urban bias became one of the intellectual cornerstones of economic reform in Africa (World Bank, 1981; Bates, 1981). While many of the mechanisms identified by the World Bank – markets, imports and exports, exchange rates, and so on – did give an economic and political advantage to certain urban social groups, the urban-bias debate tended to obscure the analysis of urban poverty. The negative impact of structural adjustment programmes, particularly on urban populations, challenges the notion of urban bias (Demery and Squire, 1996: 39–59).

Another key poverty factor has been the inability of governments to create an enabling environment to mobilize the population for development (Chambers, 1995: 172–204; Kanji, 1995: 38–55). Policymakers have failed to establish policy frameworks that would enhance the spirit of entrepreneurship and the resourcefulness of ordinary Africans. Such an enabling environment requires expanding access to credit, training and management, as well as access to appropriate technology. Governments alone cannot solve the problems described above; the private sector and NGOs must also play a significant role in job creation, training and provision of credit to community groups and informal sector operators.

An inappropriate regulatory framework

Among the weakest elements of urban management in the African context have been the absence of an 'enabling' macroeconomic environment at the national level, and the persistence of inappropriate and outdated regulatory frameworks at the municipal level. What passes for planning in most local authorities is rudimentary forms of land use, zoning, and licensing regulations, divorced from infrastructure-engineering consideration and lacking implementation mechanisms for meeting goals (Bubba and Lamba, 1991: 37–59). As a result, planning has largely been dismissed as a futile exercise, irrelevant to the practice of settlement management.

One of the reasons for the past failure of planning in Africa, particularly at regional and municipal levels, is that it has been developed as a system of procedures imposed from above. Planning has been almost exclusively concerned with complicated limitations and regulations, frequently ignoring the needs of both informal and formal sectors. New ideas are rarely submitted for approval by those they are meant to serve (Stren and Lee-Smith, 1991: 23–36). In many cities, bylaws forbid business in residential areas, making backyard slum workshops theoretically illegal. Hawkers are often chased away from city centres in the name of standards. Housing codes and zoning laws inherited from the colonial administration continue to frustrate the creativity of poor people to take care of themselves (World Bank, 1972; Cohen, 1983). Consequently, urban productivity is hampered, accentuating problems associated with poverty and unemployment.

Weak municipal institutions and a poor revenue base

The central characteristic of the urban crisis in Africa is not the scale of population growth, but the weakness of national and local government institutions in the face of rapid urban change. At national, city and municipal government levels, a lack of resources and knowledge prevent people and institutions from solving problems and managing change (Stren and Lee-Smith, 1991: 23–36; Bubba and Lamba, 1991: 37–59). These problems have been compounded at municipal levels, where lack of power and a sense of ownership prevail, and public servants are not only unable but also often unwilling to foster constructive change.

In much of Africa, central governments are the main actors in the provision of municipal services, as well as in the articulation of policies guiding urban development. However, it has been noted that the misdirection and misuse of government resources with respect to finances, delivery of infrastructure services and government regulations have led to poor performance by municipal institutions. The reasons are partly historical and partly political. One is the colonial legacy, whose laws, institutions and structures were wholly inappropriate for the resolution of such problems. Another is the inequitable distribution of resources within each country. This weakens the possibility of government action to address urban problems and limits economic opportunities for the majority of the population (Stren, 1989b: 21). As a result, cities do not function properly, and the productivity of entire countries is negatively affected.

The centralization of the public sector during the 1960s and 1970s is most evident in the changing character of financial relations between central and local government. Municipal responsibilities were reduced to tax collection on behalf of central government, while key decisions on planning and financing of infrastructure remained in the hands of central authorities (World Bank, 1991: 25; Warah, 2000a: 8–9). Since the early 1980s, with the implementation of structural adjustment programmes, the limited central government financial transfers to local authorities have virtually dried up. As a result, many municipal streets now have the appearance of a lunar landscape, with potholes and plugged drainage. Regular refuse collection has in many cases ceased, and basic maintenance of roads has become a distant memory.

Across Africa, central government interventions have paid little attention to the critical responsibilities of local institutions, such as the operation and maintenance of infrastructure, and provision of the incentives required for private economic activity. With narrow revenue bases and limited technical capacities, municipalities have been unwilling or unable to maintain infrastructure which they have not designed.

Deficiencies in infrastructure and basic services

As African cities have continued to grow, their declining economic situation has led to a dramatic deterioration in the supply of basic infrastructure and urban services. The breakdown in provision of public transport services, refuse collection, road maintenance, drainage, electricity and water supply, has in turn affected urban productivity and the wellbeing of urban residents (Stren, 1989: 36–37).

The resources necessary for the maintenance of roads, sewerage and water systems, and for the running of schools and hospitals, cannot keep up with the needs of the growing urban population. Informalization of both employment and settlement patterns has led to the horizontal growth of urban areas. This has spread existing services and infrastructure even more thinly. Adequate clean water, sanitation, energy and transport, essential to improving the lives of the poor and raising urban productivity, are extremely inadequate and deteriorating (Onibokun, 1989: 68–111; Kulaba, 1989: 203–45). The deleterious economic effects of inadequate infrastructure in Lagos, Nigeria, were described by the World Bank in this way:

> Recent Bank research on urban infrastructure in Nigeria has demonstrated that unreliable infrastructure services impose heavy costs on manufacturing enterprises. Virtually every manufacturing firm in Lagos has its own electric power generator to cope with the unreliable public supply. These firms invest 10 to 35 percent of their capital in power generation alone and incur additional capital and operating expenses to substitute for other unreliable public services. The burden of investment in power generation, boreholes, vehicles and radio equipment in lieu of working telephones is disproportionately high for small firms. In Nigeria and many other low-income countries, manufacturers' high costs of operations prevent innovation and adoption of new technology and make it difficult for them to compete in the international markets. (World Bank, 1991: 37–8)

Deficiencies in infrastructure provision also affect the health of urban residents, particularly the poor. In most African cities, provision for the regular collection and disposal of household refuge is highly inadequate, especially in poor neighbourhoods. Much of the solid waste generated within urban centres is dumped on available waste ground. For instance, only 22 per cent of the solid waste in Dar es Salaam was collected in 1988, due to the lack of refuse trucks (Kulaba, 1989: 236–7). The municipality of Addis Ababa, Ethiopia also faced a similar problem. The resources available to the municipal government to maintain its existing fleet of refuse trucks – let alone purchase new ones – were severely limited by the mid-1980s. The existing fleet, which services only 50 per cent of the population at best, suffers from endemic maintenance problems, as a result of which up to 40 per cent of the fleet is inactive at any given time. Low-income areas not serviced by access roads often wallow in pools of open sewage and mountains of stinking refuse, since trucks cannot get there and drainage channels hardly exist (Cheru, 1992a). The most common approach to waste disposal in cities like Nairobi is the practice of burning, which contributes to air pollution. In general, the inadequacy of waste management is a major contributor to disease and hampers economic development.

Sanitation is perhaps the most critical problem in many African cities. For example, in 1997 over half of the households in Addis Ababa had neither private nor shared toilet facilities, resulting in an indiscriminate use of drains, open spaces and waterways, where people also wash. Another 25 per cent share pit latrines with other families. The emptying of latrines is a problem in most towns due to the absence of desludging vehicles (vacuum trucks). Addis Ababa's first sanitary sewer system serves only the commercial areas and perhaps 15 per cent of the higher-income population. Water-borne sanitation will remain unaffordable to the vast majority of households for many years to come.

Insufficient water supply for thirsty cities

The demand for water has increased phenomenally as city populations become more concentrated. Consequently, competition for water has become more acute, not only between cities and their hinterlands but also between nations. Water tables are falling due to the overexploitation of underground water sources. Major rivers are drained dry before reaching the sea because of intensive irrigation and urban consumption. According to a recent report by the UN secretary-general, providing safe water to all in Africa cannot be anticipated before 2050.

Several of the larger cities in Africa – Johannesburg, Dakar and Nairobi, for example – have outgrown the capacity of local sources and are forced to carry water a distance of between 200 and 600 kilometres. Others, such as Abidjan, Lusaka and Addis Ababa, are drawing deeper and deeper, often overabstracting the ground aquifers (Ray, 2000: 1). This has several implications, particularly regarding environmental sustainability. But in the immediate term, the marginal cost of supplying water to these cities is rising steeply, taking this life-sustaining commodity well beyond the affordability of the average citizen. At the same time, large parts of these cities – the low-income peri-urban settlements – remain unserved by the water utilities.

The water crisis is further compounded by the failure to solve the issue of jurisdiction between central and local government. Where a central government does not allow municipal authorities to tax or borrow, and yet holds them responsible for the provision of services, delivery is not predictable. Furthermore, the water crisis is closely linked to improvement

Table 6.1 Median price of water in selected African cities

City	Country	US$/m³
Lomé	Togo	0.62
Abidjan	Côte d'Ivoire	1.19
Accra	Ghana	1.20
Nairobi	Kenya	2.18
Lagos	Nigeria	7.50

Source: UNCHS, 1998.

in the governance of cities. What is needed is a broad-based partnership involving public, private and community sectors. The private sector should bring in efficiency gains in water management. Community participation should facilitate transparency, equity and a sense of ownership, as well as aid cost recovery. The government's important role should lie in setting policy and serving as the regulatory agency.

An insufficient water supply is known to have a direct impact on the health of urban residents. In the early 1990s, cities including Nairobi, Lusaka and Addis Ababa experienced outbreaks of cholera, malaria and other communicable diseases formerly believed to be eradicated. In October 2000, thirty-two people died in Kwazulu–Natal, South Africa, as a result of cuts to the water supply of people who were too poor to pay their accounts. Although an informal trade in water supply and transportation has sprung up in response to the inefficient and decrepit public supply systems, it is the poor who must pay the extra cost of these informal services – shantytown dwellers often pay five to ten times more for water than those city residents connected to piped water. Basic services are fundamental to the poor's ability to earn a living, stay healthy and contribute to their nation's economy.

The causes of deterioration in services and infrastructure can be traced back to weak municipal institutions and the centrally directed legal and regulatory framework that guides municipal management in many African countries. Central governments have tended to institute and maintain significant financial, legal and regulatory controls, leaving little room for innovation by local authorities (Attahi, 1989: 112–46). Municipalities lack the powers required for effective political and economic decision-making, particularly in such critical areas as investment in urban infrastructure, revenue generation, and promotion of urban economic development and productivity. In Kenya, for example, local authorities serve as the agents of central government and they can only operate within the framework provided by the Ministry of Local Government (Bubba and Lamba, 1991: 37–59).

In addition to the problems arising from the relationship between central and local government, colonial standards of construction and quality of service provision have been adopted rather than their being adapted to local conditions. These standards are ill-suited to contemporary needs and lead to services that are too expensive for the majority of poor urban inhabitants (Bubba and Lamba, 1991: 53; Hardoy and Satterthwaite, 1989: 31). The focus has been on a unified urban plan, which looks good on paper but is unrealistic in practice. The use of inappropriate imported technologies in service delivery, such as refuse trucks, tends to involve high recurrent costs due to the expense of replacement parts and high use of energy, and these costs are often passed on to consumers. The high cost in turn discourages people from utilizing the system; instead consumers try to find the least expensive form of refuse disposal, or simply resort to unsanitary ways of disposing of refuse.

The numerous problems detailed above are compounded by and further exacerbate the dire environmental situation. Existing environmental infrastructure is woefully incapable of providing clean drinking water or of hygienically treating household liquid and solid wastes, much less minimizing or treating hazardous and toxic industrial waste. This situation endangers the health and productivity of the urban poor, especially women and children (World Commission on Environment and Development, 1987; Cairnacross et al., 1990; Levey, 1992: 134–49). Airborne particulate readings in the developing world are often ten times higher than peak levels allowable in the United States. Piles of uncollected and rotting refuse are disposed of in unsuitable sites; this often leads to blocked drainage channels, causing flooding, and pollutes rivers, beaches and aquifers. Each day liquid waste (including toxic and industrial waste) is disposed of using inadequate on-site methods. The incidence of malaria and cholera, often associated with poor rural areas, is now common in many urban centres in Africa. This trend seems to have been accentuated by the effects of structural adjustment in many countries as a result of the severe financial retrenchment.

The poor also experience risk from poor settlement management. Land development is not guided by environmental concerns. Often the poor have no alternative to establishing their housing on unsuitable land such as steep slopes and flood-prone areas or near dangerous industrial parks.

Poor and costly urban transport system

With increasing urbanization, African cities have not been able to meet the rapidly growing demand for urban transport and improved access to urban roads. Both the quality and the extent of transport systems have far wider impact than simply the time spent in travelling, with implications for the environment, economic efficiency and the quality of life in cities. Transport and communication systems not only link people to each other; they also provide people with access to goods, markets, schools, jobs and recreation facilities. Without a functioning transport system, most urban economies and social institutions would simply collapse.

Despite its importance, however, urban transport has received little attention from policymakers since it is not considered an integral component of human settlement planning and management. This is because transport problems have until very recently been considered the exclusive domain of technical experts, planners and builders. The tendency to view transport as a technical issue served to mystify it, thereby disempowering ordinary people, who felt they had neither the skills nor the authority to do anything about it. This rationale gave legitimacy to the idea that only the state can deliver transportation services to citizens (Williams, 1998: 1–5). Yet few state-directed transport projects addressed the more fundamental and long-term issue of sustainability.

By the early 1980s, however, state transport monopolies all across Africa were in deep financial trouble. In many countries, public transport came to a halt as the number of vehicles in service declined due to lack of foreign exchange to purchase replacement parts. The breakdown of transport systems in turn affected urban productivity, as transaction costs for both producers and consumers skyrocketed (World Bank, 1996; Godard and Ngabmen, 1998: 15–16). Besides the issue of traffic congestion and decaying road networks, existing fleets of buses owned and operated by parastatal boards remained inadequate to accommodate growing populations. Public transport monopolies have largely been inefficient and unprofitable, due to bureaucratic rigidities that inhibit response to changing conditions (for example, in getting route changes and additions to respond to new neighbourhood development).

The failure of public transport systems opened the door for rapid growth in an unlicensed privately operated transport sector to meet the growing demand (Cervero, 1988: 8–9). These informal operators enjoy certain market advantages because they have the flexibility to change their schedule in response to changing market conditions. They are often faster and run more frequently, while charging a fare comparable to that of the scheduled services. Moreover they serve as an anchor, from which the market for transit services is sustained (Lee-Smith, 1989: 276–304).

Shelter provision

The housing problem in urban Africa has assumed massive proportions, involving a maze of complex policy issues that defy clear strategic responses; these include income and employment, land tenure, access to credit, and legal reform (Hardoy and Satterthwaite, 1989). Far from instituting a realistic policy that addresses the needs of the majority, governments often engage in restrictive policies that undermine the creativity and resourcefulness of citizens. Increased squatting is an indicator of the housing mayhem, where an inappropriate government response denies 'squatter citizens' their full rights, subjecting them instead to sporadic forced eviction.

Most African governments lack comprehensive legislation on housing, making it difficult to develop an appropriate housing policy that gives direction to the roles of different actors and to the mobilization of funds. The increasing costs of building materials and of building to a high standard, coupled with inadequate credit facilities and a shortage of urban land, have made conventional housing increasingly expensive. Delays in land titling and planning approval hold up housing delivery and lead to cost overruns. The non-recognition of documents other than title deeds as security for loans has led to a situation where homeowners in site-and-service or settlement-upgrading schemes cannot obtain a mortgage to finance house improvements because they have not been issued with titles.

The absence of affordable low-cost dwellings has forced many urban dwellers to live in cramped and overcrowded informal settlements where the costs are lower, but where basic services such as water, sanitation and refuse collection are often lacking. A report commissioned by USAID in Kenya estimated that 55 per cent of the total population of Nairobi (nearly three-quarters of a million people) live in informal settlements. The area of the city covered by informal settlements is just over 5 per cent of the total area used for residential purposes (Matric Development Consultants, 1993). Densities in these settlements are high, typically 250 units per hectare, compared to 25 per hectare in middle-income areas and to 15 per hectare in high-income areas. Lack of access to essential basic services such as water further compound the health problem of squatter settlement residents. Finally, illegal settlements are usually developed on land ill-suited to housing such as hillsides, swampland and floodplain (Hardoy and Satterthwaite, 1989: 13–35).

The approaches that most governments have taken towards the housing sector since independence, and particularly towards squatter settlements, fall into three categories: laissez-faire, restrictive and supportive. Before the 1970s, most African governments pursued the laissez-faire approach, ignoring the phenomenon of squatter settlements and allocating few financial resources to them. This followed from the view that the growing housing problem was a transitory phenomenon that would disappear with high levels of economic growth.

The second, 'restrictive', approach saw governments try to arrest the growth of slums and squatter settlements through restriction. Denial of basic services such as water supplies, electricity, and education to low-income groups was one form it took. Such withholding of services is viewed by this approach as a legitimate means to discourage inhabitants from residing in the cities (Lacey and Owusu, 1989: 6). A more common measure, which prevailed up until the late 1970s, was the forcible eviction of residents from their houses, illustrated by large slum-clearance projects, under which communities were completely demolished at short notice. Despite a more permissive environment since the early 1980s, the restrictive approach still continues in some countries. For example, in a major departure from the permissive trend, the Nairobi city authorities razed two large settlements, Muoroto and Kibagare, in 1990, displacing an estimated 30,000 people (Adler, 1995: 88).

Since the mid-1970s, however, many governments have reluctantly embraced a more supportive approach. This involves site-and-services projects and undertaking slum-upgrading programmes that recognize the tenure rights of slum dwellers. Site-and-services projects require governments to release unutilized land and to provide new plots of land supplied with infrastructure and public services, such as water supplies, sewerage systems, schools, and health care facilities. Purchasers are expected to build their own houses. In some cases, credits and building materials are also provided. Similarly, slum-upgrading programmes provide infrastructure and basic services, while giving legal recognition of land tenure to slum dwellers. In reality, however, these programmes have had little effect, as they meet only a small fraction of demand. Moreover, low-income beneficiaries were usually bought out, as there was a shortage of housing for middle-income groups (Bamberger et al., 1982; Bryant, 1980: 73–85).

The housing crisis cannot be resolved independent of the land issue. It is people's lack of access to land for dwelling and a means of livelihood that is at the root of poverty as well as homelessness (Mabogunje, 1990; Kironde, 1995: 77–95). Particularly hard hit are the urban landless and the households headed by women, which predominate among the very poor. Inadequate planning for land use and outmoded inheritance and property-rights customs, particularly as they relate to women, have compounded the problem. As a result, the poor try to overcome the problem by resorting to the informal sector, which provides much more land to those seeking it than does the formal sector. Despite this fact, policymakers continue to ignore the significance of 'informal' land transactions and their impact on urban finance and delivery of services.

The growing urbanization requires an assured supply of durable and affordable building materials. Yet the chronic scarcity of raw materials has increased construction costs, putting housing beyond the reach of most urban residents (Bubba and Lamba, 1991: 51). The fact that non-renewable resources are in limited supply and renewable resources can only be replenished by nature over time imposes limits on the pace of consumption of natural resources, underscoring the need to conserve and reuse every possible resource. But such a use of resources requires enlightened government guidance and support. It also costs more money, which raises issues of international environmental justice, given the vast inequities operating in past and present environmental resource consumption internationally.

A good best-practice case of government–NGO–community partnership committed to alleviating the shortage of building material is the Maasai Housing Project in Kajado, Kenya. The project is a combined initiative involving community women's groups, the Intermediate Technology Development Group (ITDG), NGOs and government departments. The project focuses on training women, the traditional homebuilders in Maasai society, to use improved traditional methods of housing construction. ITDG developed a ferro-cement skin roofing technique, which was taught to the women. Women were also trained in stabilized soil block production, which enables them to construct homes that are leak-proof, have higher ceilings, better ventilation and natural lighting. The project has benefited about five hundred members of eleven women's groups in Kajiado District. One finding of this project was that women had more control over housing construction when traditional materials and technologies were used (UNCHS, 1996).

The problem of homelessness and poverty in urban Africa may seem unmanageable, yet solutions are incubating in the very environment where the problem exists. Up to now, the bulk of investment in shelter has come from the poor themselves, outside the realm of local and national government planning systems (Bryant, 1980: 73–85). This needs to be recognized by governments, who treat slum-dwellers as undesirable and a burden to local and national authorities. Governments should be concentrating their efforts on creating an enabling environment that supports communities in undertaking sustainable shelter projects. This will further build community empowerment and better enable governments to address other urban challenges with the support of these communities.

Inadequate financial services

The majority of African countries do not have well-developed financial institutions to underwrite housing or other infrastructural development. Where such institutions exist, they are state-owned parastatal entities, and they are usually undercapitalized and poorly managed. These institutions rarely extend credit to informal-sector operators; they usually lend to the middle and upper classes (Chana, 1999: 14–15).

Like the semi-public housing finance institutions, private commercial banks do not lend to low-income groups. Generally, the low-income groups in many African countries find formal (especially private-sector) sources of finance to be beyond their reach. Among the reasons for the exclusion of low-income groups in the formal credit sector are the perception that they have high loan-repayment default rates, and the view that the costs of administering small loans are too great. Even in South Africa, where there exists a well-developed private financial sector, the record of these institutions in extending loans to low-income groups has been very poor (Bond, 2000). Efforts to put in place a community re-investment act similar to that in the United States have been thwarted by strong lobbying of private banks.

In the absence of specialized financial institutions established exclusively to lend to poor people, Africans rely heavily on traditional methods of resource mobilization. Specifically, these are rotating credit associations where the members contribute a set amount either weekly or monthly into a common fund that individuals can draw upon to purchase, for example, materials or supplies. There also exist NGO-funded micro-credit institutions that provide group lending, but their numbers are limited relative to the growing unmet demand.

Urban Policy in Sub-Saharan Africa: An Agenda for the Next Decade and Beyond

As African cities continue to grow under conditions of economic stagnation and institutional collapse, they take on more of the qualities of their rural hinterlands. This is evidenced in the increasing importance of urban agriculture, the weakening of restrictive land-use controls and more diverse use of urban space, the spread of 'spontaneous' settlements and of petty commodity production, the deterioration of urban infrastructure and services, and the maintenance of rural economic links and of regional and cultural identities on the part of urban migrants (Jamal and Weeks, 1988: 271–92). The decomposition and recomposition of social relations of life in urban Africa take place on a daily basis irrespective of vigorous attempts by public authorities to suffocate, co-opt, or manage these diverse and often complex 'everyday forms' of resistance, improvisations, and collective actions to rewrite the rules governing urban political economy.

The success of forward-looking African urban management strategies will ultimately depend on the theoretical sharpness and practical abilities of both state and local authorities to adapt formal institutions to new and changing realities. Priority must be given to (a) raising urban productivity, and hence reducing poverty, unemployment and homelessness; (b) strengthening the links between the urban and rural areas to achieve maximum economic output, enhance complimentarity, and so on; (c) promoting social equity, economic efficiency and sustainability through better management of human and financial resources, and opening up the political process for people to participate in planning. These priorities must be based on recognition of the following principles:

- *The vibrancy of civil society* The urban poor in Africa expend tremendous energy and vitality in order to change their miserable situation. Whereas national governments and local authorities have failed to articulate new visions or provide necessary services, citizens' groups are organizing themselves to meet their shelter needs, mobilize funds to build roads and clinics, and use their own rotating credit systems to start up a whole range of businesses, from street food to furniture-making.
- *The strategic position of the urban informal sector* While urbanization in Africa is growing at a very fast pace, the growth of the urban economy and its capacity to generate sufficient employment and shelter have been limited. As a result, a substantial number of urban residents are engaged in the informal sector to meet their basic needs. Beginning in the 1970s, and gaining strength during the economic downturn of the 1980s and early 1990s, the urban informal sector has become a powerful force for employment creation in virtually all African cities (ILO, 1972; Bromley, 1978: 1033–9; de Soto, 1989). Needless to say, the lack of clear-cut urban policy with respect to land use, licensing and

registration, zoning, access to credit, and training has frustrated the initiatives and dynamism of the informal sector. The existing legal framework tends to restrict rather than encourage the success of informal sector operators. Reforming the regulatory framework to empower these vibrant social institutions should be the top priority of local authorities.
- *Gender and human settlements development* African women continue to play multiple roles in the development process of human settlements as providers of informal-sector cash income, managers of households, builders of houses, producers of services (sanitation, recycling, composting) and household necessities, reproducers rearing children, and care-takers of their community. Yet women are still at the lower end of the economic ladder. It is therefore incumbent upon African governments to recognize women's critical roles, and to ensure that women participate in the decision-making process at all levels. In particular, efforts must be made to improve women's access to productive resources such as land, and to reorient services such as training and credit in order to support women's initiatives in human settlement development.

To build on these fundamental principles, the key foci for the next decade and beyond, as agreed in the Habitat Agenda (Islamabad Conference of 1996), should be the following issues.

Improving urban governance

Poor governance – especially corruption, bureaucratic harassment and a lack of checks and balances – harms growth and the everyday lives of the poor. African cities have for too long lacked good governance, an essential ingredient in national development. The prevailing approach to urban planning and management, based on central government, places very little emphasis on the importance of private agents and citizens' groups. It allows the vested interests of an economic elite to influence unduly, or even to buy, the policies, regulations, and laws of the local authority.

The first step to improving urban governance is to redefine the principles that underpin local government statutes. This requires, first and foremost, simplification so that ordinary citizens can understand what is being talked about. African governments must also create a climate of equity, cooperation and accountability in which the talents of all urban dwellers can be applied to the problems cities face. Most systems need to be reformed in terms of the representativeness of the urban population

(Wekwete, 1999: 16). The engagement of civil society in fair and transparent decision-making in partnership with local authorities and the private sector can make the difference between well-governed and misgoverned cities, between a stagnant and a thriving urban economy.

There is a tendency to assume that if you have elected councillors and mayors, then all will be well. Experience shows that we need to go beyond that and create mechanisms which give voice to the people, force elected officials to listen to the people, and impose sanctions on elected representatives for wrong-doing. These are the basics of a model of good governance. Although governments must retain their role of planner and investor in some sectors, they should build flexibility into their organizational framework in the areas of participation, regulation, competition, decentralization and privatization (USAID, 1990a). Governments must also undertake facilitating and enabling roles in the development process through capacity-building, human-resource development, institutional development and resource mobilization. When the people are granted flexibility and a conducive environment, they can come up with solutions to their own problems.

Box 6.1 The Habitat Agenda: key commitments on governance

1. *Promote decentralization and strengthen local authorities* Recognize local authorities as the closest, and most important, partners in the implementation of the Habitat Agenda. Promote effective decentralization through democratic local authorities and their associations/networks, working to strengthen their financial and institutional capacities in accordance with the country's conditions (para. 180).
2. *Encourage civic engagement* Support institutional and legal frameworks that facilitate and enable the broad-based participation of all people and their community organizations in decision-making and in the implementation and monitoring of human settlements strategies, policies and programmes (para. 182).
3. *Ensure transparent, accountable and efficient governance* Encourage local leadership, promote democratic rule, the proper exercise of public authority and use of public resources in all public institutions at all levels to ensure responsible, accountable, just, and effective governance of towns, cities and metropolitan areas (para. 45a).

Source: UNCHS, 1996c.

One important element of good governance is that expressed through *decentralization and community participation* – that is, bringing decision-making closer to local communities. Decentralization amounts largely to establishing the role of local government in the management of settlements, which includes the delivery of basic infrastructure, provision of basic social services, and management of land use and environment. This role necessitates the development of a responsive regulatory framework (Dahiya, 1999: 25). Defining roles and responsibilities between central government and local authorities will eliminate duplication, while establishing a functional hierarchy where central government has primarily a guidance and support role.

Devolution of power from central government to local authorities must be accompanied by a clear strategy to strengthen local management processes through the use of indicators for performance evaluation and monitoring. Specifically, attention must be given to formulating integrated strategies for investment and regulation; life-cycle costing of infrastructure investments; social and environmental impact evaluations of prospective investments; strengthening legal and regulatory frameworks; improving development planning, programming and budgeting systems; and enhancing the operation and management of infrastructure systems through greater involvement of the private sector in the delivery of public services.

Effective governance that ensures local involvement in decision-making will achieve several important objectives. First, a community will have a greater sense of commitment and involvement. And it should have a greater sense as to what type and level of urban services are appropriate. This sense of ownership can be conveyed more readily to responsive governments. Second, participatory government permits different ethnic, religious, linguistic and economic groups to meet in a non-confrontational and legally sanctioned environment. Potential problems can be addressed and resolved without recourse to the violence that defines many urban agglomerations. Third, locally based bodies are more likely to deliver services that are needed by the community (UNCHS, 1992). It follows that sensitivity to environmental and aesthetic considerations will be enhanced, through community involvement in the urban planning process.

Finally, urban governance can be improved significantly if national governments grant significant financial autonomy to local authorities. Lack of financial autonomy has been one of the key factors contributing to weak technical performance at the municipal level. Municipalities have been unable to attract and retain skilled technical staff. It is therefore important that roles and responsibilities between national governments and local authorities be clarified through legislation.

Strengthening the power of local authorities

The major constraints to urban productivity have their origins in the weakness of the public sector. Despite the growing economic importance of the cities in national development, the policy and institutional framework for managing urban growth remains weak or inhospitable. An inappropriate legal and regulatory environment and inadequate infrastructure have a stifling effect on the overall economic performance of cities. Consequently, the enormous economic potential of African cities remains untapped.

First, greater recognition must be given to the important role investment in urban infrastructure can play in overall economic activity. Decrepit road and communications systems, frequent interruptions of electric power, an unnecessary and complicated legal and regulatory environment all add to the costs of doing business and are disincentives to private operators. Therefore, strengthening the capacity of local authorities to plan, invest wisely and manage scarce resources efficiently is a fundamental prerequisite for raising productivity and generating urban employment (Davey, 1993). This in turn will improve the tax base of municipalities.

Second, laws that block or hinder the efficient provision of services, particularly those that discriminate against non-traditional service providers, should be amended. The legal system should concentrate on equity and on the removal of obstacles that prevent the urban poor from receiving basic services and infrastructure. As the case study from the Jua Kali sector in Kenya demonstrates, simply changing the legal and regulatory environment can go a long way in improving urban productivity and reducing poverty.

Box 6.2 An enabling environment for the Jua Kali sector in Nairobi

Before intervention, Jua Kali artisans (small and medium-scale manufacturing enterprises) in Kenya were generally working in undefined worksites. This often led to conflicts with the local authorities and regulatory agencies. In a cooperative effort involving the Kenya Ministry of Research and Technical Training and Technology, BAT Kenya Ltd, the World Bank and a variety of NGOs, an enabling environment was created for the artisans. Now most of the Jua Kali artisans are working in legally recognized premises. Training and education have been provided and the Jua Kali entrepreneurs have worked to raise their standard of living by building better living quarters for themselves and their families. Women make up more than half of the sector's population and are encouraged to participate actively in Jua Kali associations and to enter male-dominated entrepreneurial activities. They are favourably treated in the allocation of available infrastructure and resources.

Source: UNCHS, 1996c.

The strengthening of municipal capacity to manage urban development requires building a state-of-the-art information base upon which key decisions can be made in a timely fashion. Institutionalized access to and quick transmission of information on local government rules and regulations, publication of standardized statistical data, and regular updating of the information on every aspect of the urban economy would not only help policymakers but also provide needed information to communities and the private sector for future planning.

Strengthening the competence of municipalities in the field of policy analysis also entails augmenting human resources in line with the discharge of responsibilities. This will involve training and equipment, a review of the terms and conditions of employment of municipal staff, revising remuneration levels and career advancements. The result will be better management of infrastructure and maintenance of physical stock, such as vehicles and equipment. In addition, local authorities can enhance efficiency by improving intergovernmental coordination. Efforts must be made to develop support for the horizontal exchange of best practices among mayors, city councils, city managers and the like.

Many of the necessary improvements in service provision require change, both in who provides the service and in the legal framework that governs it. Basic services like water, sewerage and power have been seen as natural monopolies which must be provided by the government or by parastatals. However, the best providers of certain services might be NGOs, community organizations or even private businesses (Nolan, 1986; Uduku, 1994). Communities may provide maintenance for systems built by local authorities, and NGOs may promote the appropriate technology.

While cost recovery is necessary, it is also essential that the poor be able to afford these services. They should not be priced out. This requires the provision of services appropriate to each situation. For water provision, the focus should be on expanding the volume rather than the quality, or on appropriate technology for the collection of rainwater. For sewerage, it may mean providing latrines or septic tanks rather than a central sewerage system (Sinnatamby, 1990: 127–57). For transport, this may mean promoting bicycles and carts rather than buses, through the creation of special lanes or credit schemes for the purchase of bicycles. In order for changes in service provision to succeed, the intended beneficiaries must be consulted. Advanced technology is of little use if it is not accepted by the community. Involving members of the community in the decision-making, planning and implementation of any project intended to benefit them can avoid potential problems.

Building the foundations for a sound municipal revenue base

In common with many US cities, urban areas in Africa suffer severe fiscal distress. This became obvious in the 1980s, characterized as the 'decade of adjustment'. Shrinking revenues were matched by expanding responsibilities. How to pay for new infrastructure investment, to provide affordable services without fiscal distress, to recover costs, and to improve administrative efficiency: these are daunting but not insurmountable challenges.

In the present era of structural adjustment, local authorities in Africa cannot hope to receive substantial resources from central authorities to fund capital projects. Increasingly, they must find innovative ways of mobilizing the resources they have. Since private capital markets are non-existent, the only alternative for improving service provision is cost recovery. The collection of fees, taxes and other revenue has to be expanded and improved significantly to meet national expenses. This will allow for the expansion of services as populations grow and demand increases. Water rates should reflect the actual cost of providing water, as should sewerage, waste-collection and transport costs.

To ensure financial accountability, local authorities must enhance development planning, programming and budgeting systems. This accountability is essential to foster a climate of trust between citizens and political leaders and bureaucrats. The collection and disbursement of revenue must be open to scrutiny and debate. Investment in modern technology (such as computers), improvement in recruitment of staff, skills development in accounting and finance, property assessment, billing, efficient issue of business permits: such reforms are part and parcel of any revenue-enhancing strategy. Financial accountability also fosters a positive economic environment for local and international investors. Good financial planning permits strategic planning and forecasting.

One way to strengthen financial accountability is through participatory budgeting. Research by Pedro Jacobi, professor at the University of São

Paulo, shows how Brazil, faced with an urban globalized economy, has experimented with fundamental changes in city management. Using the city of Pôrto Alegre as a case study, Jacobi details a process of participatory budgeting in which citizens set priorities. This process allows political leaders to create an environment which fosters the growth of social capital (Jacobi, 1999). Citizens scrutinize the past year's expenditure, agree upon current priorities, and allocate funds for new projects. An investment plan is developed and forwarded to the city's executive council. Between 15 and 25 per cent of Pôrto Alegre's annual budget is allocated according to this participatory model. Belo Horizonte, another Brazilian city, has embarked on a similar participative budgeting exercise drawing on the experience of Pôrto Alegre (Bretas, 1996: 213–22). Citizens feel a sense of ownership in transparent institutions created through consensus. The UNDP's 'Budgets as if people matter' programme is modelling this idea on a large scale. In 2001, South Africa became the first African country to initiate a People's Budget campaign. The challenge this model faces, however, is to create a responsive citizenship that recognizes participation as a crucial part of governance.

Box 6.3 The People's Budget Campaign movement in South Africa

The People's Budget Campaign (PBC) is an initiative of the Congress of South African Trade Unions (COSATU), South African National NGO Coalition (SANGOCO) and the South African Council of Churches (SACC). The PBC is a response to the deep cuts to the public spending budget since 1996, which have resulted in reduced public-sector employment, a decrease in social expenditure and low spending on social infrastructure.

The PBC is fighting for the reversal of these trends to ensure that the economy is steered in the direction of job creation, wealth redistribution, poverty eradication, social service delivery, and the redressing of all race, gender and class inequalities through an active state. It aims to achieve these goals through the production of a progressive People's Budget on an annual basis within an appropriate macroeconomic framework. The campaign will use mass mobilization and action to achieve these goals. The basic strategy of the campaign is formulated through public 'hearings' in order to canvass views from civil society on key issues and concerns to be addressed.

Source: South African National NGO Coalition (SANGOCO), unpublished paper, 2000.

Private providers must give priority to reducing corruption by establishing transparent systems for procurement, contracting and bidding for the delivery of services. Public contracts need to be awarded in a fair and open manner that allows both the nature of the project and the economic and social costs and benefits to be assessed. In addition, revenue collection must be efficient, reflecting the true costs of services offered by local governments. An overseeing mechanism or an independent financial management authority is needed to ensure that money is properly collected and used. This means that the budgetary process must also be open and transparent. Such procedures encourage citizen participation and monitoring.

Designing a strategy to tackle urban poverty

The complexity of poverty and the heterogeneity of most national cultures make it difficult to define a uniform strategy for poverty reduction. This is especially true if the objective is to approach the problem integrally and not simply through small-scale projects. Poverty-reduction programmes should be country-, city- and community-specific, tailored to the specific needs of impoverished households (Wegelin and Borgman, 1995; 131–52). The common characteristics of urban poverty, however – unemployment and underemployment, lack of adequate shelter and basic infrastructure, and, in particular, reliance on the informal sector to provide employment – make it possible to identify key areas of intervention and suggest guidelines for support strategies.

The informal sector is a case in point. Micro-enterprises have the potential to grow and generate additional employment, but their growth is seriously limited by: (1) inadequate infrastructure services; (2) a lack of general education and managerial skills; (3) the absence of business services and market information; (4) limited access to credit to purchase tools and equipment; (5) uncertainties about the future business climate; and (6) the unavailability of sites for expansion. Greater incentives, better infrastructure, and business services are all badly needed (World Bank, 1989a).

Local authorities need to review and reorientate their development-control regulations in favour of home-based enterprises (HBEs), while ensuring that their operation meets health and safety requirements. They must also develop a strategy of small-enterprise development, in which they provide advice and guidance, small loans for development and relocation opportunities, where appropriate, for HBEs. The importance of these measures is highlighted by a recent ILO-supported study in Zimbabwe. The findings describe how informal-sector operators deal with municipal ordinances which impinge on their operations: 29 per cent of those interviewed said they lobbied for favourable treatment; 13 per cent ignored the regulations; while the majority sought ways to comply, either by changing locations, ensuring adequate sanitation, or paying rates. Only a very small percentage admitted to bribing officials (Mhone, 1995; Kanji, 1995: 37–56).

Box 6.4 The Habitat Agenda: social development and poverty eradication

1. Provide all with equal opportunities for a healthy, safe and productive life in harmony with nature, their cultural heritage, and spiritual values (para. 42).
2. Promote social integration and support the disadvantaged through legislation and incentives, and encourage members and organization groups to become involved in economic, social and political decision-making (paras. 117 and 96b).
3. Promote the integration of gender perspectives in legislation, policies, planning, development and evaluation; the collection of gender-disaggregated data and information; and encourage the full and equal participation of women in decision-making (para. 46).
4. Strengthen small and micro-enterprises, particularly those developed by women, by promoting and strengthening programmes that integrate credit, finance, vocational training and technological transfer (para. 160b).
5. Encourage new partnerships between the public and the private sectors for those institutions that are privately owned and managed but public in their function and purpose; and stimulate productive employment opportunities that can generate income sufficient to achieve an adequate standard of living for all (paras. 158b and 118a).

The problems of poverty, unemployment and lack of adequate shelter and services are interrelated; they should therefore be linked through an integrated strategy. A focus on labour-intensive shelter and infrastructure programmes, with efforts to reform regulatory frameworks, will increase labour opportunities, improve urban productivity, and begin to alleviate poverty and increase equity. An integrated and sustained poverty-reduction programme might include the following:

- employment-intensive and community-based shelter provision and improvement;
- small-scale building materials production;
- employment-intensive provision and maintenance of infrastructure;

- community credit and home-based enterprises;
- audits of regulatory systems and strengthening of community-based action planning; and
- expanded educational and training opportunities for indigenous entrepreneurs.

Improving urban environmental management

The lack of adequate housing exposes low-income people to overcrowded conditions and squatter settlements without infrastructural services. Inadequate provision of water, sanitation and refuse disposal aggravate environmental and health problems in residential areas. For example, 55 per cent of Mathare residents in Nairobi lack toilet facilities, while over 61 per cent have no water supply (Friedrich-Naumann-Stiftung Foundation, 1992: 189). Since many illnesses are connected with poor services – diarrhoea, for example, is linked to poor water and sanitation, as well as to flies – it may be expected that around 70 per cent of the urban population of Kenya will become affected if present housing policies continue.

Box 6.5 The Habitat Agenda: environmental management

1. Promote geographically balanced settlement structures (para. 43k). Cities, towns and rural settlements are linked through the movement of goods, resources and people. Full advantage must be taken of the complementary contributions and linkages of rural and urban areas (para. 10).
2. Manage supply and demand of water effectively, providing for the basic requirements of human settlements development, while paying due regard to the carrying capacity of natural ecosystems (para. 141c).
3. Reduce urban pollution, especially that resulting from inadequate water supply, sanitation and drainage, and poor industrial and domestic waste management, solid waste management and air pollution (para. 43l).
4. Prevent disasters and rebuild settlements: adequate regulatory measures to avoid occurrence; reduction of impact through appropriate planning mechanisms, resources, people-centred response, rehabilitation, and reconstruction (para. 43z).
5. Promote effective, environmentally sound and energy-efficient transportation systems, and transport demand-reducing spatial development patterns and communication policies (para. 43n).
6. Institute support mechanisms to prepare and implement local environmental plans and local Agenda 21 initiatives and specific cross-sectoral environmental health programmes (para. 137l).

A strategy to promote sustainable human settlements in Africa must give emphasis to the institutionalization of preventive policies and programmes instead of reactionary and mitigative measures. In addition, the aim should be to strike a new balance between Habitat and the environmente consonant with the needs and priorities of the African people, so that they can contribute effectively to sustainable management of the biosphere. Such a project requires the following:

Legislation and enforcement

The process of enacting environmental legislation should be consultative, enlisting the participation of communities, NGOs, associations of waste pickers, local authorities and the private sector. Once legislation is enacted, local authorities should have the institutional capacity and budget to enforce the law. At the same time, market-driven incentives must be based on the 'polluter pays' principle. For example, individual households who recycle should pay less for refuse collection than those who do not.

The Sustainable Dar-es-Salaam Project (SDP) is an excellent model in environmental planning at the city level. In 1991/2, the Dar-es-Salaam City Council, with the cooperation of the United Nations Development Programme (UNDP) and the United Nations Centre for Human Settlements (UNCHS), held discussions with stakeholders within Dar-es-Salaam to establish a preliminary assessment of environmental issues. Working groups were established and nine environmental coordinators were appointed to deal with identified priorities. The working groups comprise technical advisors, representatives of government ministries, parastatals, commissions and the private sector. Since 1992 the Sustainable Dar-es-Salaam Project has initiated significant changes in the management and development of the city. These changes have been at the community level and at political and administrative levels – specifically, the development of a management process to identify crucial environmental issues and implement action plans involving public, private, NGO and community-based organization sectors.

On the basis of the lessons learned from the SDP project, the Dar-es-Salaam City Council developed a community infrastructure-upgrading programme in 1995 to assist communities in improving their own neighbourhoods. The programme works closely with communities to enhance their planning, implementation and monitoring activities and with the City Council to improve its ability to implement infrastructure projects. In Tabata, a low-income neighbourhood, the water supply system is being run and paid for by the residents themselves, and revenue generated is in turn helping to finance solid waste collection. The strong sense of community responsibility is helping to ensure long-term sustainability of the programme.[2]

Upgraded waste management

The aim here is to find alternative systems of waste disposal cheaper than the Northern model of refuse collection and conventional sewage treatment. It is important to identify local solutions that match local needs and possibilities. For example, support could be given to those engaged in recycling from the 'informal sector' – the waste-pickers. Composting for urban agriculture could also be encouraged.

A novel idea in community-based approaches to refuse collection and recycling has been developed by the municipality of Rufisque, in Senegal. The township, just outside the capital of Dakar, draws its name from the Portuguese Rio Fresco (freshwater river). In 1990, Rufisque was a depressing place with serious sanitation and refuse problems. Most compounds had inadequate or non-existent plumbing, and because of a lack of urban planning the official refuse collection lorries could not reach many areas. As a result, waste water was thrown into the street, the beach became a public toilet, and a refuse dump was spreading disease – diarrhoea topped the list of reported health complaints.

Today, Rufisque is a different place. Using a highly integrated, holistic approach – utilizing horse-drawn carts for rubbish collection, narrow-gauge plumbing pipes, the energies of young people at the Purification and Recycling Centre to treat and combine the refuse for composting, and abundantly available water lettuce for purification – the programme demonstrates the value of appropriate technology and community participation. Furthermore, the scheme is run by representative local management committees, with women and young people active at all levels. Credit initially provided by international donors will soon no longer be necessary, as it is quickly being replaced by a local revolving-credit scheme. Today, through the efforts of eight low-income communities, aided by ENDA Third World and the Canadian Host Country Participation Fund and in collaboration with the local authority, Rufisque is on its way back to becoming Rio Fresco once again.

Improved household energy use

Besides being exposed to environmental industrial pollution and increased risks from flood and landslides, residential environmental conditions in most low-income areas are considered health hazards. The cost of energy for cooking increasingly consumes a disproportionate amount of poor people's incomes. Most households use paraffin and wood charcoal. The implications for respiratory health, the risk of fires and environmental degradation are therefore quite serious. Although illegal electrical connections are common in slum areas, the poor simply cannot afford to purchase modern kitchen appliances, which would reduce the rate of pollution and reduce the risk of exposure.

Community participation in the development of household energy technology can help mitigate part of the problem. In many African countries, NGOs have taken the lead in the development and introduction of energy-saving cooking stoves made out of local materials. In Kenya, for example, the Intermediate Technology Development Group developed a more fuel-efficient cooker, the Upesi ceramic stove. Women, who are most exposed to carbon monoxide and smoke, are trained in the production of these stoves. Pollution in the kitchen has been reduced, and stove production has become an important income and employment generator. Similar projects, funded by donor agencies, are becoming increasingly popular in many parts of Africa.

Increased awareness and a developed information base

Public participation in the identification of priorities and in the formulation of policies and programmes is critical to the development of sustainable human settlements. The interface of exchange and communication between the media, the general public, NGOs, government, and the business and research communities should be widened with the aim of promoting public awareness, participation and dialogue (USAID, 1994: 25–9).

Box 6.6 The Zabbaleen Environment Programme, Cairo

The Zabbaleen of Cairo have long been engaged in the collection, recycling and reuse of domestic waste as a means of survival. Their methods involve labour-intensive sorting and door-to-door collection. They are responsible for the collection and disposal of more than 600 tons of the 2,000 tons of waste generated by Cairo's residents daily. The recycled waste is used to provide the local market with affordable products and consumer items. After years of discussion and negotiation with central and local government authorities, and having been recognized for exemplary practices by several institutions, the municipality of Greater Cairo adopted the separation of waste at source as a matter of policy. This has greatly facilitated the work of the Zabbaleen, who, with the support of the government, are now engaged in the construction of a modern industrial waste-recycling plant and the upgrading of skills of community members.

Source: UNCHS, 1996b.

Special emphasis should also be directed to building upon African indigenous practices conducive to waste reduction, recycling and reuse. All in all, efforts should be concentrated at the creation of a policy environment conducive to the development and expansion of local businesses capable of responding to the growing need for environmental services.

Box 6.7 The Habitat Agenda: 'shelter'

1. Provide security of tenure and equal access to land to all people (para. 40b).
2. Promote the right to adequate housing as an important component of the right to an adequate standard of living (paras 39 and 61).
3. Undertake legislative and administrative reforms to give women full and equal access to economic resources, including the right to inheritance and ownership of land and other property (para. 40b).
4. Promote equal access to credit (para. 48e).
5. Promote equal access for all people to safe drinking water, adequate sanitation, environmentally sound waste management and other basic services including sports, recreational and cultural facilities and amenities (para. 40c).

Improving the policy environment for shelter provision

Since the early 1980s, there has been a significant shift from government provision of urban services to creating and maintaining an 'enabling environment'. In the housing sector, this has meant a shift from direct provision of public housing to the introduction of an enabling national shelter strategy, strengthening the regulatory framework, and plans for greater involvement of the private sector and communities in settlement planning and housing production (UNCHS, 1993). Despite this encouraging trend, implementation lags far behind stated objectives. The key problem has been the weakness of government institutions to translate policies into strategies and action. While recognizing that the problems of housing production and expanding access to the poor are multifaceted and will take a long time to resolve, much more can be done to alleviate the housing crisis by simply removing barriers that stand in the way of local initiatives. These initiatives include the following:

Security of land tenure

Security of tenure is one of the basic components of the right to housing. Granting of tenure is an important catalyst in the stabilizing of communities, improving shelter conditions, reducing social exclusion, and opening up access to urban basic services. Tenure reform should therefore concentrate on the legal and institutional structures, improving professional competence and service delivery in urban planning and management of land, reforming inheritance laws, and following best practice in identifying availabile land for the urban poor (Cobbert, 1999). By taking into account local conditions, national governments and local authorities can become a catalyst for change if channels of communication are kept open between communities and public officials. Through proper consultation with all the actors, land shortages and tenure insecurity could be overcome.

The Tanzania-Bondeni Community Land Trust project in the southern part of Voi Town, Kenya is a good illustration of such an approach. Tanzania-Bondeni was a typical informal settlement. In the early 1990s, over half the settlement's 5,000 inhabitants earned less than $40 per month; the unemployment rate was 30 per cent. Most homes were temporary structures, often dilapidated and overcrowded. Health and environmental conditions were bad, and the local authority provided no infrastructure. None of the residents had any legal rights to the land, which was state-owned. The local authority approached the Ministry of Local Government and German Development Agency (GTZ) Small Towns Development Project (STDP) for assistance in improving the settlement's infrastructure (German Agency for Technical Cooperation, 1997: 16–17).

In the course of initial deliberations between the community, the local authority, and the Ministry of Local Government and GTZ–STDP, certain key principles were agreed upon, including the need to explore land tenure options for the community. An initial mobilization phase to inform the residents of the upgrading project was followed by registration of the residents, discussion of their needs and the forming of a residents' representative committee. The 'Tanzania-Bondeni Community Land Trust' (CLT) was developed in consultation with residents. The basis of the CLT concept is that land tenure rests not in the individual but in the community. At the same time, beneficiaries own the developments on their plots and they can bequeath or sell these developments. Beneficiaries formed a society under the Society's Act; the society controls the charitable trust, which holds the community's land. An elected management committee runs the day-to-day affairs of the CLT. To date a development plan has been drawn up, roads have been opened and water supply has been brought to the area.

Despite its participatory approach, however, the CLT was deficient in one respect: it was not gender sensitive. According to one of the NGOs working in the community, Kituo Cha Sheria (Legal Aid Centre), the lack of a specific focus on women's interests has led to the marginalization of women as community traditions kept men in place as the main decision-makers (Benschop and Trujillo, 1999: 7–8). This shows that women do not automatically benefit from tenure models designed to benefit a community. Indeed, in countries where patriarchal customs still dominate, communal land tenure systems could be said to be disadvantageous to women. Where specific attention is paid to this problem and, for example, women's cooperatives within a community are supported, the benefit for women seems to be much greater and the risk of their marginalization much smaller. A community land trust model can therefore work very well, but only if the special needs of women are taken into consideration.

Box 6.8 The Cape Town Serviced Land Project

Urbanization in the Cape region of South Africa has been severely distorted by apartheid policies, which were designed to keep as many Africans out of the region as possible. In consequence, planning and development in the region were undertaken in a selective manner, ensuring that the only shelter available for Africans was in squatter areas. The large number of squatters, combined with government efforts to reduce squatting, led to escalating tensions as competition for land and for access to services increased.

Started in 1993, the Serviced Land Project (SLP) encouraged severely alienated and less motivated squatter communities of the Cape region to participate in a people-centred process aimed at developing underdeveloped land as well as upgrading squatter areas. This development process included the creation of twenty-four Residents' Development Committees, the establishment of seven Project Committees, the drafting of a business plan providing for the creation of 35,000 residential sites with secure title, and the planning and promotion of a business and commercial centre within the project area (7,500 residential sites have already been created). Earthworks for over 15,000 sites are nearing completion and bulk services for another 7,500 are to be installed. The first stage of the project provided over 12,500 person-days of employment as well as construction-training skills to 99 people living in the project area. In recognition of the project's significance to South Africa's Reconstruction and Development Program (RDP), the SLP was designated (by President Mandela) a Presidential Project of the RDP.

The granting of secure tenure does, however, also set in motion a whole train of logical consequences that will need to be dealt with by local authorities. These may include, for example, the need for efficient and reliable methods of recording land title, cadastral systems, as well as the administrative mechanisms and means to record and update property rights. Further downstream, issues concerning the provision of basic services arise, especially the provision of potable water and sanitation, as well as the essential institutional and technical elements required to support an affordable and practical shelter strategy. Planning policy, zoning, appropriate building standards and transportation policy are all issues that will need to be addressed.

Housing finance

The absence of well-developed formal financial arrangements is a major constraint on the development of a healthy housing market and increased urban productivity. The services of most commercial banks and government-owned housing finance corporations are out of the reach of most citizens, particularly the poor. If and when such services are available, mortgage rates are exorbitantly high. In Kenya, for example, the annual mortgage rate is 22 or 23 per cent for a period of between ten and twenty years (USAID, 1991: 39). It is therefore incumbent upon national governments to improve the housing finance system by making sure that relevant institutions are accessible and that they offer services that meet the demands of low-income groups. It is within the power of national governments and local authorities to facilitate access by the poor and small-scale enterprises to commercial banks, or to support the creation of community savings banks similar to the famous Grameen Bank in Bangladesh.

Housing finance mechanisms and institutions can also be developed through community-based organizations, which have to be transparent and accountable to target urban poor families. In Ethiopia, for example, the Norwegian Save the Children organization supported the establishment of the Saving and Credit Cooperative (SACC) at community level for low-income people. They linked the cooperative to the financial formal sector by setting up a National Bank department (Savings and Credit Cooperative Development Office, SACCDO) to register and supervise individual SACCs (Save the Children–Ethiopia, 1993: 2).

Improving access to building materials

There is a need to diversify the production of indigenous materials to include small-scale producers and those in the informal sector. This should involve a discrete programme of training and support through small-enterprise development agencies and the availability of credit facilities for the disbursement of small loans. Such agencies should draw heavily on proven private-sector expertise (UNCHS, 1991b). Further measures should be taken to enable low-income groups to access low-cost building materials – for example, cooperative bulk-purchase arrangements organized by NGOs – or to establish building-material 'banks.'

Revising zoning and building regulations

Outdated building and planning regulations, which generally impose high standards, push the cost of housing upward and out of the reach of the poor. This problem can be solved by simplifying procedures, increasing flexibility in the approval of building materials and in standards, reducing minimum plot size, and accepting the multiple use of dwellings.

Promoting public–private partnership

While major strides have been made in promoting community participation in shelter provision, the same cannot be said about public–private participation in the African context. Too much government intervention in the shelter field has ruled out a significant contribution by the private sector. Efforts must be made to review the legal and regulatory environment and to develop incentives for the private sector to engage in the provision of low-cost housing.

Expanding the scope for greater participation by NGOs and CBOs

Local authorities often do not recognize community organizations as playing an important role in community mobilization. They frequently fail to utilize such organizations in a variety of key projects where they have clear comparative advantage. In many African countries, NGOs are participating in a wide range of activities in both urban and rural areas: environment, energy, health, water and sanitation, shelter, education, family planning, and women's issues. Many of the best-practice models cited in this chapter were initiated by NGOs, both local and international, often with the collaboration of community-based organizations (CBOs). The key role of municipal authorities should be the facilitation of communities' initiatives, and, with NGOs, the overall coordination of provision of urban services. To this end, it is necessary to review the regulatory framework to ensure that government effectively interacts and builds effective, cooperative alliances with communities (Menendez, 1991: 41–52; UNCHS, 1991b). Local authorities could also provide training and funding to community groups.

Enabling an efficient and cost-effective transport system

Urban transport is the glue that holds together human settlements. Poor or inadequate transport leads to a low quality of life and is often cited as the single most negative aspect of urban existence. Considering the importance of transport and communications in the urban economy, decentralizing urban transport decision-making to the local level can better ensure all urban residents are adequately served by effective transport services at affordable prices (Godard and Ngabmen, 1998: 15–16).

In the case of urban Africa, greater private-sector participation and competition in the provision and operation of urban transport services is a necessity (World Bank, 1996). This would entail creating a conducive environment for the paratransit private transport sector that spans the spectrum – from single-passenger taxicabs to minibuses, and almost everything in between – in terms of speed, comfort, geographical coverage, and carrying capacity. For the approach to work, an appropriate institutional framework is needed that delineates the roles of the private and public sectors whilst enhancing their cooperation. Quite often, paratransit functions as a 'gap filler' – entering streets that are too narrow to accommodate full-size buses, plying cross-town routes left unserved by public operators, and providing complementary feeder connections to rail stations (Cervero, 1998: 8–9; Lee-Smith, 1989: 276–304).

With regard to transport systems, priority should be given to reducing unnecessary travel through appropriate patterns of land use – those that reduce transport demand and promote public transport (Plumbe, 1998: 25–6). Efforts must also be made to implement measures that discourage the growth in private motorized traffic and reduce congestion, which is damaging environmentally, economically and socially. Such measures should include pricing, traffic regulation, parking and land-use planning, traffic abatement schemes, and effective alternative transport methods, particularly in the most congested areas (Nichols, 1998: 6–7).

Conclusion

Any attempt to grasp the complexity and dimensions of growing urbanization and poverty in Africa requires flexibility and a keen interest on the part of local authorities to intensify support for horizontal exchanges of best practices. Given the interrelated nature of many of the issues discussed in this chapter, local authorities must move away from narrowly focused sectoral perspectives towards more inclusive multidisciplinary approaches.

Finally, the extent to which innovative approaches in African urban management will translate into tangible results depends largely on the appropriateness of overall national economic policy. Inappropriate macroeconomic policies and investment decisions by central governments at the national level will diminish, if not destroy, the effectiveness of the best-thought-out urban management strategies at the local level.

Notes

1. People employed part-time who are seeking full-time paid employment, or who are employed at jobs below their capabilities.
2. UNCHS, best practices website at www.bestpractices.org.

CHAPTER 7

Rebuilding War-torn Societies and Preventing Deadly Conflicts

The last decade of the twentieth century was marred by unprecedented levels of political violence amidst ongoing and emerging crises in the Third World. The African continent, in particular, has been a region where protracted conflicts have claimed the lives of millions of people. The roots of these conflicts date back to the colonial period. Under colonialism, regional ethnic groups were broken up and forced to cohabit with other ethnic groups within the artificial borders of the new states. In the 1960s, the newly independent African states inherited those colonial boundaries, together with the challenge that legacy posed to their territorial integrity and to their attempts to achieve unity. The challenge was compounded by the fact that the framework of colonial laws and institutions inherited by some states had been designed to exploit local divisions, not overcome them. As a result, post-independence governments tried to achieve national unity through the centralization of political and economic power and the suppression of political pluralism. Priority was given to law and order to maintain relative peace and tranquillity. Predictably, political monopolies often led to corruption, nepotism and the abuse of power. Forging genuine national unity from among disparate and often competing communities has remained elusive.

Colonial divisions were further reinforced by the Cold War machinations of both East and West. Across Africa, undemocratic and oppressive regimes were supported and sustained by the competing superpowers in the name of their broader foreign-policy goals. Some of Africa's longest and most deadly conflicts were fuelled by superpower rivalries. With the end of the Cold War, however, the ethnic pieces put together by colonial glue and reinforced by the Old World Order are now pulling apart and reasserting their autonomy.

The persistence of civil strife continues systematically to divert scarce national resources from development, and hence from Africa's ability to gain benefits from globalization. Ending violent conflicts in chronically unstable African countries, and building a foundation for preventing future violent conflict, are the prerequisites for sustainable social and economic development. Moreover, violent conflict poses a number of problems for Africa's transformation agenda. These include:

Unprecedented loss of civilian life

In Africa, wars have caused the deaths of almost five million civilians since 1955, and it is estimated that as many have become handicapped for life. Since 1970, more than thirty wars have been fought in Africa, the vast majority of them intra-state in origin. In 1996 alone, fourteen of Africa's fifty-three countries were afflicted by armed conflicts, accounting for more than half of all war-related deaths worldwide and resulting in more than 8 million refugees, returnees and displaced persons (United Nations, 1997a). In Rwanda, over 800,000 people were massacred in a hundred days in 1994, the vast majority of whom were women and children. During Mozambique's sixteen-year civil war, 490,000 children died from war-related causes. Another 200,000 children were orphaned or abandoned by adults. At least 10,000 children served as soldiers during the conflict.

Massive displacement of people

Over the past decade, the African continent hosted about half of the world's displaced people. In 1999 one-fifth of Africans lived in countries severely disrupted by wars or civil conflicts, and 90 per cent of the casualties were civilians. There were more than 3 million refugees and 16 million internally displaced persons (World Bank, 2000: 15). The Horn of Africa alone has produced over 4 million refugees, a number surpassed by the wars in Angola and Mozambique. Displacement is now common in Central Africa as a result of the conflict in the Democratic Republic of the Congo (DRC), and in West Africa due to the ongoing conflict in Sierra Leone, Guinea and Liberia. The internally displaced, who are much less visible than refugees who cross international borders, comprise another 15 to 20 million people. A worrisome and woefully neglected feature of this pattern is the unusually large proportion of widows and orphans among the displaced.

Disintegration of the social fabric

Physical disruption of the habitat and displacement of people often lead to partial or total disintegration of social structures based on family, clan or tribe. For centuries, these structures have provided cultural roots, preserving Africa's rich heritage. As a result of war, women and children now make up a disproportionate percentage of those communities recovering from conflict. A significant number of these women are heads of households, responsible not only for immediate family members but also for elderly relatives.

As a result of Rwanda's genocide 70 per cent of the population today is female and 50 per cent of all households are headed by women (Warah, 2000b: 17). The population of post-conflict Angola is similar: it has become a nation of war widows struggling to feed families. With the diminution of indigenous culture, people become vulnerable to cultural 'substitutes' such as militarism, warlordism, religious fanaticism, and political or tribal extremism. How to reconstitute community social capital is perhaps a bigger challenge than the reconstruction of physical infrastructure.

Squandered human and economic resources

Militarization has diverted valuable and scare resources for war purposes, and too often has forced development into the background. A frightening consequence is the emergence of a 'war ethic' among the general population: people become more accustomed to making or coping with war than creating peace or engaging in productive activities. Hospitals, schools, roads, bridges, communication networks and other infrastructure that takes decades to build is wantonly destroyed. In the case of Mozambique, over 40 per cent of schools and health centres have been destroyed. The economic losses total $15 billion, equal to four times the country's GDP in 1990 (UNICEF, 1996; Kranna, 1994). Food production and marketing systems are also a common casualty. Some of the most talented and skilled people are forced to seek new livelihoods in more favourable environments.

Ecological degradation

War forces insecure people to flee from their villages, leaving land unprotected and exacerbating the process of desertification. Furthermore, the spill-over effect of conflict can have a devastating impact on the natural resource base of refugee-receiving neighbouring countries. This can clearly be seen in western Tanzania and southeastern Malawi, which became home for thousands of Mozambican refugees who were fleeing brutal attacks from the Mozambique Resistance Movement (RENAMO) during the height of the Mozambique conflict (Colleta, 1997: 2).

It is no surprise that the worst civil-war-fuelled humanitarian disasters in Africa – Liberia, Ethiopia, Zaïre, Somalia, Mozambique and Angola – have occurred in countries where dictators played the Cold War game and crushed political dissent in their countries. This left no option for change except through armed rebellion. These countries have seen their development interrupted, and in some cases set back by decades. Conflicts are also rooted in the enormous economic inequalities that have persisted in each of these countries. Once war ends, re-establishing the development process at the level attained before the commencement of hostilities and building durable peace are very difficult, especially under conditions of economic collapse and with a weak state.

This chapter examines the root causes of conflict in Africa and then considers the challenge of conflict-prevention and peacemaking in post-conflict countries. It argues that peacemaking and post-conflict reconstruction are best achieved by addressing structural injustices. Peacemaking has everything to do with the ongoing management of social and political conflicts through good governance. It encompasses the entrenching of respect for human rights and political pluralism, and the elimination of economic injustice.

The Political, Economic and Social Context of Conflict

Through much of the Cold War period military rule was the predominant form of government in Africa. Before 1990 only eight African countries had multiparty systems of government. Since the Egyptian revolution in 1952, there have been more than eighty-five violent or unconstitutional changes of government in the continent; some ninety government leaders have been deposed, and some twenty-six presidents and prime ministers have lost their lives as a result of political violence. Out of the thirty-one countries that have experienced violent changes of government, Benin, Burundi, Ghana, Nigeria, Sudan, Sierra Leone and Uganda have all had at least five military takeovers (Africa Institute of South Africa, 1998: 98–9). Both East and West helped accelerate Africa's militarization by supporting repressive military juntas in the face of widespread poverty and neglect of infrastructure and social services.

With the end of the Cold War, two strikingly different realities began to emerge in Africa. On the one hand, many long-running conflicts in the continent came to a close when guerrilla insurgencies decisively defeated despotic regimes, as was the case in Ethiopia and Eritrea. Other countries, such as Somalia, Liberia, Sierra Leone and Rwanda, descended into anarchy, self-destruction and genocide. The fall of Siyaad Bare's regime in January 1991 in Somalia, and the 1990 execution of military leader Sergeant Samuel Doe in Liberia by militiamen from Charles Taylor's National Patriotic Front of Liberia, illustrate this point. Valuable American allies during the Cold War, these two countries splintered along tribal and clan lines as competing warlords waged destructive warfare, which claimed the lives of thousands of civilians, leaving properties and infrastructure destroyed on a massive scale. In July 1997, Charles Taylor was elected president, ending more than seven years of civil conflict (Human Rights Watch/Africa, 1997). Taylor has now transformed himself from a local warlord to a regional one, fuelling the war in Sierra Leone so that he can personally benefit from diamond trafficking. The country remains in a shambles, with development prospects poor and dwindling, as the international community increasingly isolates Taylor and the people of Liberia continue to suffer the aftermath of war.

Many observers in the West, including the popular media, try to present the humanitarian crisis in countries like Rwanda, Liberia, and Somalia as nothing unusual, just a natural part of the African way of life. Readers of these events were warned in 1994 of 'the coming anarchy' – a new security threat for the Western world after the end of the Cold War (Kaplan, 1994). The Africa correspondent of the *Washington Post*, Keith Richburg, for his part, went further, giving thanks that his ancestors were brought to America as slaves so that he does not have to experience the kind of brutal and inhumane treatment of Africans by other Africans that he witnessed while covering Africa for his newspaper (Richburg, 1998).

The tendency to view African conflict in 'ethnic terms' was clearly evident in the differing reactions of the international community to the tragedies that unfolded in Somalia and Rwanda, on the one hand, and in Bosnia, on the other. Support for dispatching a UN military force to the killing fields of Somalia and Rwanda generated little interest in an international community obsessed with Yugoslavia. Had it not been for the few courageous NGOs, such as the Red Cross and Médecins Sans Frontières, who kept their flags flying in Mogadishu, the world would have completely ignored the plight of the Somali people.

It is a grave error to describe the genocide in Rwanda and the senseless killings in Somalia as mere 'ethnic conflict'. Clans do not generate conflicts and destruction. It is the politicization of clan and ethnic relations that accentuates conflict and destruction. This is exactly what happened in Somalia and Rwanda. Most of the warlords in Liberia and Somalia had little claim to legitimacy of any sort, even among their own clans. They were men who manipulated their clan and ethnic links and their access to arms in order to recruit marginalized youth to fight the former regimes, and to support their struggle for power after the regimes collapsed. They managed to consolidate their political authority, but only after sending millions of innocent people to their deaths and instilling a fear of renewed conflict in the hearts of their people.

Similarly, systematic mass extermination of 800,000 Tutsis was an attempt by the Hutu extremists, specifically the presidential guards and their leader Juvenal Habyarimana, to hold on to power. They attempted to suffocate the demand for multiparty democracy coming from the country's democratic movement, made up of both Hutu and Tutsi people. Within a few hours of the shooting down of Habyarimana's plane, widely seen by European officials as an act carried out by the presidential guards themselves as the pretext for the slaughter, Hutu extremists carried out the systematic 'ethnic cleansing' of Tutsis.

Efforts at resolving conflicts, rebuilding societies and working to prevent future deadly strife in Africa must be informed by an understanding of their historical context, with the aim of addressing the underlying structural causes. While identity affiliations have always existed, the colonial heritage of Africa is responsible for shaping vastly inequitable relations between identity groups, and thereby entrenching structural injustice. The genocide in Rwanda is an excellent reminder of the need to address the structural roots of conflict (Uvin, 1997: 91–115). It is clear that the primary cause for conflict is the absence of justice. Resolving conflicts, securing lasting agreements, and building peace must be done in such a way as to address fundamental issues of democracy, equal justice, equal opportunity to benefit from development, and the rule of law.

Africa's Dismal Record in Conflict Resolution

Africa has lacked the necessary commitment and organized effort required to resolve conflicts. The glaring lack of continental and subregional institutional mechanisms and the absence of a common security infrastructure make prevention and resolution of conflicts difficult tasks. Inadequate human and material resources – prerequisites for timely intervention in conflict – and no established approaches to security issues are factors that further bedevil efforts to secure peace.

Past attempts have tended to ignore the root causes of conflict, and consequently have achieved little success in bringing sustained peace. Realpolitik-based negotiation strategies have tended to produce processes of exclusion that, rather than shift parties from entrenched positions, instead reward powerful groups. Resulting agreements have often served to further polarize antagonists – as in Angola, for example. Parties to conflict have rarely developed far-reaching, alternative strategies – for example, peace-building strategies that aim to include civil society in the process, thereby ensuring ownership of outcomes and potentially better chances of sustaining peace.

The role of international interests, notwithstanding the end of the Cold War, cannot be ignored. In the era of globalization, it is no longer only superpower interests in war and peace that must be considered in any transformation strategy. Business – such as the buying and selling of diamonds and other natural and mineral resources – can fuel war, and even inadvertently become a new cause.[1]

At the intergovernmental level, the Organization of African Unity (OAU) is, morally and practically, bankrupt. It is incapable of providing effective leadership for the resolution and prevention of deadly conflict in Africa (M'buyinga, 1982). The Commission for Mediation, Conciliation and Arbitration remained largely inactive through much of the 1970s and 1980s, a period when the continent literally bled to death.

The OAU's outdated principle of non-interference in the internal affairs of member states and the acceptance of colonial borders as sacrosanct has made it irrelevant in the eyes of most African peoples. The OAU's relationship with the communist regime in Ethiopia is illustrative. In the face of an international outcry over the resettlement and villagization policies of the Ethiopian government and its handling of the 1984 famine, the OAU did not once condemn brutal acts of forced displacement. Nor did it offer its good offices to mediate the conflict between guerrilla forces and the government. So long as Colonel Mengistu continued to train and support anti-colonial and anti-apartheid forces from Zimbabwe, Namibia and South Africa, he was held in high regard by the OAU and the majority of member governments. The forced resettlement of peasants and nationalization of property were considered internal Ethiopian matters with which the OAU should not meddle.

Similarly, during the Rwandan and Somali conflicts in the early 1990s, the OAU passively watched the two countries descend into anarchy, genocide, looting and self-destruction. Even after more than two years of Somali turmoil, the OAU had made no significant statement to the international community about humanitarian needs, national reconciliation processes or peacekeeping in Somalia. No delegation of respected African elders had been dispatched to resume dialogue between conflicting factions. Only two governments, Ethiopia and Eritrea, took an active role, dispatching delegations to Mogadishu during the height of the civil war and facilitating the January and March 1993 talks on national reconciliation.[2]

In the wake of the Rwandan and Somali debacles and widespread public criticism, the OAU finally decided to establish a Mechanism for Conflict Prevention, Management and Resolution during its annual meeting in June 1993 (Organization of African Unity, 1992). In 1996, a Conflict Management Centre was established in the OAU Secretariat to develop and sustain this capability. The primary objective of the Centre is to anticipate and prevent conflicts. The Centre, with its electronic communication and situation room, will exist as long as donor funding continues to flow. No attempt has been made to anchor conflict-prevention capability at the national level or to enlist the participation of non-governmental bodies, civil society groups, universities or human rights organizations.

As in the past, current OAU strategies are not fully exploiting or developing the leadership potential available at sub-state and regional levels. To date, the organization has not explored the merits of peace proposals initiated by local emissaries equipped with innovative and well-thought-out approaches to conflict resolution. The contributions of indigenous civil society institutions, such as the Church, women's organizations, intellectuals and African universities, are also ignored. Even the hastily put together African Women's Committee on Peace and Development has only a limited role to play in OAU's peace initiatives, being expected to function as an Advisory Body to the Secretary-General of the OAU (Organization of African Unity, 1998: 23). Instead, the OAU has relied on Western military advisors, who play a key role in shaping the work of the Centre.

Box 7.1 Women as peacemakers: a case from Mali

In Mali, the National Women's Movement for Securing Peace and National Unity (MNF–PUN) used grassroots approaches for building peace, which went beyond traditional meetings between military officers, high-level politicians and diplomats. Working at the local level, MNF–PUN played a key role in bringing the warring parties in Mali together, with the eventual result being the 1991 National Pact. In their efforts, the women worked to humanize the conflict by bringing the victims into focus and acting as mediators. Currently, MNF–PUN's members are working to defuse tensions among various ethnic groups, in particular encouraging other local women to take a proactive role in conflict resolution.

Source: cited in Mazurana and McKay, 1999.

The failure of the OAU to project any vision has encouraged a situation whereby particular governments have tended to monopolize attempts to resolve conflicts in Africa; few others have been involved in peace efforts. Furthermore, most peace efforts by governments have not been sufficiently informed about the effects of war on the continent. Such information could help to advance discussion beyond the 'just causes' arguments espoused with vigour by various factions, directing their attention, and perhaps more importantly that of the public, to the consequences of war and the need for non-military solutions to outstanding political problems. The fact that war is immensely profitable for many remains a stark challenge.

Angola and Sierra Leone clearly illustrate the problem. Despite international condemnation of the atrocities committed by Sierra Leone's Revolutionary United Front (RUF), Presidents Charles Taylor of Liberia and Bless Campoure of Burkina Faso are actively involved in fuelling the violence in Sierra Leone (Sesay, 1996: 35–52). The two leaders and several businessmen close to them, in close collaboration with RUF's leaders, are profiting from the control of the diamond trade. In the case of Angola, for example, the son of the late French president François Mitterrand, Jean-Christophe Mitterrand, was arrested in January 2001 on suspicion of fostering arms deals in Angola despite an international embargo. As in Sierra Leone, business interests are prolonging the war in Angola.[3]

Finally, past attempts by the OAU to resolve conflict have taken no account of the gender dimension of conflict and its resolution. Conflict affects men and women differently (Dirasse, 1995). Men predominate among armies and militias, and as civilians are often targeted for attack, while women form the majority (60–80 per cent) of the millions of internally displaced and refugee populations resulting from armed conflict and its aftermath. In the absence of men, women bear the burden of maintaining their families under situations of physical insecurity, vulnerable to looting and asset seizure (ILO, 1997: 16–19). Both men and women experience trauma as a result of violence, flight and bereavement, but often in different ways. Women also experience specific trauma resulting from the pervasive war act of sexual violence (Nduna and Goodyear, 1997; Human Rights Watch/Africa, 1996).

Amid such seemingly insurmountable paralysis, Nigeria under President Olesegun Obasanjo, and South Africa under Thabo Mbeki, have tried to pressure the OAU to become more proactive in conflict prevention and resolution efforts (Le Pere et al., 1999: 3–8). Both governments have been very active in a number of initiatives. The Lusaka Peace Accord to end the Angolan civil war was brokered by South Africa's foreign minister,

Nkosazana Dlamini-Zuma, while Nigeria's leadership in the Economic Community Monitoring Organization (ECOMOG) is well known. Both countries were also instrumental in the recent signing of a US-brokered peace agreement between Ethiopia and Eritrea. Nigeria- and South Africa-led initiatives could provide the necessary impetus for an overhaul and renewal of the OAU, SADC, and the Economic Community of West African States (ECOWAS) security structures. This will only come about if these countries continue to prioritize such activities and work to strengthen institutional capacity for proactive peace building and conflict prevention.

Most importantly, perhaps, civil society must have a central, meaningful role in the efforts to build peace and prevent future strife. Governmental, regional and international initiatives will be far more successful if they incorporate the valuable foundation-building work taking place within civil society. The inclusion of civil society groups in all aspects of conflict resolution and recovery is critical.

In this regard, traditional African approaches to conflict resolution cannot be ignored. The summary report of the 1999 All-Africa Conference on African Principles of Conflict Resolution and Reconciliation emphasizes that where agreements break down and hostilities repeatedly resume it is necessary 'to deploy methods that can penetrate the very foundation of relationships among the people, within their own locale, in a manner they can directly relate with'.[4] This often involves making use of traditional mechanisms of conflict resolution, something civil society is more likely to be in touch with. Those working to establish African solutions to African problems would be well advised to take note of the important work being done to revive African traditional methods of conflict resolution and peace building – for example, the Network for the Promotion of African Principles of Conflict Resolution and Reconciliation (REPARCOR). Such efforts illustrate the growing awareness that wisdom lies in many traditions. Africa's revival will require re-establishing certain traditions, while constructing new ones from the old that can thrive in the era of globalization.

The Role of the International Community: Partners in Crime?

With the end of the Cold War, the Western powers simply abandoned the African autocrats who once served them as reliable allies. The departure of the cold warriors and a significant erosion in the living standards of the majority of Africans provided the impetus for the growth of popular resistance and a challenge to the authority of decaying regimes. While some autocratic leaders, sensing their vulnerabilities, quickly embraced multiparty elections, others decided to hold on to power in the hope of weathering the political storm that eventually engulfed them. In extreme cases, such as Somalia and Liberia, Cold War dinosaurs gave way to warlords, bringing their own version of anarchy and self-destruction.

The United Nations, which could have provided the lead in conflict prevention in many of these crisis-ridden countries, has repeatedly failed to respond in a timely fashion. This is largely due to the unwillingness of some Security Council members to intervene, citing issues of sovereignty and the danger of operating in conflict-ridden African countries. When the Security Council finally approved an emergency airlift of food and the deployment of 500 UN troops in late July 1992, the secretary-general, Boutros Boutros Ghali, who personally pressed the council for urgent action, implied that the world's failure to respond to Somalia's plight was rooted in racism.[5]

Indifference towards African conflicts went hand in hand with the failure of the United Nations to intervene expeditiously and effectively in crisis spots by failing to commit the needed resources. In Rwanda, for example, the genocide occurred as a result of the decision by the United Nations to withdraw its peacekeeping forces, against the advice of the head of the UN forces in the country. In a cable sent to UN headquarters on 11 January 1994 (three months before the genocide), General Dallaire, head of the UN Mission, transmitted to his superiors in New York a detailed plan for the genocide prepared by individuals very close to the government. The UN peacekeeping office in New York, which was then headed by the current secretary-general, Kofi Annan, conveniently ignored his warnings.[6] In April 1994, following the killing of ten Belgian soldiers serving with the UN Mission in Rwanda (UNAMIR), the force was reduced to a small staff of 270 just when the genocide of Tutsi and moderate Hutu was taking place (Woodhouse, 1996: 130). Apologies by President Clinton and UN Secretary-General Kofi Annan two years after the genocide were wholly inadequate for both the victims and their surviving relatives (Aronoff, 1998: A25).

Many Western governments, that of the United States in particular, remain uncommitted to sending their soldiers to die in Africa. At the same time, they are somehow willing participants in peacekeeping operations in places like Bosnia and Kosovo that are considered strategically important. Though it is never said publicly, the implicit message is that deaths of Western soldiers in the defence of white civilian lives in Europe can be justified, which is not the case with African conflicts. Africa's low position on the agenda of the great powers explains both Western reluctance and the resulting pressure on African governments to find 'African solutions for African problems' through subregional peacekeeping. Hence, the responsibility for restoring order in Liberia, Sierra Leone and the Democratic Republic of the Congo (DRC) has been left to ill-equipped and ill-prepared regional organizations, such as ECOWAS and SADC. Regional powers like Nigeria and South Africa are expected to take a more proactive role in organizing subregional peacekeeping operations (Spence, 2000: 142). However, regional solutions can be hindered by regional politics, as is the case in the DRC's and ECOMOG's intervention in the Liberian civil war.

When the United Nations undertakes peacekeeping operations, such initiatives should largely involve troops from the continent in which they are deployed. Advice, training in peacekeeping techniques, and a degree of logistical support has been forthcoming from Western governments, but the direct involvement of troops and a commitment to appropriate the necessary funds have been ruled out. The one exception has been the dispatching of a contingent of British troops to Sierra Leone. Their presence has been effective, not only in saving lives, but also in creating the conditions for negotiation between the warring factions.

Key Principles for Resolving and Preventing Conflict in Africa

If sustained peace is the goal, conflict resolution in Africa must move beyond military response, and focus on addressing the root causes of conflict. At the most fundamental level, the absence of justice is frequently the principal reason for the absence of peace. Ethnic discrimination, denial of basic rights, extreme economic inequality and other manifestations of injustice are forms of 'structural' violence, according to peace theorist Johan Galtung. Structural violence plants the seeds of physical violence and, in many cases, deadly conflict.

An examination of African civil wars shows that the gross economic and political inequalities that prevail in many African countries must be addressed if the territorial integrity of those countries is to be preserved. For example, despite the internationally negotiated settlement of their civil wars, Angola and Sierra Leone continue to struggle. A negotiated settlement does not necessarily bode well for a lasting peace if it fails to address the substantive causes of violence.

The primary objective of external and local efforts to prevent and resolve African crises should therefore be the *establishment of peace with justice*. Without this, efforts to resolve conflicts and sustainably rebuild societies are meaningless. In contrast to the realpolitik conflict-management approaches that have generally served to obstruct Africa's transformation, a bottom-up approach is offered. Among the issues that require immediate attention are the following:

Seeking political solutions

Any effort to build and sustain peace will depend upon the active participation of civil society. At the same time, all groups or parties that can affect the peace must be included in the process. Marginalizing any one group means marginalizing their cause. In many African cultures where pride and honour are highly cherished properties, humiliating one group kills any prospect for permanent peace in the country. In Somalia, for example, the decision by the United Nations Operation in Somalia (UNOSOM) officials and the USA to isolate General Farah Aidid probably did more harm to the population than the political cost of including him in the peace process.

Analysis and experience from other conflict-ridden parts of the world provide examples of a wide range of non-military means for resolving conflicts. These include promoting confidence-building measures; establishing humanitarian norms and codes of conduct; establishing trust through cooperation on shared development problems and projects; and identifying specific mechanisms for sustaining peace initiatives. These options can only exist in a democratic environment. Thus the bond between peace and democracy must be strengthened.

Empowering civil society

Leaders like Bare in Somalia, Mobutu in the former Zaïre, and Mengistu in Ethiopia succeeded in driving popular forces underground, squandering national resources, and suffocating progressive organizations – not difficult, given the weakness, marginalization and fragmentation of civil society. Serious attempts to find indigenous forms of governance that present a viable alternative to warlords will need to take into account the clan and community leaderships that represent the main centres of power. Attention should also be given to intellectuals and other influential groups who might be able to contribute to the revival of civil society. The full participation of popular organizations and grassroots movements at all levels will also be necessary. The empowerment of civil society should be a top priority for the international community in seeking to bring peace to countries such as Sierra Leone and Angola. Unfortunately the opposite is sometimes done – consider USAID's withdrawal of support from Liberia to punish Taylor, despite the negative effect such an action would have on Liberian civil society.

Redressing gender disparities

The burden of living in and rebuilding war-torn societies often falls on women and girls whose male relatives are fighting indefinitely in wars, or have been killed in battle. Once the conflict ends, many women find that they have no access to the land or property left behind by male members of the family, due to discriminatory customary laws. Consequently, women often have no land on which to grow food to feed their families. Worse, they may even be rendered homeless, as they no longer have any claim to the property left behind by their husbands or fathers. These important issues must be addressed in post-conflict rebuilding efforts.

Box 7.2 Rwanda's matrimonial regimes and succession law

In March 2000, the Rwandan National Assembly passed the Matrimonial Regimes, Liberties and Succession law to empower women and girls to inherit land and own property. The law is the first of its kind in Rwanda's history, allowing women to become heads of the family. The law comes in the wake of various international and national campaigns to adopt gender-sensitive legislation in war-torn countries. Women and girl children became the focus of attention after the genocide in Rwanda, as they constituted a large majority of returnees and orphans.

Source: cited in *Habitat Debate*, vol. 6, no. 2 (2000) and adapted from *The East African*, 10–16 April 2000.

Rehabilitation of the economy

The task of sustaining peace in post-conflict societies must go hand in hand with human development and ecological restoration. In many cases, the traditional economy has been replaced by one based on relief supplies. Basic institutions essential to modern economy and society have virtually disappeared. There is no waged income, no financial structure, no formal administration, and little access to essential services. Most of the trained individuals required to run the institutions of modern society have disappeared or fled the country. This drain of skilled and educated people must somehow be reversed.

Any political solution to the crisis in conflict-ridden African countries must be accompanied by an economic development plan that offers employment alternatives for combatants. In the absence of real changes in people's lives, zero-sum mentalities will prevail instead of moderation, thus undermining the chances of peace. Therefore, people must see the benefit of peace in an improved standard of living, better education and housing, and access to health and basic food items. Otherwise society will begin to wonder what peace is for, if not to improve living standards.

Improving the quality of governance

Civil and political liberties are also linked to improved governance, less corruption, and more effective public spending and delivery of government services. They also constitute in themselves a fundamental aspect of well-being. Poor governance – especially corruption, bureaucratic harassment and a lack of checks and balances – harms growth and the everyday lives of the poor. It allows the vested interests of an economic elite to influence unduly, or even to buy, the policies, regulations and laws of the state. The social costs are enormous. Allowing people to influence decisions that affect their lives is vital for increasing transparency, the necessary bulwark against corruption and bureaucratic abuse. It also counters efforts by economic elites to manipulate state policies for their narrow advantage. The engagement of civil society in fair and transparent decision-making in partnership with reformers in the executive, the legislature, the judiciary and the private sector can make the difference between a well-governed and a misgoverned state, between a stagnant and a thriving society.

The greatest need is for capacity building in the area of national and local governance. In the post-crisis reconstruction of states, sectors of the international community are preoccupied with democratic governance – a condition that they believe is met through free and fair elections. Much less emphasis is placed on efficient and effective governance. Yet without viable systems, the principles of democracy cannot be 'operationalized'. It is hard to imagine how Laurent Kabila could have held elections within months of taking power in the Democratic Republic of the Congo, as expected by the United States, when the country's administrative and logistical capacity to conduct elections was virtually nonexistent.

Civilian control of the military

The military obviously plays a central role in the conduct of wars. But it can also play an important role in post-war peace-building processes in terms of democratization, state formation and nation building. In order to fulfil this function, the military must agree to the demilitarization of politics, including the establishment of civilian control and accountability to civil society (Durotoye and Griffiths, 1997: 133–60). In return, societies often need to rely on the military to provide temporary support to the police in maintaining law and order. Indeed, the presence of security institutions is a necessary, but not sufficient, condition for peace building to take place.

Building local knowledge and capacity for conflict prevention

The international community should abandon the delusion that it is responsible for resolving crisis and managing conflict in African countries. For better or worse, peacemaking and peace building are not sustainable unless locals shape the form and content of the processes. A wide cross-section of society must participate, including civil servants, scholars, women's organizations, labour unions, and activists in non-governmental organizations. This process should be distinguished, however, from the current international practice of simply training Africans to carry out their own military solutions. Needless to say, the new policy should not involve abandoning African people to the risk of genocide where there is no appropriate African readiness to respond.

Building local capacity for conflict prevention and resolution

The key to sustaining peace in Africa is localization of the means for conflict resolution. Neither the OAU nor far-away central government and international donors is in a position to measure or anticipate potential conflicts in distant localities. Local government agencies or nongovernmental agencies close to a conflict area may recognize signs of trouble, but are unlikely to possess the skills or resources required to pre-empt a potential conflagration. They often rely on directives and support from an equally ill-equipped national government. Instituting confidence-building mechanisms among the protagonists in such cases can be the first line of defence against potentially deadly civil strife and ethnic conflict. This requires the training of local government officials to respond well in advance of a crisis, the establishment of early warning systems, and involving civil society in the monitoring system.

Efforts to build local, national and subregional efficiency in preventing conflict must begin with the identification of structural risk factors. It is important to understand the causes of conflict, which might include economic stagnation, inequitable distribution of resources, undemocratic political system, weak social structure, suppression of minority rights, flows of refugees, ethnic tensions, religious and cultural intolerance, and the proliferation of weapons. Such understanding will establish better conditions for early actions and measures to address the root causes of armed conflicts (Swedish Ministry of Foreign Affairs, 1999: 13).

A first step is to create awareness through research and public education. A systematic build-up of knowledge, preparedness to act in response to early signals of nascent crisis, and improved coordination between various policy areas are central elements of a conflict prevention strategy. Such a stragegy must support local negotiation efforts and problem-solving approaches, rather than simply prescribing outcomes based on Western experience. Teaching people to build bridges is more useful than building bridges for them. A well-informed and involved public is essential for the establishment of a durable and just peace. It is hard to understand how ordinary Hutus, who shared birthdays and weddings with their Tutsi neighbours, could turn around and systematically slaughter them after listening to anti-Tutsi propaganda transmitted by radio. A well-informed Hutu population would have rejected the call to arms ordered by the extremist group.

Efforts should be directed towards strengthening the capacity of government and civil society through the transfer of skills and knowledge. Research on the identification of structural risk factors should focus on the following aspects of conflict resolution:

- *Ethnicity* Examination of the surge in subnational identities and religious loyalties. The focus here should be on examining local and national policy decisions that result in the exclusion of ethnic groups. For example, local government decisions regarding grazing rights might favour one ethnic group over the other, and could lead to deadly conflict.
- *Democratization* This looks beyond the immediate clashes and assesses long-term measures for establishing stability. Whereas democracy can be a method of redressing conflict in Africa, the institutions associated with democracy can also ignite inter-ethnic violence, with the potential to spill over and escalate into war unless genuine channels are provided for opening up the political process and allowing access to decision-makers.
- *Economic development* Tension can arise between democracy and the demands of economic revitalization. Economic adjustment, although necessary, can trigger strikes and civil unrest. Economic liberalization lacks a procedure for conflict resolution.
- *Equitable use of natural resources* Access to resources such as water and grazing could breed conflict over the means used to change human practice and achieve environmental balance. Conflict over grazing and watering rights in one corner of a country could quickly escalate to engulf the whole society.

From Bullet to Ballot: Post-conflict Reconstruction

The building of peace and reconstruction have assumed centre stage in the development policies of Western bilateral donors and multilateral organizations. The World Bank, for example, defines the process in this way:

> Post-conflict reconstruction supports the transition from conflict to peace in an affected country through the rebuilding of the socio-economic framework of the society. Reconstruction is the basic building block for establishing the enabling conditions for a functioning peacetime society in the framework of governance and rule of law. (World Bank, 1998: 14)

Reconstruction, according to the World Bank, does not refer only to the reconstruction of physical infrastructure. Conflict management and reconciliation are threads that must run through this framework to achieve a sustainable result.

The transition from war to sustainable peace is multifaceted and the outcome is uncertain and varies from place to place. This is because the nature of war determines the nature of peace; the solutions proposed must directly address the factors that produced and sustained the conflict (World Bank and Carter Centre, 1997: 4).

The period following the initial cessation of hostilities is particularly challenging. Establishing a functioning civil administration, guaranteeing security to returnees and displaced persons, and providing basic food and shelter are daunting tasks. How these are handled will shape the tempo and efficacy of reconstruction, demobilization, reintegration and peace-building efforts. But to treat the issues of humanitarian assistance, reintegration and reconciliation as activities autonomous from the important task of enhancing human rights and building a participatory system of government is mistaken and dangerous.

Demobilization and ensuring comprehensive disarmament

Demobilization requires a complete cessation of hostilities through a monitored cease-fire agreement, the victory of one of the parties, or the agreement of the warring parties that they can no longer meet their objectives with military means. Whatever the impetus for the cessation of hostilities, however, the outcome is always uncertain and varies from country to country.

In Ethiopia, for example, the demobilization of troops in 1991 was a very complicated exercise and the political and economic situation allowed little time for careful preparation. As an advisor to the Transitional

Government at the time, I took the view that the rapid demobilization of well over half a million troops without a massive infusion of donor funds would lead to anarchy and chaos. After the fall of the Mengistu regime in May 1991, many of the soldiers were dispersed in disarray. Some fled to neighbouring countries, often taking their weapons with them. After a short period of preparation, in which former military training centres were turned into assembly points, the Transitional Government of Ethiopia called for demobilization. Within two months, the registration of all those that reported was completed. An additional 50,000 soldiers demobilized themselves and returned to their communities without a 'package', with or without their weapons.

The demobilization in Eritrea, on the other hand, had a different dynamic. Once the Eritrean People's Liberation Front (EPLF) had defeated the Ethiopian (Dergue) army, many of the fighters wanted to begin earning a living immediately. Demonstrations against the government's call for fighters to continue to work without pay after the referendum in May 1993 pushed the leadership to speed up the demobilization. On the other hand, most of the fighters had been in the EPLF for so long that they saw little prospect for themselves outside its structure. The process of reintegration took a long time.

Box 7.3 Demobilization: the Ugandan experience

The Ugandan government's demobilization programme focused on the reallocation of public expenditure from military interests in favour of social sectors. The programme was promoted by a public expenditure review in 1992 that revealed that defence spending amounted to about 40 per cent of the annual budget, crowding out investment in the social sectors. The government requested the World Bank to become the lead agency to mobilize resources for such a programme. The Bank restructured an ongoing International Development Association credit programme to include a component for assisting the socioeconomic reintegration of demobilized soldiers and their dependants into productive civilian life. The programme was targeted at about 50,000 veterans and their dependants (representing about a 50 per cent reduction in the force) over a three-year period.

The programme provided veterans with a fresh set of civilian clothing; transportation to their home districts; a transitional safety net of cash and in-kind payments (e.g. agricultural tools, building materials) over a six-month readjustment period; job training; and enhanced health benefits, especially for the disabled and chronically ill. Primary-school fees were also paid for veterans' children for one year. The average cost of this package was about $1,000 per veteran.

Under the programme, about 33,000 veterans and more than 100,000 dependants have been successfully integrated into their home communities. About $35 million was mobilized through a Bank-coordinated multi-donor effort to achieve this result. As a direct result of the programme, over the 1992–94 period defence expenditure was reduced from 38 per cent to 22 per cent of overall recurrent expenditure, making room for a substantial increase in social expenditures.

Source: World Bank, 1995: 61–3.

Without effective and comprehensive disarmament, many post-conflict countries in Africa would soon return to their grim routine of brutal warfare, looting and self-destruction. The intensity and scale of the carnage witnessed in such places as Rwanda, Liberia and Somalia during the past decade are closely related to the availability of military technology. An AK-47 rifle or a grenade launcher in the hands of a militia member can do more harm in a split second than a dozen villagers, armed with bows and arrows, can achieve in a month of warfare.

The cost of incomplete and half-baked disarmament was clearly evident in Somalia, following the United States-led 'Operation Restore Hope' in 1992. The confrontation between the US forces and one of the warlords, General Farrah Aidid, was in large part a consequence of the disarmament policy pursued by the American commanders who preceded the UN team. On the one hand, the Americans insisted that disarming Somalia's factional militias, which had waged war since the fall of dictator Mohammed Said Barre in January 1991, was never part of their primary mission. On the other hand, they took steps to remove visible heavy weapons from the capital in advance of the arrival of UN forces. This action raised expectations among Somalis that the Americans would totally disarm the warlords and militias before turning control over to the UN. But the warlords were never fully disarmed; they simply moved their heavy equipment outside the famine zone where US troops would be operating. It was these arsenals that the warlords later used to wage war against UN forces (Richburg, 1993: 9–10). The killing of twenty-five Pakistani peacekeepers on 6 June 1993 and eighteen Americans in October 1993 finally ended US involvement in Somalia. America's reluctance to send US troops to Rwanda, Sierra Leone and the DRC was partly influenced by the experience in Somalia (Woodhouse, 1996: 129).

Even if disarmament does not lead to a lasting peace, it can reduce the degree of human carnage. Any disarmament or political agreement will rest upon not only the restoration of civilian administration but also the emergence of economic alternatives for the thousands of militia members conditioned to survive by force. Such considerations must underpin the ongoing transition from war to peace. Unfortunately, the key Western governments who are preaching about building peace are the same ones that are engaged in rearming and training defence forces in the so-called post-conflict countries such as Ethiopia, Eritrea and Mozambique. A recent exposé by the *Washington Post* on the role of US special forces in Africa flies in the face of Washington's well-publicized and high-profile peace-building and democratic initiatives in the continent.

The reintegration of refugees, displaced persons and ex-combatants

Of fundamental importance in building peace is the demobilization and absorption into productive activities of the armed youth that continue to constitute a major threat to security and to the development of civil society. Providing profitable alternatives to violence, addressing the special needs of child soldiers and accommodating other vulnerable groups, such as the internally displaced, refugees and widows, are critical dimensions of demobilization and reintegration (Kingma, 1997).

Efforts to extend relief and humanitarian assistance to refugees, the internally displaced and newly demobilized soldiers must be a step towards development, and must be delivered in ways that promote, rather than compromise, long-term development objectives. Successful integration and rehabilitation require a mix of activities – some take immediate effect while others are long-term actions that need to evolve smoothly into development efforts.

Needless to say, demobilization and reintegration are complex and costly undertakings. Countries emerging out of conflict, lacking the financial means and an effective institutional base, are not in a position to undertake the massive task of rehabilitation and reconstruction on their own. Such an undertaking requires well-planned and well-coordinated donor intervention with the aim of strengthening key institutions of civil society, and for the state to undertake long-term reconstruction, development and peace-building.

Reconstruction and rehabilitation

Reconstruction and rehabilitation should be undertaken as integral components of a broad peace-building and development strategy. In many countries emerging out of years of war, much of the pre-war infrastructure and employment no longer exists. The effect of war can be measured not only by its cost in human lives, but in terms of the livelihoods of tens of thousands of urban workers and millions of peasant farmers in the rural areas. Helping people and economies to get back on their feet after conflict is vital for building long-term peace. The survival of any disarmament or peace agreement will rest upon the availability of economic alternatives for the thousands of militia members conditioned to survive by force. This entails targeted interventions with immediate impact on the lives of ex-combatants and returnees: for example, access to land, to credit, to livestock, and to alternative sources of income.

Post-war rebuilding is an extremely slow, costly and uncertain process. Efforts to restore adequate shelter, water and basic infrastructure to innumerable ruined cities and the abandoned countryside will take decades. Reconstruction should thus have both an urban and a rural dimension. Most rural residents can be helped to stay in their own villages and to earn an income by participating in the rehabilitation and reconstruction of infrastructure. The aim of such a project would be to identify food-assisted labour-intensive works which will generate short-term and medium-term employment to the unemployed. Appropriate measures might include the following:

- *Addressing unemployment* through well-designed public works programmes to upgrade the physical infrastructure in both rural and urban areas. In the rural areas, such activities would include building secondary roads, irrigation channels, small dams and reservoirs, expanding clean water supplies and introducing rural electrification and conservation work (Webb et al., 1991b). In addition, public works programmes should provide minimum packages for those who want to resume farming – the restocking of cattle herds and the provision of seeds and tools. In the urban areas, public works projects should focus on the rehabilitation of existing urban infrastructure (roads, schools, public buildings, etc.) in order to reverse the physical/infrastructural decay of the major towns. The construction of well-designed market stalls should be given priority to assist informal-sector entrepreneurs for a nominal fee.
- *Expanding and initiating income-generating activities* in the informal sector. Ways must be found for the unemployed to obtain materials, training and credit to start up businesses. People must be redeployed to assist in the resettlement of refugees and displaced persons until they begin to care for themselves. For example, the International Labour Organization

(ILO) is currently implementing a multidisciplinary action programme on the development of skills and entrepreneurship in those countries emerging from armed conflict. Vocational training is available through a variety of local providers, including NGOs, religious groups and artisans. Development of small enterprises is organized through local economic development agencies, which assist with business support services. In Mozambique, the ILO provided skills training for 9,000 ex-combatants, who, on completion of the training, were given toolkits to start their own businesses. More than 70 per cent of those trained became employable and more than 600 micro-enterprises were created, resulting in more than 2,000 new jobs (ILO, 1997: 19).
- *Youth capacity building* Many young men and boys between the ages of 12 and 25 have few skills other than those necessary for combat. The 'vacuum' created in their lives when conflict ends must be filled immediately. The alternative is unemployment, hunger, disease and a probable return to anti-social behaviour (United Nations, 1996).

Apart from providing gainful employment, these measures contribute directly to building confidence among the population. Each must be initiated in consultation with local communities to ensure they develop in culturally appropriate ways.

Establishing and strengthening civil and political administration

Reconstruction programmes are often very ambitious and tend to disregard the relative incapacity of government and of national NGOs, and the fact that the private sector barely exists. In other circumstances, however, implementing agencies manifest an inability to utilize available institutional resources efficiently and effectively. This is especially true in the case of nationally executed programmes. In many cases, it is becoming apparent that governments simply do not have the capacity to absorb external project financing on a big scale. This can be due to a number of factors (Moreno, 2000: 19–20):

- Collapse of government institutions or a serious decline in their administrative capacity.
- Lack or erosion of human resources.
- An environment that does not enable the participation of other potential partners (civil society) or that suffers from the relative inexperience of NGOs.
- Lack of transparency and accountability of institutions and weak administrative capacities and systems.

- Problems in establishing coherent inter-institutional and inter-sectoral linkages.
- Poor definition of strategic priorities, resulting in inadequate decisions regarding investments that have little or no impact on the transition process.

The case of oil-rich Angola demonstrates the impact of poor capacity on effective demobilization and reintegration efforts. It has not been possible to ascribe a central role to the government in economic reconstruction. Angola still lacks the rudimentary civil administration required to restore economic capacity and to coordinate and implement reconstruction and peace-building projects. The absence of effective local nongovernmental organizations working on the ground further compounds the problem.

Nationally executed projects require not only effective and committed government but also a strong and active civil society. It is desirable to define manageable sets of priority actions and identify the training needs of the various partners involved in the implementation of the programmes. The sustainability of the programme depends on a strong sense of government ownership and leadership. Existing structures need to be strengthened and new ones created. Community participation must be encouraged and supported. Finally, an integrated approach should be adopted, incorporating mechanisms and sectoral working groups that can engage the relevant institutions in an active and organic capacity.

Decentralization of authority to increase the participation of civil society and community groups not only increases responsiveness; it can also deepen community ownership of the process of rebuilding after the war. Decentralization also relieves government of the burden of being spread too thinly, allowing it to focus instead on a few critical areas.

Establishing a regional security structure

The reluctance of the West to intervene in African conflict spots, and the growing use of mercenary forces by contending parties to gain the upper hand on the battle front, have given way to a number of subregional initiatives to prevent conflicts in Africa. While some of these initiatives operate under existing subregional architectures, such as ECOWAS, IGAD and SADC, others are being taken by countries who want to prevent neighbouring conflicts from engulfing them. The Kampala conference on Security, Stability, Development and Cooperation in Africa (CSSDCA), which emerged from the African Leadership Forum of 1991, also endorsed African solutions to African conflicts (African Leadership Forum, 1991).

Among regional initiatives taken in the early 1990s have been the efforts of ECOWAS in the conflict in Sierra Leone and Liberia. Although ECOMOG, largely staffed and led by Nigeria, was accused of committing atrocities due to the inexperience and poor training of its soldiers, it was largely credited for ending the Liberian civil war. Moreover, these actions set the stage for eventual UN intervention in the Sierra Leone conflict. Without Nigeria's leadership, there would be no ECOMOG, as Nigeria largely paid for the operations, at great cost to its economy (Sesay, 1996: 47).

In the Horn of Africa, Prime Minister Melese Zenawi of Ethiopia and President Issayas Afewerki of Eritrea tried to build a subregional security structure by transforming IGAD to take on a regional security dimension. Initially, much effort went into resolving the internal crisis in both Sudan and Somalia, long before the involvement of UNISOM in Somalia. Unfortunately, the refusal of the Islamic fundamentalist regime in the Sudan to accept peace overtures and the collapse of the Somali state dimmed any hope of a regional approach to conflict resolution. The sudden outbreak of war between Ethiopia and Eritrea – the key architects of the regional conflict prevention paradigm – was the straw that broke the camel's back. The fact that the leading proponents of the idea of 'African solutions for Africa's problems' descended into a war that no one expected only underscores the need for such a strategy to take root in Africa.

Despite these mainly encouraging developments, however, regional security architecture faces the same kind of problem as regional economic coordination. Subregional divisions and disunity still continue to hamper efforts to manage conflicts in the DRC, Sudan, Somalia and Sierra Leone. In the DRC, the involvement of Uganda, Rwanda, Zimbabwe and Namibia in the conflict has done little to ease tensions. In Angola, the involvement of neighbouring countries in helping UNITA break the Lusaka Peace Accord has been a critical factor in the war's continuation. In an extraordinary effort to stop the covert support that UNITA was receiving from the government of Congo Brazzaville, the government of Angola dispatched several thousand troops and fighter planes in October 1997 to overthrow the democratically elected President Pascal Lissouba. In his place, the Angolans installed former military strongman General Denis Sassou-Nguesso.

Regional security concerns should not rule out the use of economic sanctions by African states against a belligerent government or guerrilla factions. The current UN sanctions on Jonas Savimbi of UNITA are an excellent example. Since war has a negative spillover effect (economic, social, political, ecological) on neighbouring countries, it is within the rights of affected countries to put pressure on the warring factions to come to a peace agreement. Sanctions (similar to those imposed by the governments of the Great Lake region on Burundi) should be regarded as a legitimate part of regional peacekeeping strategy.

Conclusion

Much of the discussion in this chapter relates strongly to the subject of renewing and restoring democracy in Africa, discussed in Chapter 2. Support for the development of democratic institutions is particularly important from the perspective of conflict prevention. Making and consolidating peace has everything to do with the management of social and political conflicts through good governance. This encompasses the entrenching of respect for human rights and political pluralism, accommodating diversity, and strengthening the institutions of state and civil society. There is no single, simple or short-term approach to resolving crises in Africa. As stated throughout this book, the absence of justice is the principal reason for the absence of peace. Acute injustice typically gives rise to popular struggles, which are met by systematic repression.

The most effective conflict-prevention strategies in Africa are those described inappropriately as 'post-conflict peace building'. These include: socioeconomic development and the meeting of basic human developmental needs, capacity building in the area of governance, respect for human rights and political pluralism, and structural accommodation of cultural diversity. A particularly important issue in conflict prevention is how to redress massive economic inequalities. Reconciliation is impossible unless the root causes of injustice are addressed squarely. The absence of participatory government lies at the heart of many of the intra-state conflicts in Africa today. The long-term consolidation of peace requires that this situation be remedied using a participatory system of government that is not imported and that responds to the aspirations and cultural values of the people in the affected country. All members of society, without discrimination, must participate fully in political, civil, economic, social and cultural life, with a view to preventing a return to violence.

Resolution of the deeper causes of conflict, therefore, requires changes in the social and political order. This frequently requires constitutional, electoral and judicial reform, reconstruction of the police and armed forces, and payment of compensation to victims of arbitrary injustice. Constitutional innovation should not shy away from the need to grant autonomy, even secession, to groups who express the desire to form their own nation-state. However, one must recognize that democratization has the potential to produce conflict within countries in transition. One major reason for this is the inability of new institutions to manage effectively the significant growth in participatory politics and the ensuing competing claims.

Finally, the implementation of democracy, respect for human rights, and peace building will not be successful unless each is anchored in strong and effective local and national government institutions and a strong legal framework. Public officials will not be able to carry out their mandate if they are working in a context of weak government institutions and courts. It is difficult to conceive of development, peace building and democratization in the absence of a viable, accountable and active state. Equally important is the need to strengthen the organizations of civil society. The building of peace and meaningful political participation by citizens requires strong popular organizations that will enable different sectors of society to assert and fight for their particular social rights. Effective participation requires grassroots education to create more active, self-confident and competent citizens. By expanding their visions and raising their consciousness, citizens can undermine the vicious circle of mass exclusion and marginalization, and build a strong foundation for sustained peace.

Notes

1. 'Fuelling Africa's Wars', *The Economist*, 13 January 2001, pp. 44–5.
2. 'Highlights of Peace Accord Reached between 15 Somali Factions on March 27, 1993', *Humanitarian Monitor*, June 1993, p. 15.
3. 'Fuelling Africa's Wars', p. 44.
4. All-Africa Conference on African Principles of Conflict Resolution and Reconciliation, 1999: vii.
5. 'The Security Council's Unhumble Servant', *The Economist*, 8–14 August 1992, p. 31.
6. Cited in Adelman and Suhrke, 1999.

CHAPTER 8

Concluding Remarks: A Wake-up Call to Fellow Africans

The last quarter of the twentieth century brought tremendous advances in the way human beings organize production, work, trade and many other activities. Accelerating advancements in science and technology, transformations in world trade and investment regimes, and global compacts on environmental and social policies have been far reaching. These advances have been accompanied by dramatic shifts in global politics, starting with the collapse of communism in Eastern Europe and the end of the Cold War between the two superpowers. The unravelling of the Soviet system also unleashed an unprecedented demand for democracy and rule-based political systems across the globe, including in Africa. This has been complemented by a new global ethics on human rights and the environment, now widely entrenched throughout the world.

These global economic and political shifts, with their contradictory tendencies, pose a great challenge to the African continent. Africa has been ill-prepared to adjust itself simultaneously to complex global dynamics, new opportunities and the management of internal and external threats. 'Except in Africa!' is the phrase used to describe this disjuncture. Africa appears to be travelling in reverse towards anarchy and self-destruction. Even the spread of democracy, which for so long has eluded Africans, has become a negative force when introduced into an environment of abject poverty, high illiteracy, and weak state and civil society institutions. In such cases, IMF-imposed austerity measures have exacted more sacrifice from the very poor the organization claims to help. Many countries are still immersed in bloody civil conflicts, with seemingly no way out. Moreover, the global economic boom of the past decade and a half has completely bypassed Africa, and the continent has the lowest human development index of any region in the world. This situation is in stark contrast to that of the industrialized countries, which have benefited enormously from globalization, and, to a lesser extent, that of parts of East Asia and Latin America.

All the projections concerning Africa look grim and irreversible. The cover page title 'Hopeless Africa' in the 13 May 2000 issue of *The Economist* was not far from the truth. Yet the portrayal of hopelessness and despair need not become a self-fulfilling prophecy if we Africans care to do something about it instead of constantly begging the international community to come to our rescue. External assistance can become a catalyst for change only when such assistance is received to complement Africa's own plan for transformation. Such a strategy is an absolute necessity, particularly when weighed against our past history. Caring about Africa is an ancestral obligation that we cannot escape from, no matter where in the world we choose to reside.

Africa's marginal position in the new global hierarchy provides a compelling occasion to reorganize our political systems and economies, to defend Africa's sovereignty, and to strengthen the continent's capacity to become more assertive in international affairs. To bemoan and complain about the negative effects of global forces without taking the necessary counter-measures at national and regional levels will do little to ease the pain of marginalization. As the esteemed Brazilian educator Paulo Freire succinctly put it, 'the oppressors will never make change; the oppressed themselves must bring the change they desire'. In the preceding chapters, the broad process of the African Renaissance has been elaborated. A few additional pointers are in order:

Decolonizing the African mindset

Foreign aid from the West, which was supposed to lift Africa from underdevelopment and undemocratic rule, has in fact done more to keep Africa down, and to disempower her peoples. It has severely altered the African psyche, with greater impact than a century of missionary education – a testament, perhaps, to the power of money and technology. John F. Kennedy's famous inaugural address, 'Ask not what your country can do for you; ask what you can do for your country' – has been wrongly interpreted by African leaders. Their motto of leadership reads: 'Ask not what we can do collectively for our continent; ask again and again what our former colonial masters can do for us.' The beggar mentality of the elites, their almost holy worship and adulation of Europeans, no matter what their rank and level of education, and the elite's rejection of anything African – from locally produced consumer products to African doctors and professors – are all testimony to how deeply ingrained the 'dependency' mentality is. Reversing this colonial mental trap is the first and most important step towards the full emancipation of the continent. To deny the possibility of 'self-transformation' is to give credence to the widely held racist Western view that Africans are an inferior race with very little appreciation of the values of democracy and progress.

The first mark of an independent Africa is political leadership. Nobody will take Africa seriously if its leaders refuse to take responsibility for their own actions or inactions. We should be able to stand up and claim credit when we do things right and accept responsibility for our wrongdoings. *The quality of leadership in each African country matters.* Honesty can get us much closer to our dream of an African Renaissance than money. Respect for Africa comes through deeds and actions: commitment to social justice; commitment to innovation, hard work and merit based on performance; commitment to protecting our sovereignty; commitment to African unity; and commitment to promote and defend democracy and the rule of law.

Scaling up the technological ladder

We know that the technological innovations that are driving the current globalization process have completely bypassed the African continent. The only way to narrow the knowledge gap is not through begging or by asking for preferential treatment from the advanced countries, but by investing in education, and in basic research and development. Strengthening African universities and dissuading Africa's best and brightest from leaving the continent are important measures.

Becoming assertive in international negotiations

The present international trade and finance system works against the interests of Africa. This is indisputable. What Africans must do now is stop complaining about how unjust the international system is and instead become more assertive in future negotiations and fundamentally reform the current international rules that perpetuate uneven development. This will also require African leadership in the G77 and in other forums, in order to set out a solid Third World position in major areas of international negotiation.

The marginalization of African countries in international trade is due to the fact that most countries face considerable administrative, institutional and financial problems at several levels. First is the lack of ownership of the rules and provisions contained in trade agreements. In the context of the WTO, for example, many African countries feel no sense of 'ownership' mainly because they did not actively participate in their establishment. Ownership of the rules is an important element in the functioning of a rules-based system such as the WTO, where the central organization has limited enforcement power. Building among members a solid sense of ownership of such rules begins with participation in their establishment.

Second, African countries lack the capacity to engage meaningfully in the wide range of WTO issues under discussion. The Geneva-based delegations of these countries are often small and lack the personnel with technical backgrounds that are needed to participate effectively. Also, the links between WTO delegations and their governments at home are not well developed. Furthermore, the involvement of stakeholders, such as the business community and civil society, is minimal. Finally, because of the complexity of the entire system, African countries have made commitments beyond their administrative and institutional capacity. For Africa to become an effective advocate for change in global economic governance, African governments must do much more to strengthen their capacity in all the relevant specializations. This includes developing analytical, lobbying and negotiation skills, and establishing an incentive structure to retain African specialists in trade, investment and other relevant areas.

Furthermore, African countries must adopt a common stand in WTO and other multilateral negotiations. They must be prepared to put forward alternative concepts and formulations on issues of importance to them. It is essential that they try to evolve a collective or common stand on key issues such as their treatment as nations, the definition of investment, performance requirements and investment incentives, transfer of technology, financing for development, and obligations to investors.

The various recommendations presented in this book, when pulled together, may not constitute a hegemonic response to the marginalizing tendencies of globalization. But were African countries to succeed in implementing most of these suggestions, the continent would have a strong foundation from which to move forward with dignity and strength. The advantages of national and collective African strategies will be amplified even more if efforts are made by African governments to take a leading role in strengthening South–South cooperation in order to enhance the bargaining power of Third World countries, as well as expand trade and investment among themselves. Until this task is accomplished, the African Renaissance will remain a pipe dream.

References

Abdullahi An-Na'im (1995), 'Which Way, Islam: Democracy or Oppression? The Case of Sudan', in Mia Melin (ed.), *Democracy in Africa: On Whose Terms?*, Stockholm: Forum South.

Achola, P.P.W. (1990), *Implementing Educational Policies in Zambia*, World Bank Discussion Paper no. 90, Washington, DC: World Bank.

Adams, A. (1981), 'The Senegal River Valley', in J. Heyer et al., *Rural Development in Tropical Africa*, New York: St. Martin's Press.

Adelman, Howard and Astri Suhrke (eds) (1999), *Path of a Genocide: The Rwandan Crisis from Uganda to Zaïre*, Piscataway, NJ: Transactions Publishers.

Adler, Graham (1995), 'Tracking Poverty in Nairobi's Informal Settlements: Developing an Institutional Strategy', *Environment and Urbanisation*, vol. 7, no. 2, p. 88.

Africa Institute of South Africa (2000), 'The Brain Drain: Will the Outflow of Skilled People Kill the African Renaissance?', *Africa Insight*, vol. 30, no. 2, Special Issue.

Africa Institute of South Africa (1998), *Africa at a Glance 1997/8*, Pretoria: Africa Institute of South Africa, pp. 98–9.

African Leadership Forum (1991), *The Kampala Document: Towards a Conference on Security, Stability, Development and Co-operation in Africa*, Kampala, May 19–22.

Ahmed, R., and N. Rustagi (1987), 'Marketing and Price Incentives in African and Asian Countries: A Comparison', in D. Elz (ed.), *Agricultural Marketing Strategy and Price Policy*, Washington, DC: World Bank.

Ake, Claude (1988), 'Building on the Indigenous', in Swedish Ministry for Foreign Affairs, *Recovery in Africa: A Challenge For Development Co-operation in the 1990s*, Stockholm: Swedish International Development Agency.

Ake, Claude (1996), *Democracy and Development in Africa*, Washington, DC: Brookings Institution.

All-Africa Conference on African Principles of Conflict Resolution and Reconciliation (1999), Final Report, 8–12 November, p. vii.

Apiyo, Lawrence O. (1998), 'Land-grabbing and Evictions in Kenya', *Habitat Debate*, vol. 4, no. 1, pp. 18–19.

Aredo, Dejene (1990), 'The Evolution of Rural Development Policies in Ethiopia', in S. Pausewang, F. Cheru, S. Brune and E. Chole (eds), *Ethiopia: Rural Development Options*. London: Zed Books, pp. 45–57.

Armah, Ayi Kwei (1968), *The Beautyful Ones Are Not Yet Born*, Ibadan: Heinemann.

Aronoff, Yael S. (1998), 'An Apology is Not Enough', *Washington Post*, 9 April, p. A25.

Attahi, Kofi (1989), 'Côte d'Ivoire: An Evaluation of Urban Management Reforms', pp. 112–146, in R. Stren and R. White (eds), *African Cities in Crisis*, Boulder, CO: Westview Press.

Baker, Jonathan (1992), *Small Towns in Africa*, Uppsala: Scandinavian Institute of African Studies.

Baker, Jonathan (1995), 'Survival and Accumulation Strategies at the Rural–Urban Interface in North-west Tanzania', *Environment and Urbanisation*, vol. 7, no. 11, pp. 117–32.

Bamberger, Michael, Bishwapura Sanyal and Nelson Valverde (1982), *Evaluation of Sites and Services Projects: The Experience from Lusaka, Zambia*, World Bank Staff Working Paper no. 548, Washington, DC: World Bank.

Barad, Robert (1990), 'Unrecorded Transborder Trade and its Implications for Regional Economic Integration', in World Bank, *The Long-term Perspective Study on Sub-Saharan Africa*, Proceedings of a Workshop on Regional Integration and Co-operation, vol. 4, Washington, DC: World Bank, pp. 102–8.

Barber, Benjamin (1994), 'Jihad vs. McWorld', *Atlantic Monthly*, March.

Barnet, Richard and Johan Cavanagh, (1994), *Global Dreams: Imperial Corporations and the New World Order*, New York: Simon & Schuster.

Barraclough, Solon L. (1991), *An End to Hunger? The Social Origins of Food Strategies*, London: Zed Books.

Bates, Robert (1981), *Markets and States in Tropical Africa: The Political Basis of Agricultural Policies*, Berkeley: University of California Press.

Becker, C., A. Hamer, and A. Morrison (1994), *Beyond Urban Bias in Africa*, Portsmouth, NH: Heinemann, and London: J. Currey.

Beckman, Bjorn (1989), 'Empowerment or Repression? The World Bank and the Politics of African Adjustment', in Peter Gibbon, Yosuf Bangura and Are Ofstad (eds), *Authoritarianism, Democracy and Adjustment*, Seminar Proceedings no. 26, Uppsala: Scandinavian Institute of African Studies, pp. 83–105.

Bediako, Tom (1995), 'NGOs and Trade Unions in the Democratisation Process', in Mia Melin (ed.), *Democracy in Africa: On Whose Terms?*, Stockholm: Forum South, pp. 205–14.

Bennetta, Jules-Rosette (1981), *Symbols of Change: Urban Transitions in a Zambian Community*, London: Alex Publishing.

Benschop, Marjolein and Trujillo, Catalina (1999), 'Security of Tenure: Why Focus on Women?' *Habitat Debate*, vol. 5, no. 3, pp. 7–8.

Bernstein, H (1992), 'Agricultural Modernisation in Sub-Saharan Africa', *Journal of Peasant Studies*, no. 7, p. 9.

Berry, Sara (1988), 'Concentration without Privatisation? Some Consequences of Changing Patterns of Rural Land Control in Africa', in R.E. Downs and S.P. Reyana (eds), *Land and Society in Contemporary Africa*, Hanover and London: University Press of New England, pp. 53–75.

Bond, Patrick (2000), *Elite Transition: From Apartheid to Neoliberalism in South Africa*, London: Pluto Press.

Bratton, Michael and Nicolas van de Walle (1997), *Democratic Experiment in Africa: Regime Transitions in Comparative Perspective*, New York: Cambridge University Press.

Braxton, Gloria (1998), 'Promoting Greater Civic Awareness and Participation in Zambia', *African Voices*, vol. 7, no. 1, Winter/Spring.

Bretas, Paulo Roberto (1996), 'Participative Budgeting in Belo Horizonte', *Environment and Urbanisation*, vol. 8, no. 1, pp. 213–22.

Bromley, Ray (1978), 'Introduction: The Urban Informal Sector: Why is it Worth Discussing?' *World Development*, vol. 6, nos. 9/10, pp. 1033–9.

Brophy, Heather (1998), 'Civic Education Fosters Dialogue and Action in Mozambique', *African Voices*, vol. 7, no. 1, Winter/Spring.

Brown, Michael Barratt and Pauline Tiffen (1992), *Short Changed: Africa and World Trade*, London: Pluto Press.

Brown, William (2000), 'Restructuring North–South Relations: ACP–EU Development Co-operation in Liberal International Order', *Review of African Political Economy*, vol. 27, no. 85, pp. 367–84.

Bruce, J.W. (1988), 'A Perspective on Indigenous Land Tenure Systems and Land Concentration', in R.E. Downs and S.P. Reyana (eds), *Land and Society in Contemporary Africa*, Hanover and London: University Press of New England, pp. 23–52.

Bryant, Carolie (1980), 'Squatters, Collective Action, and Participation: Learning from Lusaka', *World Development*, vol. 8, pp. 73–85.

Bryceson, D.F. and V. Jamal (1997), *Farwell to Farms: De-agrarianization and Employment in Africa*, Research Series 1997/10, Leiden: Africa Studies Centre.

Bubba, Ndina and Lamba, Davinder (1991), 'Local Government in Kenya', *Environment and Urbanisation*, vol. 3, no. 1, pp. 37–59.

Buhera, Grace (2000), 'The Significance of Africa Growth and Opportunity Act for the SADC Region', Southern African Research and Documentation Centre (SARDC).

Butegwa, F. (1991), 'Women's Legal Right of Access to Agricultural Resources in Africa: A Preliminary Inquiry', *Third World Legal Studies*, pp. 45–57.

Cairnacross, Susan, et al. (1990), *The Poor Die Young: Housing and Health in the Third World*, London: Earthscan.

Callaghy, Thomas (1984), *The State–Society Struggle: Zaire in Comparative Perspective*, New York: Columbia University Press.

Callaghy, Thomas (1990), 'Lost between State and Market: The Politics of Economic Adjustment in Ghana, Zambia, and Nigeria', in J. Nelson (ed.), *Economic Crisis and Policy Choice*, Princeton, NJ: Princeton University Press, pp. 257–66.

Camdessus, Michel (1998), 'Africa is a "Continent on the Move"', *IMF Survey*, June.

Canadian Coalition for Global Economic Democracy (1996), *Multilateral Debt Reduction: A Proposal Framework*, Toronto, 12 January.

Castells, Manuel (1993), 'The University System: Engine of Development in the New World Economy', in Angela Ranson (ed.), *Improving Higher Education in Developing Countries*, EDI Series, Washington, DC: World Bank.

Cervero, Robert (1998), 'Paratransit: The Gap Fillers', *Habitat Debate*, vol. 4, no. 2, pp. 8–9.

Chambers, Robert (1983), *Rural Development: Putting the Last First*, London: Longman.

Chambers, Robert (1991), *The State and Rural Development: Ideologies and an Agenda for the 1990s*, IDS Discussion Paper 269, Falmer: University of Sussex, p. 20.

Chambers, Robert (1995), 'Poverty and Livelihoods: Whose Reality Counts?' *Environment and Urbanisation*, vol. 7, no. 1, pp. 172–204.

Chana, Tara (1999), 'Affordable Housing: The Kenyan Experience', *Habitat Debate*, vol. 5, no. 2, pp. 14–15.

Chazan, Naomi and Donald Rothchild (1988), *Precarious Balance: State and Society in Africa*, Boulder, CO: Westview Press.

Cheery, G. (1974), *The Evolution of British Town Planning*, London: Leonard Hill.

Cheru, Fantu (1987), *Dependence, Underdevelopment and Unemployment in Kenya: School Leavers in a Peripheral Political Economy*, Lanham, MD: University Press of America.

Cheru, Fantu (1988), 'Food Security and Institutional Development in SADCC', in Carolie Bryant (ed.), *Poverty, Policy, and Food Security in Southern Africa*, Boulder, CO: Lynne Reinner, pp. 250–73.

Cheru, Fantu (1989), *The Silent Revolution in Africa: Debt, Development and Democracy*, London: Zed Books.

Cheru, Fantu (1992a), *Social Dimensions of Economic Reform: Proposal to Initiate Urban Community-based Rehabilitation in the Major Towns of Ethiopia*, Addis Ababa, mimeo.

Cheru, Fantu (1992b), *The Not So Brave New World: Rethinking Regional Integration in Post-apartheid Southern Africa*, South African Institute of International Affairs, Bradlow Paper no. 6, Johannesburg: SAIIA.

Cheru, Fantu (1996), *UNDP/World Bank/UNCHS Urban Management Program*, Project Summary Assessment Report for inclusion in the Global, Inter-regional and Regional Evaluation Report, New York: UNDP.

Cheru, Fantu (1997), 'The Silent Revolution and the Weapons of the Weak: Transformation and Innovation from Below', in James Mittelman and Stephen Gill (eds), *Innovation and Transformation in International Relations*, Cambridge: Cambridge University Press, pp. 153–70.

Cheru, Fantu (2000), 'Debt Relief and Social Investment: Linking the HIPC Initiative to the HIV/AIDS Epidemic in Africa: The Case of Zambia', *Review of African Political Economy*, no. 86, pp. 519–35.

Cheru, Fantu (2001), *Why So Much Hype for So Little Relief? The HIPC Debt Relief Initiative, G7 Governments and the Politics of Appeasement*, report submitted to the 57th Session of the UN Commission on Human Rights, Geneva.

Cheru, F. and J. Bayili (1991) *Burkina Faso: Assessment of Micro-Economic Policy and its Impact on Grassroots and Non-Governmental Organizations*, Consultant Report, Washington, DC: African Development Foundation.

Cheru, Fantu and Winston Mathu (1989), *Integrated Land Use and Rural Development Project in Ethiopia*, New York: United Nations Sudano–Sahelian Office.

Cheru, Fantu, Phillip Rawkins, Mona Keseba, Mary-Elisabeth Gonzalez and Eric de Silva (1997), *Global, Inter-Regional and Regional Programs: An Evaluation of*

Impact, United Nations Development Program, Office of Evaluation and Strategic Studies, New York: UNDP.

Chhibber, A. (1989), 'The Aggregate Supply Response: A Survey', in S. Commander (ed.), *Structural Adjustment and Agriculture: Theory and Practice in Africa and Latin America*, London: ODI and Heinemann.

Clapham, Christopher (1969), *Haile Selassie's Government*, London: Longman.

Cleaver, K. and G. Schreiber (1994) *Reversing the Spiral: The Population, Agriculture and Environment Nexus in Sub-Saharan Africa*. Washington, DC: World Bank.

Cloud, K. and B. Knowles (1991), 'Where Can We Go From Here? Recommendations for Action', in J. Davidson (ed.), *Agriculture, Women, and Land: The African Experience*, Boulder, CO: Westview Press, pp. 250–64.

Cobbert, William (1999), 'Towards Securing Tenure for All', *Habitat Debate*, vol. 5, no. 3.

Cohen, John and N.I. Isaksson (1987), 'Villagization in Ethiopia's Arsi Region', *Journal of Modern African Studies*, vol. 25, no. 3, pp. 435–64.

Cohen, Michael (1983), *Learning by Doing: World Bank Lending for Urban Development, 1972–82*, Washington, DC: World Bank.

Colleta, Nat J. (1997), *Demilitarisation, Demobilisation, and the Social and Economic Integration of Ex-combatants: Lessons from the World Bank Africa Experience*, paper prepared for USIAD Conference Promoting Democracy, Human Rights, and Reintegration in Post-Conflict Societies, Washington, DC.

Colonial Office Advisory Committee for Education in the Colonies (1948), *Education for Citizenship*, Col. no. 216, London: HMSO.

COMESA (Common Market for Eastern and Southern Africa) (1995), *Review Study of the Implementation of the Common Market for Eastern and Southern Africa (COMESA) Monetary Harmonization Programme, Volume 1, Main Report.*

COMESA (n.d.), *Doing Business in the PTA/COMESA Region: A Practical Guide for Economic Operations*, jointly presented by PTA Secretariat and the International Trade Center UNCTAD/GATT.

Cooksey, B. (1986), 'Policy and Practice in Tanzanian Secondary Education since 1967', *International Journal of Educational Development*, vol. 6, no. 3, pp. 183–202.

Coousins, B., D. Weiner, and N. Amin (1992), 'Social Differentiation in the Communal Lands of Zimbabwe', *Review of African Political Economy*, no. 53, pp. 5–24.

Cornia, Giovanni Andrea, Richard Jolly and Francis Stewart (1987), *Adjustment With a Human Face*, Oxford: Clarendon Press.

Cosbey, Aaron (1998), 'The TRIPs Agreement and Developing Countries', *Global Dialogue*, vol.3, no. 1, March, pp. 12–15.

Craig, J.E. (1990), *Comparative African Experiences in Implementing Educational Policies*, World Bank Discussion Paper no. 83, Washington, DC: World Bank.

Craig, John (2000), 'Evaluating Privatisation in Zambia: A Tale of Two Processes', *Review of African Political Economy*, vol. 27, no. 85, pp. 357–66.

Crummey, Donald (1994), 'Ethnic Democracy? The Ethiopian Case', paper presented at the 37th annual meeting of the African Studies Association, Toronto.

Dahiya, Bharat (1999), 'The Impact of Decentralisation Policies in India', *Habitat Debate*, vol. 5, no. 4.

Dalmalm, Asa (1995), 'A Slowly Changing Core of Culture: The Impact of Traditional

Religion and Christianity', in Mia Melin (ed.), *Democracy in Africa: On Whose Terms?* Stockholm: Forum South.

Davey, Kenneth J. (1993), *Elements of Urban Management*, Urban Management Program, Discussion Paper no. 11, Washington, DC: World Bank.

Davidson, Basil (1983), *Modern Africa*, London: Longman.

Davidson, Jean (1991), *Agriculture, Women, and Land: The African Experience*, Boulder, CO: Westview Press.

Davis, Rob (1992), 'The Significance of Theoretical Debates on Regional Co-operation and Integration in the Transformation of Southern Africa', modified version of paper originally presented at Ruth First Memorial Symposium, Cape Town: University of the Western Cape.

Davis, Rob (2000), 'Forging a New Relationship with the EU', in T. Bertelsmann-Scott, Gregg Mills and E. Sidiropoulos (eds), *The EU–South Africa Agreement*, South African Institute of International Affairs: Johannesburg, pp. 5–16.

de Soto, Hernando (1989), *The Other Path: The Invisible Revolution in the Third World*, New York: Harper & Row.

Dejene, Alemneh (1987), *Peasants, Agrarian Socialism and Rural Development in Ethiopia*, Boulder, CO: Westview Press.

Delgado, C.L., J. Hopkins, and V.A. Kelly (1998), *Agricultural Growth Linkages in Sub-Saharan Africa*, Research Report 107, Washington, DC: International Food Policy Research Institute.

Demery, L. and L. Squire (1996), 'Macroeconomic Adjustment and Poverty in Africa: An Emerging Picture', *World Bank Research Observer*, vol. 11, no. 1, pp. 39–59.

Devas, Nick and Carole Rakodi (1993), *Managing Fast Growing Cities: New Approaches to Urban Planning and Management in the Developing World*, London: Longman.

Diamond, Larry (1983), 'Class, Ethnicity and the Democratic State: Nigeria, 1950–1966', *Comparative Studies in Society and History*, vol. 25, no. 3, pp. 457–89.

Diouf, Makhtar (1990), 'Evaluation of West African Experiments in Economic Integration', in World Bank, *The Long-term Perspective Study of Sub-Saharan Africa*, Background Papers on Proceedings on Regional Integration and Co-operation, vol. 4, Washington, DC: World Bank, pp. 21–6.

Dirasse, Laketch (1995), 'Gender Issues and Displaced Populations', in N. Heyzer et al. (eds), *A Commitment to the World's Women: Perspectives on Development for Beijing and Beyond*, New York: UNIFEM.

Drozdiak, William (2001), 'EU Drops Tariffs for Poorest Nations: Tactic Promotes Global Trade Talks', *Washington Post*, 28 February, p. E1.

Durning, Alan (1989a), *Action at the Grassroots: Fighting Poverty and Environmental Decline*, Worldwatch Paper no. 88, Washington, DC: Worldwatch Institute.

Durning, Alan B. (1989b), *Poverty and the Environment: Reversing the Downward Spiral*, Worldwatch Paper no. 92, Washington, DC: Worldwatch Institute.

Durotoye, Yami and Robert J. Griffiths (1997), 'Civilising Military Rule: Conditions and Processes of Political Transmutation in Ghana and Nigeria', *African Studies Review*, vol. 40, no. 3, pp. 133–60.

Ekins, Paul (1992), *A New World Order: Grassroots Movements for Global Change*, London: Routledge.

Ezenwe, Uka (1990), 'Evaluating the Performance of West African Integration Movements', in World Bank, *The Long-term Perspective Study of Sub-Saharan Africa*, Background Papers on Proceedings on Regional Integration and Co-operation, Volume 4, Washington, DC: World Bank, pp. 27–33.

Fanon, Franz (1963), *The Wretched of the Earth*, New York: Grove Press.

FAOSTAT (United Nations Food and Agriculture Organisation Statistical Database, 2000. FAO Trade and Production Statistics. http: //apps.fao.org/default.htm.

Feder, Greshon, Richard E. Just, and David Zilberman (1985), 'Adoption of Agricultural Innovation in Developing Countries: A Survey', *Economic Development and Cultural Change*, vol. 33, no. 2.

Fieldhouse, D.K. (1986), *Black Africa, 1945–1980*, London: Unwin Hyman.

Fisher, Stanley, Ernesto Hernandez-Cata, and Moshin Khan (1998), *Africa: Is This the Turning Point?* IMF Paper on Policy Analysis and Assessment 98/6, June, Washington, DC: International Monetary Fund.

Friedrich-Naumann-Stiftung Foundation (1992), *Blueprint for a New Kenya: Post Election Action Program*, Nairobi: FNSF.

German Agency for Technical Co-operation (GTZ) (1997), 'Tanzania–Bondeni Community Land Trust', *Habitat Debate*, vol. 3, no. 2, pp. 16–17.

Gilbert, Alan and Gugler, Josef (1982), *Cities, Poverty and Development*, Oxford: Oxford University Press, pp. 49–65.

Gills, Barry Gills and Joel Rocamora (1992), 'Low Intensity Democracy', *Third World Quarterly*, vol. 13, no. 3.

Ginzberg, Eli (1971), *Manpower for Development: Perspectives on Five Continents*, New York: Praeger.

Godard, Xavier and Hubert Ngabmen (1998), 'Urban Transport in Sub-Saharan Africa', *Habitat Debate*, vol. 4, no. 2, pp. 15–16.

Government of Ethiopia (1987), *Agricultural Pricing and Marketing Policy of Ethiopia: A Synopsis*, Addis Ababa, December.

Government of Ethiopia (1990), *Report by President Mengistu Haile Mariam to the 11th Plenum of the Central Committee of the Workers Party of Ethiopia*, resolutions adopted by the plenum, Addis Ababa, March.

Government of Kenya (1974), *Third Development Plan, 1974–78*, Part I, Nairobi: Government Printer.

Government of Malawi (1998), *Malawi Decentralisation Policy*, Department of Local Government Administration, Lilongwe.

Government of Zambia (1997), *HIV/AIDS in Zambia: Background, Projections, Impacts, and Interventions*, Ministry of Health, Central Board of Health: Lusaka.

Green, Reginald (1981), *Magendo in the Political Economy of Uganda: Pathology, Parallel System or Dominant Sub-mode of Production*, IDS Discussion Paper no. 64, Falmer: Institute of Development Studies.

Hancock, Graham (1989), *Lords of Poverty: the Power, Prestige and Corruption of the International Aid Business*, New York: Atlantic Monthly Press.

Hanlon, Joseph (1978), 'Does Modernisation Mean Mechanisation?', *New Scientist*, August.

Harbeson, John W. (2000), 'Externally Assisted Democratisation: Theoretical Issues and African Realities', in John Harbeson and Donald Rothchild (eds), *Africa in World Politics*, Boulder, CO: Westview Press, pp. 235–57.

Harbison, Frederick Harbison and Meyers, Charles A. (1964), *Education, Manpower and Economic Growth: Strategies in Human Resources Development*, New York: McGraw-Hill.

Hardoy, J. and Satterthwaite, David, (1989), *Squatter Citizen*, London: Earthscan.

Harris, L. (1980), 'Agricultural Co-operatives and Development Policy in Mozambique', *Journal of Peasant Studies*, vol. 7, no. 3.

Havnevik, Kjell J and Mats Harsmar (1999), The *Diversified Future: An Institutional Approach to Rural Development in Tanzania*, Expert Group on Development Issues, Stockholm: Swedish Ministry of Foreign Affairs.

Hawkins, Tony (2000), 'Africa Tears Down Trade Barriers', *Financial Times*, 30 October.

Hayami, Y., and J.P. Platteau (1996), 'Resource Endowments and Agricultural Development: Africa vs. Asia', paper prepared for the IEA Round Table Conference on the Industrial Foundation of Economic Development in East Asia, Tokyo.

Heinemann, Moser C. (1995), 'Urban Social Policy and Poverty Reduction', *Environment and Urbanisation*, vol. 7, no. 1, pp. 159–71.

Hill, P. (1972), *Rural Hausa: A Village and a Setting*, Cambridge: Cambridge University Press, p. 191.

Himonga, C.N. (1991), 'Rural Women's Access to Agricultural Land in Settlement Schemes in Zambia: Law, Practice and Socio-economic Constraints', *Third World Legal Studies*, pp. 59–73.

Hirschmann, David (1995), 'Democracy, Gender and US Foreign Assistance: Guidelines and Lessons', *World Development*, vol. 23, no. 8, pp. 1291–302.

Hoben, Allen (1975), *Land Tenure among the Amhara of Ethiopia*, Chicago: University of Chicago Press.

Hodges, Tony (1983), 'Mozambique: The Politics of Liberation', in G. Carter and P. O'Meara (eds), *Southern Africa: The Continuing Crisis*, Bloomington: Indiana University Press.

Hollnsteiner, Mary R. (1979), 'Mobilising the Rural Poor through Community Organisation', *Philippine Studies*, vol. 27, no. 3, pp. 383–4.

Human Rights Watch/Africa (1996), *Shattered Lives: Sexual Violence during the Rwandan Genocide and its Aftermath*, New York: Human Rights Watch.

Human Rights Watch/Africa (1997), *Liberia: Emerging From the Destruction*, New York: Human Rights Watch.

Hyde, Karin (1989), *Improving Women's Education in Sub-Saharan Africa: A Review of the Literature*, PHREE Background Paper Series, Doc#PHREE/89/15, Washington, DC: World Bank.

Hyden, Goran (1981), *Beyond Ujamaa in Tanzania: Underdevelopment and an Uncaptured Peasantry*, Berkeley: University of California Press.

IFAD (1994), 'Land Degradation Accelerating in Africa', International Fund for Agricultural Development, press release, 4 May.

Ihonvbere, Julius O. (1996), *Economic Crisis, Civil Society and Democratisation: The Case of Zambia*, Trenton, NJ: Africa World Press.

Ihonvbere, Julius O. (1997), 'Organised Labour and the Struggle for Democracy in Nigeria', *African Studies Review*, vol. 40, no. 3.

Iliffe, J. (1987), *The African Poor: A History*. Cambridge: Cambridge University Press.

ILO (1972), *Employment, Incomes and Equality: A Strategy for Increasing Productive Employment in Kenya*, Geneva: ILO.

ILO (1981), *The Paper Qualification Syndrome and the Unemployment of School Leavers*, ILO Jobs and Skills Program for Africa (JAPSA), Addis Ababa: ILO, p. 11.

ILO (1985), *Informal Sector in Africa*, Jobs and Skills Program for Africa, ILO: Addis Ababa, pp. 13–15.

ILO (1997), 'Giving Peace – and People – a Chance', *World of Work*, no. 20, pp. 16–19.

IMF (1991), *International Financial Statistics Yearbook 1991*, Washington, DC: International Monetary Fund, pp. 120–21.

IMF (1998), 'Distilling the Lessons from the ESAF Reviews' (draft report).

IMF/IDA (2000a), *Poverty Reduction Strategy Papers: Progress in Implementation*, report prepared by the Staffs of the IMF and the World Bank, Washington, DC.

IMF/IDA (2000b), *Heavily Indebted Poor Countries Initiative and Poverty Reduction Strategy Papers: Progress Report*, a Joint Memorandum by the President of the World Bank, James D. Wolfensohn and the Managing Director of the IMF, Horst Kohler, 7 September.

International Institute for Labor Studies (1981), *Lagos Plan of Action for the Economic Development of Africa 1980–2000*, Geneva: IILS.

Jacobi, Pedro (1999), *Challenging Traditional Participation in Brazil: The Goals of Participatory Budgeting – The Case of Porto Alegre*, Report no. 32, Washington, DC: Woodrow Wilson International Centre for Scholars.

Jamal, Vali and John Weeks (1988), 'The Vanishing Rural–Urban Gap in Sub-Saharan Africa', *International Labour Review*, vol. 127, no. 3, pp. 271–92.

Jibowo, A.A. and A.P. Allen (1980), 'Resistance and Response to Change Pressure: The Case of Land Tenure Arrangements and the Isoya Rural Development Project, Oyo State, Nigeria', *Eastern Africa Journal of Rural Development*, vol. 31, no. 1/2, p. 47.

Jolly, Richard (1969), *Planning Education for African Development: Economic and Manpower Perspectives*, Nairobi: East Africa Publishing House.

Joseph, Richard (1997), 'Democratisation in Africa after 1989: Comparative and Theoretical Perspectives', *Comparative Politics*, vol. 29, no. 3.

Kanji, Nazneen (1995), 'Gender, Poverty and Economic Adjustment in Harare, Zimbabwe', *Environment and Urbanisation*, vol. 7, no. 1, pp. 37–56.

Kaplan, Robert (1994), 'The Coming Anarchy', *Atlantic Monthly*, February.

Karabel, Jerome and A.H. Halsey (1977), *Power and Ideology in Education*, New York: Oxford University Press.

Keare, Douglas H. and Scott Parris (1982), *Evaluation of Shelter Programs for the Urban Poor: Principal Findings*, World Bank Staff Working Paper no. 547, Washington, DC: World Bank.

Kebede, Hanna (1990), 'Women and Rural Development', in S. Pausewang et al. (eds), *Ethiopia: Options for Rural Development*, London: Zed Books.

Kelly, Michael J. (1991), *Education in a Declining Economy: The Case of Zambia, 1975–85*, Washington, DC: World Bank.

Kenya Colony and Protectorate (1948), *A Ten-year Plan for the Development of African Education*, Nairobi: Government Printer.

Kenya Colony and Protectorate (1949), *African Education in Kenya* (the Beecher Report), Nairobi: Government Printer.

Kherallah, Meylene, C. Delgado, Eleni Gabre-Madhin, Nicola Minot and Michael Johnson (2000), *The Road Half Travelled: Agricultural Market Reform in Sub-Saharan Africa*, Food Policy Report, International Food Policy Research Institute: Washington, DC: pp. 9–10.

Kimenyi, Mwangi S. (1993), 'The Necessity for Economic Reform', *Finance*, 31 January.

Kingma, Kees (1997), 'Post-war Demobilisation and Reintegration of Ex-combatants into Civilian Life', Bonn International Centre for Conversion (BICC), paper prepared for USAID Conference on Promoting Democracy, Human Rights, and Reintegration in Post-Conflict Societies, Washington, DC, 30–31 October.

Kinyanjui, Kabiru (1974), *The Distribution of Educational Resources and Opportunities in Kenya*, Discussion Paper no. 208, University of Nairobi, Institute of Development Studies.

Kinyanjui, Kabiru (1980), *Education and Development in Africa: Theories, Strategies, and Practical Implications*, Working Paper no. 375, University of Nairobi, Institute of Development Studies.

Kironde, J.M. Lusugga (1995), 'Access to Land by the Urban Poor in Tanzania: Some Findings from Dar-es-Salaam', *Environment and Urbanisation*, vol. 7, no. 1, pp. 77–95.

Kiros, Fasil G. (1990), *Implementing Educational Policies in Ethiopia*, Discussion Paper no. 85, Washington, DC: World Bank.

Kitching, Gavin (1980), *Class and Economic Change in Kenya: The Making of an African Petite Bourgeoisie*, New Haven, CT: Yale University Press.

Knowles, B. (1991), 'Where Can We Go From Here? Recommendations for Action', in J. Davidson (ed.), *Agriculture, Women and Land: The African Experiencer*, Boulder, CO: Westview Press.

Kombe, Jackson W. (1994), 'The Demise of Public Urban Land Management and the Emergence of the Informal Land Markets in Tanzania: A Case of Dar-es-Salaam', *Habitat International*, vol. 18, no. 1, pp. 23–43.

Kranna, Michael (ed.) (1994), *The True Costs of Conflict*, New York: The New Press.

Kulaba, Saitiel (1989), 'Local Government and Management of Urban Services in Tanzania', in R. Stren and R. White (eds), *African Cities in Crisis: Managing Rapid Urban Growth*, Boulder, CO: Westview Press, pp. 203–45.

Lacey, Linda and Owusu, Steven E. (1989), 'Squatter Settlements in Monrovia, Liberia: The Evolution of Housing Policies', in R. Stren and R. White (eds), *African Cities in Crisis: Managing Rapid Urban Growth*, Boulder, CO: Westview Press, p. 6.

Laishley, Roy (1992), 'Commodity Prices Deal Blow to Africa', *Africa Recovery*, vol. 6, no. 1, April.

Lambrechts, Kato (1999), 'Losing the Soul of Lomé?', *Global Dialogue*, vol. 4, no. 1, April, pp. 1–3.

Laporte, Geert (1993), 'Integration: From Words to Deeds', *The Courier*, no. 142, November–December, pp. 60–62.

Le Pere, Garth, Kato Lambrechts and Anthoni van Nieuwkerk (1999), 'The Burden of the Future: South Africa's Foreign Policy Challenges in the New Millennium',

Global Dialogue, vol. 4, no. 3, pp. 3–8.

Lee, Margaret C. (1989), *SADCC: The Political Economy of Development in Southern Africa*, Winston-Derek Publishers: Nashville, TN, p. 272.

Lee-Smith, Diana (1989), 'Urban Management in Nairobi: A Case Study of the Matatu Mode of Public Transport', in R. Stren and R. White (eds), *African Cities in Crisis: Managing Rapid Urban Growth*, Boulder, CO: Westview Press, pp. 276–304.

Leftwich, Adrian (1993), 'Governance, Democracy and Development in the Third World', *Third World Quarterly*, vol. 14, no. 3.

Levey, Caren (1992), 'Gender and the Environment: The Challenge of Crosscutting Issues in Development Policy Planning', *Environment and Urbanisation*, vol. 4, no. 1, pp. 134–49.

Leys, Colin (1996), *The Rise and Fall of Development Theory*, Bloomington: Indiana University Press.

Lipton, Michael (1977), *Why Poor People Stay Poor: The Urban Bias in Public Policy*, Cambridge, MA: Harvard University Press.

Lipton, Michel (1988), 'The Place of Agricultural Research in the Development of Sub-Saharan Africa', *World Development*, vol. 16, no. 10.

Lirenso, Alemayehu Lirenso (1990), 'Villagization Policies and Prospects', in S. Pausewang et al. (eds), *Ethiopia: Options for Rural Development*, London: Zed Books, pp. 135–43.

Mabogunje, A.L. (1974), 'Toward an Urban Policy in Nigeria', *Nigerian Journal of Economic and Social Studies*, vol. 16, no. 1.

Mabogunje, Akim L. (1990), *Perspectives on Urban Land and Urban Management Policies in Sub-Saharan Africa*, World Bank Technical Paper no. 196, Washington, DC: World Bank.

Mabogunje, Akim L. (1991), *A New Paradigm for Urban Development Strategies in Developing Countries*, Washington, DC: World Bank.

McCormick, John (1989), *Reclaiming Paradise: The Global Environmental Movement*, Indiana University Press: Bloomington.

MacGaffey, Janet (1983), 'How to Survive and Become Rich Amidst Devastation: The Second Economy in Zaire', *African Affairs*, no. 82, pp. 351–64.

MacGaffey, Janet (1988), 'Economic Disengagement and Class Formation in Zaire', in Donald Rothschild and Naomi Chazan (eds), *The Precarious Balance: State and Society in Africa*, Boulder, CO: Westview Press, pp. 171–88.

Mackenzie, F. (1993), 'Gender and Land Rights in Murang'a District, Kenya', *Journal of Peasant Studies*, vol. 21, no. 1.

Mamingi, N. (1997), 'The Impact of Prices and Macroeconomic Policies on Agricultural Supply: A Synthesis of Available Results', *Agricultural Economics*, vol. 16, no. 1, pp. 17–34.

Mandebvu, O.S. (1994), 'Technical Education and National Development: Meeting the Challenge Through the Training of Technical Education Teachers in Zimbabwe', paper prepared at the Fourth Annual Conference of the Southern African Comparative and History of Education Society, Gaborone, Botswana.

Manuh, Takyiwaa (1998), 'Women in Africa's Development', *Africa Recovery*, no. 1, p. 10.

Marris, Peter and Somerset, Tony (1971), *African Businessmen: A Study of Entrepreneurship and Development in Kenya*, London: Routledge.

Martin, Guy (1989), 'The Preferential Trade Area (PTA) for Eastern and Southern Africa: Achievements, Problems and Prospects', *Africa Spectrum*, no. 2.

Matric Development Consultants (1993), *Nairobi's Informal Settlements: An Inventory*, Report prepared for USAID/REDSO/ESA: Nairobi.

Mayer, Marina (1999), 'The EU–South Africa Trade Deal: Implications for Southern Africa', *Global Dialogue*, vol. 4, no. 2, pp. 10–13.

Mazrui, Ali (1990), 'Islamic Revivalism and Expansionism', *Africa Events*, February.

Mazurana, Dyana E. and Susan R. McKay (1999), *Women and Peace Building*, International Centre for Human Rights and Democratic Development, Montreal.

Mbekeani, Kennedy (1999), 'Free Trade between South Africa and the EU: A Raw Deal for the BLNS Countries', *Global Dialogue*, vol. 4, no. 3.

Mbilima, D. (1989), 'Regional Organisation in Southern Africa', in Alan W. Whiteside (ed.), *Industrialisation and Investment in Southern Africa*, London: James Curry, pp. 36–7.

M'buyinga, Elenga (1982), *Pan Africanism or Neo-colonialism: The Bankruptcy of the OAU*, London: Zed Books.

Medrad, Jean-François (1982), 'The Underdeveloped State in Tropical Africa: Political Clientelism or Neo-patrimonialism', in Christopher Clapham (ed.), *Private Patronage and Public Power: Political Clientelism in the Modern State*, London: Frances Pinter.

Menendez, Aurelio (1991), *Access to Basic Infrastructure by the Urban Poor*, Economic Development Institute Report no. 28, Washington, DC: World Bank, pp. 41–52.

Mengisteab, Kindane (1997), 'New Approach to State Building in Africa: The Case of Ethiopia's Ethnic-based Federalism', *African Studies Review*, vol. 40, no. 3, December.

Menkhaus, Ken (1998), 'Somalia: Political Order in a Stateless Society', *Current History*, May.

Mhone, Guy (1995), *The Impact of Structural Adjustment on the Urban Informal Sector in Zimbabwe*, Discussion Paper no. 2, Geneva: ILO.

Middleton, John and Terry Demsky (1989), *Vocational Education and Training: A Review of World Bank Investment*, World Bank Discussion Paper no. 51, Washington, DC: World Bank.

Migot-Adholla, S., P. Hazell, B. Blaarel, and F. Place (1991), 'Indigenous Land Rights Systems in Sub-Saharan Africa: A Constraint on Productivity?', *World Bank Economic Review*, vol. 5, no. 1, pp. 155–7.

Mittelman, James (1996), *Globalisation: Critical Reflections*, Boulder, CO: Lynne Rienner.

Monga, Celestin (1996), *The Anthropology of Anger: Civil Society and Democracy in Africa*, Boulder, CO: Lynne Rienner.

Moreno, Edwardo Lopez (2000), 'The Road to Peace is Paved with Flawed Intentions', *Habitat Debate*, vol. 6, no. 2, pp. 19–20.

Moser, Caroline (1995), 'Urban Social Policy and Poverty Reduction', *Environment and Urbanization*, vol. 7, no. 1.

Moss, Elliot R. (1984), 'Institutional Destruction Resulting from Donor and Project Proliferation in Sub-Saharan African Countries', *World Development*, vol. 12, no. 4.

Mtizwa-Mangiza, Naisson (1999), 'Strengthening Rural–Urban Linkages', *Habitat Debate*, vol. 5, no. 1, pp. 1–5.

Mukalo wa Kwayera (1993), 'Post-election Analysis', *Society*, no. 3.

Muriu, Muthoni (2000), 'The Partnership Agreement between the ACP and the EU: All Things to All Persons?', *African Agenda*, vol. 3, no. 3, May–June, pp. 5–7.

Mutharika, Bengu (1991), Interview, *Southern African Economist*, April/May.

Mutua, Rosalind W. (1975), *Development of Education in Kenya: Some Administrative Aspects, 1846–1963*, Nairobi: East African Literature Bureau.

Nabudere, Dani W. (1991), 'Africa's Development Experience under the Lomé Convention', paper prepared for Pan-African Conference on Thirty Years of Independence: Results and Prospects, Windhoek, Namibia.

National Christian Council of Kenya (1966), *After School What? A Report on Further Education, Training and Employment of Primary School Leavers*, Nairobi: NCCK.

Nduna, Sydia and Lorelei Goodyear (1997), *Pain Too Deep for Tears: Assessing the Prevalence of Sexual and Gender Violence among Burundian Refugees in Tanzania*, New York: International Rescue Committee.

Nhalapo, Welile (2000), 'South Africa's Chairmanship of the NAM and the South Summit', *Global Dialogue*, vol. 5, no. 1, May.

Nichols, Matthew (1998), 'Driving Ourselves to Death: The Environmental Impact of Transport', *Habitat Debate*, vol. 4, no. 2, pp. 6–7.

Nolan, Amy (1986), 'A Growing Role for the Private Sector in the Provision of Public Services in Third World Cities', Washington, DC: USAID/PRE.

Nomvete, Bax D. (1993), 'Regional Integration in Africa: A Path Strewn with Obstacles', *The Courier*, no. 142, November–December, pp. 50–59.

Nyoni, S. (1995), 'Is Democracy Possible? The Role of Grassroots Movements', in M. Melin (ed.), *Democracy in Africa: On Whose Terms?* Stockholm: Forum South, pp. 187–96.

Obudho, Robert A. and Sala El-Shaks (eds) (1975), *Urbanisation, National Development, and Regional Planning in Africa*, New York: Praeger.

Odanga, Adhiambo and Heneveld, Ward (1995), *Girls and Schools in Sub-Saharan Africa: From Analysis to Action*, Washington, DC: World Bank.

Oja, Olatunde J. (1985), *African International Relations*, Ann Arbor: University of Michigan Press.

Okoth-Ogendo, H.W.O. (1976), 'African Land Tenure Reform', in Judith Heyer et al. (eds), *Agricultural Development in Kenya*, Nairobi: Oxford University Press, p. 175.

Oldeman, L.R. (1998), *Soil Degradation: A Threat to Food Security?*, Report 98/01, Wageningen: International Soil Reference and Information Centre.

Onibokun, Adepoju (1989), 'Urban Growth and Urban Management in Nigeria', in R. Stren and R. White (eds), *African Cities in Crisis: Managing Rapid Urban Growth*, Boulder, CO: Westview Press, pp. 68–111.

Onis, Ziya (1991), 'The Logic of the Developmental State', *Comparative Politics*, October.

Organization of African Unity (1992), *Report of the Secretary-General on Conflicts in Africa: Proposals for an OAU Mechanism for Conflict Prevention and Resolution*, Council of Ministers, CM/1710 (l. VI) Organization of African Unity, June, Addis Ababa: OAU.

Organization of African Unity (1998), *Resolving Conflicts*, vol. 2, no. 4, March–April, p. 23.

Ostergaard, Tom (1993), 'Classical Models of Regional Integration: What Relevance for Southern Africa?', in Bertil Oden (ed.), *Southern Africa After Apartheid: Regional Integration and External Resources*, Seminar Proceedings no. 28, The Scandinavian Institute of African Studies: Uppsala, Sweden.

Ottaway, Marina (1975), 'Land Reform and Peasant Associations in Ethiopia', *Rural Africana*, Fall.

Ottaway, Marina (1994), *Democratization and Ethnic Nationalism: African and Eastern European Experiences*, Washington, DC: Overseas Development Council.

Oxfam International (1999), *Education Now: Break the Cycle of Poverty*, London: Oxfam.

Oxfam International (n.d.), *Multilateral Debt: The Human Costs*, position paper.

Pankhurst, Alula (1990), 'Resettlement: Policies and Practice', in S. Pausewang et al. (eds), *Ethiopia: Options for Rural Development*, London: Zed Books.

Pankhurst, H. and S. Jacobs (1991), 'Land Tenure, Gender Relations and Agricultural Production: The Case of Zimbabwe's Peasantry', in J. Davidson (ed.), *Agriculture, Women, and Land: The African Experience*, Boulder, CO: Westview Press, pp. 202–27.

Pausewang, Siegfried, et al. (eds) (1991), *Ethiopia: Options for Rural Development*, London: Zed Books.

Plank, David N. (1993), 'Aid, Debt, and the End of Sovereignty: Mozambique and its Donors', *Journal of Modern African Studies*, vol. 31, no. 3, pp. 407–30.

Plumbe, Tony (1998), 'Curitiba: A Replicable Best Practice?', *Habitat Debate*, vol. 4, no. 2, pp. 25–6.

Poinsot, Jacqueline, Alai Sinou and Jaroslav Sternadel (1989), *Les Villes d'Afrique noire: politiques et operation d'urbanisme et d'habitat entre 1650 et 1960*, Paris: La Documentation Française.

Pradervand, P. (1989), *Listening to Africa: Developing Africa from the Grassroots*, New York: Praeger.

Provisional Government of Ethiopia (1975), 'Public Ownership of Rural Lands Proclamation', 29 April.

Psacharopoulos, George (1990), *Why Educational Policies Can Fail: An Overview of Selected African Experiences*, World Bank Africa Technical Department, Discussion Paper no. 82, Washington, DC: World Bank.

Quisumbing, A., L.R. Brown, H.S. Feldstein, L. Haddad and C. Pena (1995), *Women: The Key to Food Security*, Washington, DC: International Food Policy Research Institute.

Raghavan, Chakravarthi (1991), *Recolonization: GATT and the Uruguay Round*, London: Zed Books.

Rahmato, Dessalegn (1985), *Agrarian Reform in Ethiopia*, Trenton, NJ: Red Sea Press.

Rahmato, Dessalegn (1987), *Famine and Survival Strategies: A Case Study from North-east Ethiopia*, Addis Ababa: Institute for Development Research.

Rahmato, Dessalegn (1989), 'Rural Settlements in Post-revolution Ethiopia', paper prepared for the Conference on Population Issues in National Development, Office of National Committee for Central Planning: Addis Ababa.

Rahmato, Dessalegn (1990), 'Co-operatives, State Farms and Smallholder Production', in S. Pausewang et al. (eds), *Ethiopia: Options for Rural Development*, London: Zed Books, pp. 100–110.

Rahmato, Dessalegn (1993), 'Agrarian Change and Agrarian Crisis: State and Peasantry in Post-Revolution Ethiopia', *Africa*, vol. 63, no. 1.

Raney, Laura, K. Subbarao, Halil Dundar and Jennifer Haworth (1994), *Women in Higher Education: Progress, Constraints, and Promising Initiatives*, World Bank Discussion Paper no. 244, Washington, DC: World Bank.

Rau, Bill (1991), *From Feast to Famine: Official Cures and Grassroots Remedies to Africa's Food Crisis*, London: Zed Books.

Ravenhill, John (1990), 'Overcoming Constraints to Regional Co-operation in Africa: Co-ordination Rather than Integration', in World Bank, *The Long-term Perspective Study of Sub-Saharan Africa*, vol. 4, Proceedings of a Workshop on Regional Integration and Co-operation, Washington, DC: World Bank.

Ray, Kalyan (2000), 'Water for Thirsty Cities', *Habitat Debate*, vol. 6, no. 3.

Republic of Kenya (1972), A *Guide to Industrial Investment in Kenya*, Ministry of Commerce and Industry, Nairobi: Government Printer.

Richburg, Keith (1993), 'The US and Somalia: Passing the Torch', *Humanitarian Monitor*, June, pp. 9–10.

Richburg, Keith (1998), *Out of America: A Black Man Confronts Africa*, San Diego: Harcourt.

Ritchie, Mark (1990), 'GATT, Agriculture and the Environment', *The Ecologist*, November.

Robson, P. (1980), *The Economies of International Integration*, London: Allen & Unwin.

Rodney, Walter (1982), *How Europe Underdeveloped Africa*, Washington, DC: Howard University Press.

Rodrik, Dani (1999), *The New Global Economy and Developing Countries: Making Openness Work*, Policy Essay no. 24, Washington, DC: Overseas Development Council.

Rodrik, Dani (2001), 'Trading in Illusions', *Foreign Policy*, March–April, pp. 55–62.

Rosenblum, Mort and Doug Williamson (1987), *Squandering Eden: Africa at the Edge*, New York: Harcourt Brace Jovanovich.

Rueschemeyer, Dietrich, Evelyne Huber Stephens, and John Stephens (1992), *Capitalist Development and Democracy*, Chicago: University of Chicago Press.

Saangare, Louis (1990), 'Rationalization of Intergovernmental Organizations for Purpose of Regional Co-operation', in World Bank, *The Long-term Perspective Study of Sub-Saharan Africa*, Background Papers on Proceedings on Regional Integration and Co-operation, vol. 4, Washington, DC: World Bank, pp. 111–112.

Saasa, Oliver S. (1993), 'The Effectiveness of Regional Transport Networks in Southern Africa – Some Post-apartheid Perspectives', in Bertil Oden (ed.),

Southern Africa After Apartheid: Regional Integration and External Resources, Seminar Proceedings no. 28, Uppsala: Scandinavian Institute of African Studies.

Sachs, Jeffrey (2000a), 'A New Map of the World: Today's World is Divided Not by Ideology, but by Technology', *The Economist*, 24 June, pp. 81–3.

Sachs, Jeffrey (2000b), 'The Charade of Debt Sustainability', *Financial Times*, 26 September.

SADCC (1980), *Southern Africa: Towards Economic Liberation – A Declaration by the Government of Independent States of Southern Africa*, Lusaka: SADCC.

Saito, K., H. Mekonnen, and D. Spurling (1994), *Raising the Productivity of Women Farmers in Sub-Saharan Africa*. World Bank Discussion Paper no. 230, Washington, DC: World Bank.

Salih, Mohamed (1994), *Inducing Food Insecurity: Perspectives on Food Policies in Eastern and Southern Africa*, Seminar Proceedings no. 30, Uppsala: Scandinavian Institute of African Studies.

Samoff, Joel (1987), 'The Reconstruction of Schooling in Africa', *Comparative Education Review*, vol. 37.

Sandbrook, Richard (1986), 'The State and Economic Stagnation in Tropical Africa', *World Development*, vol. 14, no. 3, pp. 319–32.

Sandbrook, Richard (1988), 'Liberal Democracy in Africa', *Canadian Journal of African Studies*, vol. 22, no. 2.

Satterthwaite, David (1995), 'The Underestimation and Misrepresentation of Urban Poverty', *Environment and Urbanisation*, vol. 7, no. 1, pp. 3–10.

Save the Children–Ethiopia (1993), *A Brief Exposure of Income Generation Program in Ethiopia*, paper prepared for the Africa Regional Workshop on Credit and Income Generation, Addis Ababa.

Sawyerr, Akilagpa (1998), 'Does Africa Really Need Her Universities? *Codesria Bulletin*, no. 3/4.

Schiff, M., and A. Valdes (1992), *The Plundering of Agriculture in Developing Countries*, Washington, DC: World Bank.

Schmitter, Philippe C. and Terry Karl Lynn (1991), 'What Democracy Is and Is Not', *Journal of Democracy*, Summer.

Schultz, Theodore W. (1961), 'Investment in Human Capital', *American Economic Review*, no. 51.

Scott, James C. (1993), *Everyday Forms of Resistance*, Occasional Paper Series no. 15, International Peace Research Institute, Meigaku, Yokohama.

Sesay, Max A. (1996), 'Civil War and Collective Intervention in Liberia', *Review of African Political Economy*, no. 67, pp. 35–52.

Sheffield, James R. (1967), *Education, Employment and Rural Development*, Nairobi: East African Publishing House.

Sinnatamby, Geham (1990), 'Low Cost Sanitation', in Jorge E. Hardoy, Sandy Cairncross and David Satterthwaite (eds), *The Poor Die Young*, London: Earthscan, pp. 127–57.

Soto, Alvro de and Graciana del Castillo (1994), 'Obstacles to Peace-building', *Foreign Policy*, no. 94.

Sparr, Pamela (ed.), (1994), *Mortgaging Women's Lives: Feminist Critiques of Structural Adjustment*, London: Zed Books.

Spence, Jack (2000), 'A New International Order: Lessons of Kosovo', *South African International Affairs*, vol. 7, no. 1.

Spencer, D.S.C. (1994), *Infrastructure and Technology Constraints to Agricultural Development in the Humid and Sub-humid Tropics of Africa*, Environment and Production Technology Division Discussion Paper no. 3, Washington, DC: International Food Policy Research Institute.

Stavenhagen, Rodolfo (1997), 'Peoples' Movements: The Antisystemic Challenge', in Robert Cox (ed.), *The New Realism: Perspectives on Multilateralism and World Order*, London: Macmillan and United Nations University Press.

Stren, Richard (1989a), 'The Administration of Urban Services' in R. Stren and R. White (eds), *African Cities in Crisis*, Boulder, CO: Westview Press, pp. 36–7.

Stren, Richard (1989b), 'Urban Local Government in Africa', in R. Stren and R. White (eds), *African Cities in Crisis*, Boulder, CO: Westview Press.

Stren, Richard and Lee-Smith, Diana (1991), 'New Perspectives on African Urban Management', *Environment and Urbanisation*, vol. 3, no. 1, pp. 23–36.

Swedish Ministry of Foreign Affairs (1999), *Preventing Violent Conflict: A Swedish Action Plan*, Stockholm, DS.

Tekere, Moses (2000), 'A Strategic Response to Post-Lomé IV Trade: ACP–EU Arrangements', *African Agenda*, vol. 3, no. 3, May/June.

Teklu, Tesfaye, Joachim von Braun and Elsayed Zaki (1991), *Drought and Famine Relationships in Sudan: Policy Implications*, Research Report 88, Washington, DC: International Food Policy Research Institute.

Timberlake, Lloyd (1986), *Africa in Crisis: The Causes, the Cures of Environmental Bankruptcy*, London: Earthscan.

Uduku, N.O. (1994), 'Promoting Community-based Approaches to Social Infrastructure Provision in Urban Areas of Nigeria', *Environment and Urbanisation*, vol. 6.

UNAIDS (1997), *Tuberculosis and AIDS*, Geneva: UNAIDS.

UNAIDS (2000), *Report of the Global HIV/AIDS Epidemic*, Geneva: UNAIDS, June 28.

UNCHS (1991a), *Development of National Technological Capacity for Production of Indigenous Building Materials*, Nairobi: UNCHS.

UNCHS (1991b), *Global Shelter Strategy to the Year 2000*, Nairobi: UNCHS.

UNCHS (1992), *Community Participation in Zambia: The Danida/UNCHS Training Program*, Nairobi: UNCHS.

UNCHS (1993), *Public/Private Partnership in Enabling Shelter Strategies*, Nairobi: UNCHS.

UNCHS (1996a), *An Urbanising World: Global Report on Human Settlements 1996*, London: Oxford University Press.

UNCHS (1996b), Compilation of Best Practices under evaluation for formal presentation at the Habitat II conference in Istanbul, draft document, January 15, 1996, case submission no. 123: community-led Massai housing project.

UNCHS (1996c), *The Habitat Agenda: Goals, Principles, Commitments and Global Plan of Action*, Istanbul, 3–4 June.

UNCHS (1998), Urban Indicators Program, draft document submitted in preparation for Istanbul +5.

UNCTAD (1995), *Foreign Direct Investment in Africa, 1995*, Current Studies, Series A, no. 28, Geneva: UNCTAD.

UNCTAD (2000a), *African Development in a Comparative Perspective*, Geneva: UNCTAD.

UNCTAD (2000b), *Trade and Development Report 2000*, Geneva: UNCTAD.

UNCTAD (2000c), *World Investment Report 2000: Cross-Border Mergers and Acquisitions and Development*, Geneva: UNCTAD.

UNDP (1991a), *Cities, People and Poverty: A UNDP Strategy Paper*, New York: UNDP.

UNDP (1991b), *Internal Review of the Impact of the UNDP/World Bank/UNCHS Urban Management Program, 1986–1991*, prepared by Rob Work, consultant for New York: UNDP.

UNDP (1992), *Urban Management Program (Phase 2)*, Project document, Int/92/005/a/01/56, New York: UNDP.

UNDP (1997), *Human Development Report 1997*, New York: Oxford University Press.

UNDP (2000), *Human Development Report 2000*, New York: Oxford University Press.

UNDP–Malawi (2000), *UN Common Country Assessment of Malawi*, November, Lilongwe: UNDP–Malawi.

UNECA (1991), *Foreign Direct Investment as Source of Development Finance for Africa*, E/ECA/UNTCf75.1, August, Addis Ababa: UNECA.

UNECA (1996), *Economic and Social Survey of Africa, 1995–1996*, Addis Ababa: UNECA.

UNECA (1997), *Rationalisation of ECA-Sponsored Institutions: Renewal for Improved Service*, E/ECA/CM.25/5, 27 March, Addis Ababa: UNECA.

UNECA (2000), *Economic Report on Africa 1999: The Challenges of Poverty Reduction and Sustainability*, Addis Ababa: UNECA.

UNECA/African NGOs (1990), *African Charter for Popular Participation in Development and Transformation*, Addis Ababa: UNECA.

UNESCO (1961a), *Final Report, Conference of African States on the Development of Education in Africa*, Paris: UNESCO.

UNESCO (1961b), *Outline of a Plan for African Educational Development*, Paris: UNESCO.

UNESCO (1993a), *Trends and Projections of Enrolment by Level of Education, by Age and by Sex, 1960–2025*, Paris: UNESCO.

UNESCO (1993b), *World Education Report 1993*, Paris: UNESCO.

UNESCO (1996a), *Statistical Yearbook 1996*, Paris: UNESCO.

UNESCO (1996b), *World Science Report 1996*, Paris: UNESCO.

UNESCO (1997), *Statistical Yearbook 1997*, Paris: UNESCO.

UNESCO (1998), Seventh Conference of Ministers of Education of African Member States, *Development of Education in Africa: A Statistical Review*, Paris: UNESCO.

UNHCHR (1993), *National Institutions for the Promotion and Protection of Human Rights*, Fact Sheet no. 19, Geneva: April.

UNICEF (1996), *State of the World's Children 1996*, New York: Oxford University Press.

UNIFEM/UNCHS (1998), 'Inter-Regional Consultations on Women's Rights to Land and Property Under Situations of Conflict and Reconstruction', Kigali, Rwanda: 16–18 February.

United Nations (1987a), *United Nations Programme of Action for African Economic Recovery and Development, 1986–1990*, Report of the Secretary-General, document A/42/560, New York: United Nations.

United Nations (1987b), *Africa One Year Later: Progress in the Implementation of the UN Program of Action for African Economic Recovery and Development, 1986–1990*, New York: United Nations.

United Nations (1991a), *Final Review and Appraisal of the Implementation of the United Nations Program of Action for African Economic Recovery and Development, 1986–1990*, General Assembly, A/AC.238/L.2/Add.1/Rev.1, New York: United Nations.

United Nations (1991b), *World Economic Survey 1991*, Department of International Economic and Social Affairs, ref. Ell 99175/STIESA/222, New York: United Nations.

United Nations (1991c), *World Investment Report 1991*, United Nations Centre on Transnational Corporations, STICTC/118, New York: United Nations.

United Nations (1996), *The Impact of Armed Conflict on Children: Report of the Expert of the Secretary-General*, New York: United Nations.

United Nations (1997a), *The Causes of Conflict and the Promotion of Durable Peace and Development in Africa*, Report by the UN Secretary-General to the Security Council, New York: United Nations.

United Nations (1997b), *World Economic and Social Survey 1997*, United Nations, Ell 997150/STIESA/256, New York: United Nations.

United Nations Commission for Africa (1990), *African Alternative Framework to Structural Adjustment Programmes for Socio-Economic Recovery and Transformation: Selected Policy Instruments*, Addis Ababa: UNCA.

United States General Accounting Office (2000), *Debt Relief Initiatives for Poor Countries Faces Challenges*, GAO/NSIAD-00–161, Washington, DC: General Accounting Office.

USAID (1990a), *Decentralizing Urban Development Programs: A Framework for Analysing Policy*, Office of Housing and Urban Programs, Working Paper, Washington, DC: USAID.

USAID (1990b), *The Informal Sector in Housing and Urban Development: A Review and a Road Map*, Working Paper prepared by the Co-operative Housing Foundation, Washington, DC: USAID.

USAID (1991), *The Development of Credit Markets in Kenya for Urban Infrastructure and Housing Finance*, Working Paper prepared by William L. Stringer, for the Office of Housing and Urban Programs: Washington, DC: USAID.

USAID (1994), *The Role of the City in Environmental Management*, prepared by David Foster for the Office of Environment and Urban Programs, Washington, DC: USAID.

Uvin, Peter (1997), 'Prejudice, Crisis, and Genocide in Rwanda', *African Studies Review*, vol. 40, no. 2, pp. 91–115.

Viner, Jacob (1950), *The Customs Union Issue*, New York: Carnegie Endowment for International Peace.

Wade, Robert (1990), *Governing the Market: Economic Theory and the Role of Govern-*

ment in East Asian Industrialization, Princeton, NJ: Princeton University Press.

Wall, Tim (1992), 'Soviet Demise Brings Africa New Challenges', *Africa Recovery*, vol. 6, no. 1, April, pp. 14–19.

Wangwe, S.M. (1990), 'A Comparative Analysis of the PTA and SADCC Approaches to Regional Economic Integration', in World Bank, *The Long-term Perspective Study on Sub-Saharan Africa*, Proceedings of a workshop on Regional Integration and Co-operation, vol. 4, Washington, DC: World Bank, pp. 34–9.

Warah, Rasna (2000a), 'Nairobi Descends into Darkness and Despair', *Habitat Debate*, vol. 6, no. 3, pp. 8–9.

Warah, Rasna (2000b), 'Rwanda Passes Succession Law', *Habitat Debate*, vol. 6, no. 2, p. 17.

Watkins, Kevin (1991), 'Agriculture and Food Security in the GATT Uruguay Round', *Review of African Political Economy*, no. 50.

Webb, Patrick, Joachim Von Braun, and Yisehac Yohannes (1991a), 'Famine in Ethiopia: Policy Implications of Coping Failure at National and Household Levels', Washington, DC: International Food Policy Research Institute, mimeo.

Webb, Patrick, Joachim von Braun, and Yisehac Yohannes (1991b), *Labour-intensive Public Works for Food Security: Experiences in Africa*, Working Papers on Food Subsidies 6, Washington, DC: International Food Policy Research Institute.

Weber, Max (1947), *The Theory of Social and Economic Organization*, New York: The Free Press.

Weede, Erich (1993), 'Rent-seeking or Dependency as Explanations of Why Poor People Stay Poor', in Michell Seligson and John T. Passe-Smith (eds), *Development and Underdevelopment*, Boulder, CO: Lynne Rienner.

Wegelin, Emil and Karin Borgman (1995), 'Options for Municipal Interventions in Urban Poverty Alleviation', *Environment and Urbanisation*, vol. 7, no. 2, pp. 131–52.

Weintraub, D. (1975), *Land and Peasants in Imperial Ethiopia*, Assen: Van Gorcum.

Wekwete, Kadmiel (1999), 'The African Urban Governance Crisis', *Habitat Debate*, vol. 5, no. 4, p. 16.

Williams, Brian (1998), 'The Missing Link: Towards Sustainable Urban Transport', *Habitat Debate*, vol. 4, no. 2, pp. 1–5.

Woodhouse, Tom (1996), 'Commentary: Negotiating a New Millennium? Prospects for African Conflict Resolution', *Review of African Political Economy*, no. 68, vol. 23, p. 130.

World Bank and the Carter Centre (1997), *From Civil War to Civil Society: The Transition from War to Peace in Guatemala and Liberia*, Washington, DC: World Bank.

World Bank (1972), *Urbanization: Sector Working Paper*, Washington, DC: World Bank.

World Bank (1981), *Accelerated Development for Sub-Saharan Africa: An Agenda for Action*, Washington, DC: World Bank.

World Bank (1989a), *Ghana: Urban Sector Review*, Report no. 734–GH, Washington, DC: World Bank.

World Bank (1989b), *Inter-Regional Trade in Sub-Saharan Africa*, Washington, DC: World Bank.

World Bank (1989c), *Sub-Saharan Africa: From Crisis to Sustainable Growth*, Washington,

DC: World Bank.

World Bank (1990), *Science Education and Development in Sub-Saharan Africa*, World Bank Techmical Paper No. 124, by Manuel Zymelman, Washington, DC: World Bank.

World Bank (1992), *World Bank Adjustment Lending and Economic Performance in Sub-Saharan Africa in the 1990s: A Comparison with Other Low-income Countries*, Washington, DC: World Bank.

World Bank (1991), *Urban Policy and Economic Development: An Agenda for the 1990s*, Washington, DC: World Bank.

World Bank (1994a), *Adjustment in Africa: Reform, Results and the Road Ahead*, Washington, DC: World Bank.

World Bank (1994b), *Higher Education: The Lessons of Experience*, Washington, DC: World Bank.

World Bank (1995a), *Findings Africa Region*, no. 39.

World Bank (1995b), *Priorities and Strategies for Education: A World Bank Review*, Washington, DC: World Bank.

World Bank (1995c), *Annual Report 1995*, Washington, DC: World Bank.

World Bank (1996), *Sustainable Transport: Priorities for Policy Reform*, Washington, DC: World Bank.

World Bank (1997), *Rural Development: From Vision to Action*, A Sector Strategy Paper, Washington, DC: World Bank.

World Bank (1998), *Post-conflict Reconstruction: The Role of the World Bank*, Washington, DC: World Bank.

World Bank (2000), *Can Africa Claim the 21st Century?* Washington, DC: World Bank.

World Bank (2001), *African Development Indicators 2001*, Washington, DC: World Bank.

World Commission on Environment and Development (1987), 'The Urban Challenge', in *Our Common Future*, New York: Oxford University Press.

World Economic Forum (1998) *African Competitiveness Report 1998*, Geneva: World Economic Forum.

Zakaria, Fareed (1997), 'The Rise of Illiberal Democracy', *Foreign Affairs*, November/December.

Index